Robotics Models Using LEGO WeDo 2.0

Design, Build, Program, Test, Document and Share

Diego Galvez-Aranda
Mauricio Galvez Legua

Apress®

Robotics Models Using LEGO WeDo 2.0: Design, Build, Program, Test, Document and Share

Diego Galvez-Aranda
Bryan, TX, USA

Mauricio Galvez Legua
Ate, Ancash, Peru

ISBN-13 (pbk): 978-1-4842-6845-2
https://doi.org/10.1007/978-1-4842-6846-9

ISBN-13 (electronic): 978-1-4842-6846-9

Managing Director, Apress Media LLC: Welmoed Spahr
Acquisitions Editor: Aaron Black
Development Editor: James Markham
Coordinating Editor: Jessica Vakili

Distributed to the book trade worldwide by Springer Science+Business Media New York, 1 NY Plazar, New York, NY 10014. Phone 1-800-SPRINGER, fax (201) 348-4505, e-mail orders-ny@springer-sbm.com, or visit www.springeronline.com. Apress Media, LLC is a California LLC and the sole member (owner) is Springer Science + Business Media Finance Inc (SSBM Finance Inc). SSBM Finance Inc is a **Delaware** corporation.

For information on translations, please e-mail booktranslations@springernature.com; for reprint, paperback, or audio rights, please e-mail bookpermissions@springernature.com.

Apress titles may be purchased in bulk for academic, corporate, or promotional use. eBook versions and licenses are also available for most titles. For more information, reference our Print and eBook Bulk Sales web page at http://www.apress.com/bulk-sales.

Any source code or other supplementary material referenced by the author in this book is available to readers on GitHub via the book's product page, located at www.apress.com/978-1-4842-6845-2. For more detailed information, please visit http://www.apress.com/source-code.

Printed on acid-free paper

To my parents, Elsa and Mauricio,
and my sisters, Fernanda and Graciela,
for always supporting me. Vamos!

—Diego Galvez-Aranda

Table of Contents

About the Authors

Diego Galvez-Aranda obtained his degree in electrical engineering from the National University of Engineering in Lima, Peru.

Thanks to his father, during his childhood, Diego grew up building LEGO Technic models, awakening his interest in engineering. During his undergraduate days, Diego started a blog called "Not Just Bricks" in which he started posting various projects and building instructions that he developed using the LEGO WeDo and LEGO Mindstorms set.

Thanks to his blog, he started a "Robotics in Schools" project. The main idea behind the project was to implement robotics classes at various schools across Peru and elaborate support materials for teachers to apply robotics in their classes.

Simultaneously, Diego was invited to write several articles in *HispaBrick Magazine* about the LEGO WeDo set. In the magazine, he wrote 12 articles on how to program various LEGO WeDo projects from the entry level.

In 2012, together with a group of friends, Diego founded the "Lego Robotics Club" at his university. As part of the "Robotics Club," he competed in the World Robot Olympiad (WRO) 2012, 2013, 2014, and 2015, getting the first place in the 2012, 2013, and 2014 editions.

Diego believes in robotics as a powerful tool to enhance the learning experience of children in different areas. Currently, he is pursuing a PhD in electrical engineering at Texas A&M University in Texas, USA. His thesis work involves machine learning and molecular simulations of rechargeable Li-ion batteries.

Mauricio Galvez Legua is an electronic engineer graduated from the National University of Engineering in Lima, Peru with more than 30 years as a teacher in Institutes and Universities in Peru. He has a master degree in "Evaluation and Accreditation of Educational Quality".

He was in charge of the implementation of educational robotics in the peruvian Ministry of Education.

He is currently a professor at the Faculty of Electrical and Electronic Engineering of the National University of Engineering. He teaches courses on digital systems, microprocessors/ microcontrollers, programming C, computer architecture, data networks, operating systems and Robotics.

About the Technical Reviewer

Edwar Alvarado Zavaleta obtained his degree in electrical engineering from the National University of Engineering in Lima, Peru. He was in charge of the implementation of educational robotics in the Ministry of Education, Peru.

Edwar is continuously teaching robotics in various schools and preparing virtual material that is used as support material for teachers and students through the virtual platform "Robotronic" that helps them to use robotics in their classes. He also coached several high-school teams that competed in the World Robot Olympiad (WRO).

Edwar collaborated on the development of the building instructions shown in this book.

About the Graphic Designers

Fernanda Galvez Aranda is an environmental engineer from La Molina National Agrarian University in Lima, Peru. She has attended multiple drawing and painting workshops showing her artwork.

In this book, Fernanda has designed the illustration concepts, considering the goals of the book and the environment in which the animals that inspired the prototypes live.

Fernanda has created and drawn by hand the main characters, all their positions, and all the objects which they have interacted with.

Graciela Galvez Aranda is a biologist from Ricardo Palma University in Lima, Peru. As a student, she has worked in management and graphic design in companies related to education.

Her studies in science have given her a different view of robotics, since she believes it studies nature as a way to understand it better.

In this book, Graciela has digitized the hand-drawn drawings of each character and helped give them life with colors.

Also, she has done the covers of each chapter like they were from fairy tales, trying to ensure there was harmony between nature and the prototypes.

Introduction

This book has been written with the purpose of documenting my experience in the design and construction of robotic prototypes and is aimed at children who like to put things together and take things apart, who are restless, and who express in their behavior a need to understand how "our world works." That curiosity was fueled in large part by LEGO kits, which were companions on adventures throughout my childhood. I was fascinated by how I could "build" objects, animals, and machines, following building guides. My hands began to be those of a "digital artisan," which allowed me to build my own ideas. Over time, and given my degree in electronic engineering, I started sharing my knowledge to the next generation of creators. Through robotics courses for children, I developed a teaching methodology called "five phases in prototyping," which is the basis of this book.

The book is aimed at young LEGO enthusiasts who want to prototype solutions to challenges using mechanical and computer science engineering. Teachers and parents will also find the book a helpful guide to introducing the world of robotics in a dynamic and fun way. Its fundamental purpose is to introduce concepts of design, construction, and prototype programming in a fun way. The book uses simple language to make it easy to understand for children. We chose projects based on animals (not robots) in clear allusion to the importance of maintaining the bond with our natural world and respect for nature and environment.

Each book's chapter will follow the "five phases in prototyping" to create robots inspired by animals, challenging you to replicate a bio-inspired motion, such as crawling, quadruped walking, biped walking, flapping wings, and swimming. Through the five phases in prototyping, you will encourage your problem-solving skills by analyzing situations, designing solutions, and checking how they work, stimulating your imagination and creativity.

WHAT TO KNOW BEFORE YOU START?

Learning

- Is strongly related to **doing**.
- Is an active **knowledge-building** experience.
- We learn when we are **curious**: We investigate, explore, make, and test.

I wonder how planes can fly?

Technology

- Is the set of **skills**, **methods**, or **processes** used for the design and construction of machines or services to satisfy human needs.

Science

- Nowadays, the work is mental and no longer only **physical**.
- **Intelligence** is the **work tool**.
- The knowledge is obtained through **observation** and **experimentation**.

Technology

Science

Engineering

- Apply **scientific knowledge** (math, physics, chemistry, etc.) to develop **technology** (models and techniques) and solve problems affecting the humanity.
- **Invention** is making an idea come true.

Automated systems evolution

Metal Age

Stone Age

Mechanization

· Humans have evolved from the beginning of time, adapting to the environment, using tools, mastering metals, building machines (mechanization), and giving them a basic level of intelligence (automation) to have autonomous machines (robotization).

Automation

Robotization

Robotics

- Robotics is the **design** and **construction** of **machines** with a certain degree of **intelligence**, capable of replacing human beings in certain activities.
- Robotics is an **interdisciplinary field**, involving the interaction of several other fields such as **mechanics, electronics,** and **informatics.**

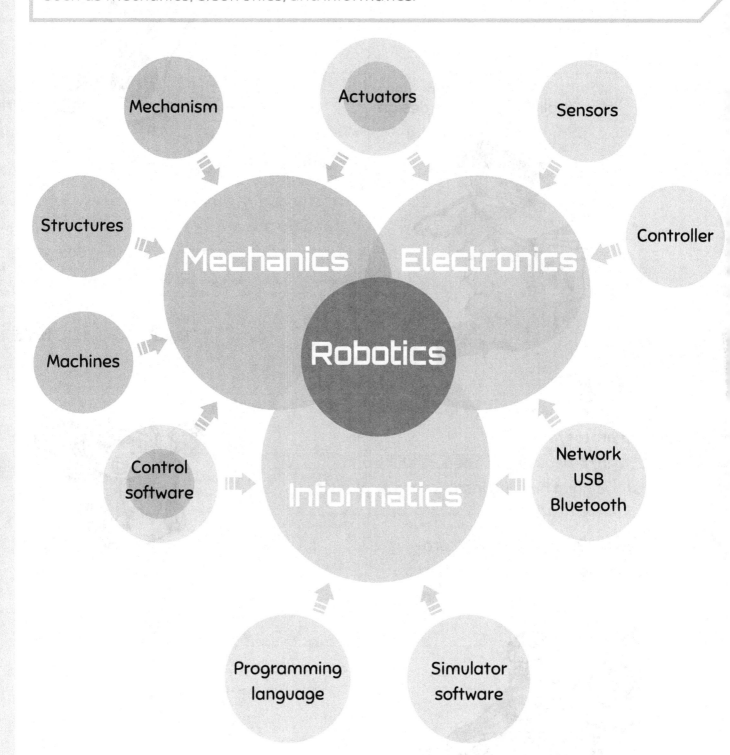

Phases in prototyping

· Encourages **problem-solving** skills by analyzing situations, designing solutions, and checking how they work
· Stimulates **imagination** and **creativity**
· **Five phases:** Design, Build, Program, Test, and Document & share

It is time to introduce you to some of my friends!

Hi! I'm **"Brolin"** and I like to **design** solutions inspired in nature.

Design phase

· It starts with **"imitation,"** copying examples that you observe in reality, evolving through **"imagination"** to create your own designs.

Hola! I'm **"Rafa"** and I like to **build** the things that "Brolin" designs!

Build phase

· Is the implementation of the design, which is called **prototype**.
· You make use of your manual skills and understanding of **building instructions** or **plans**.

Hi! I'm **"Dawn"** and I enjoy **programming**; I can spend hours coding in front of the computer!

Program phase

· It is **"telling"** your prototype what to do according to its design.
· It is described by a **sequence of steps** that define the behavior of your prototype (program).

6

Test phase

· Visual verification that your prototype **works as planned**.

· If the prototype does not work, this may be due to **errors** in the **program** phase, the **build** phase, or the **design** phase. If so, you should return to the corresponding phase and **solve** the problem.

My turn! I like **testing** all the cool stuff that my friends create.

Hello! I'm **"Zuzu"** and I like to share all the inventions my friends make.

Document & share phase

· Once your prototype is working without any errors, then you can **document** it so that in the future you can **repeat** it and/or **improve** it.

· This also allows you to **share** your work spreading knowledge, so others can try your prototype.

Phases in prototyping

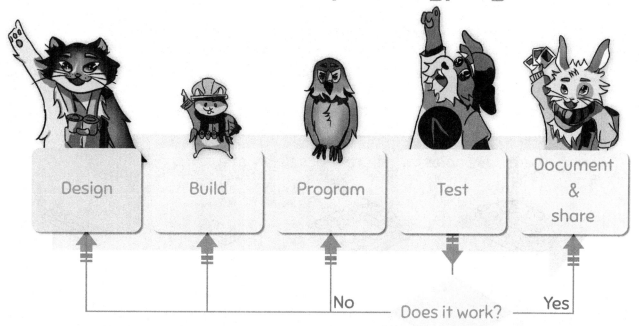

| Design | Build | Program | Test | Document & share |

No — Does it work? — Yes

Mechanics

- Mechanics allow the design of the prototype **physical structure**.
- Structural parts, **simple machines**, and **motion transmission** systems are examples of the use of mechanics.

LEGO pieces

- In your LEGO WeDo set, you will find pieces of different **colors**, **sizes**, and **types**. Each of them allows you to build different prototypes.
- In the following sections, you will explore all the **mechanical pieces** that come in your WeDo set.

Bricks

- Can be connected to other bricks by using the **studs** located on the top face.

Plates

- Similar to bricks but they are **three times thinner**.
- Come in different **shapes**, not only rectangular.
- Some of them have **holes** for different assembly methods.

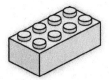
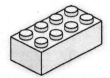

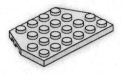
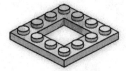

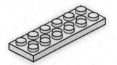
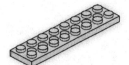

Beams

- Similar to bricks but with holes at the sides.
- Are always **1 unit in width** and from 2 to 16 **units in length**.

Axles

- They are used to transfer **rotational** motion. Usually work together with **gears** and **beams**.
- Can be also used as **structural support elements**.
- Axle length is measured by **counting** the **studs** from a beam.

6

  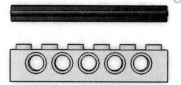

Bushings

- They are used to **hold** the position of the **axles**.

Connectors

- They are used to **assemble** two **beams** together.

Pulleys

- They are used to **transfer** rotational motion. It must be used together with a **rubber band** or a **string**.

Gears

- They are used to transfer **rotational motion** through their **teeth**.

- Two particular types of gears are **worm gear** and **gear rack**.

Wheels

- They are used to **reduce friction**, making the transportation of heavy objects easier.
- Must be used together with **axles**.

Slope bricks

- Let you get away from the **blockiness** of regular bricks by adding slopes.
- Come in different **sizes** and **heights**.
- Their function is mostly **decorative** to add details in your buildings.

     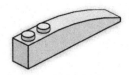

Mechanism

- A set of pieces that are connected between them to **transfer** and/or **transform energy** and **motion**.

Informatics

- Informatics allow you to create **programs** through a programming language to "**bring life**" to your prototypes.

Algorithm

- **Algorithm** is a finite and ordered **sequence of tasks** to follow in order to solve a problem. To design an algorithm, you first have to **identify** and **analyze the problem** you want to solve.

Flowchart

- A **flowchart** is a diagram that represents a **sequence of tasks** (algorithm).
- A **flowchart** shows each task as a box, and the order sequence is defined by connecting the boxes with arrows.

Program

- A **program** is a **set of instructions** that a computer understands and executes.
- Programs are written using a **programming language**, allowing the **communication** between the given instructions and the computer.

Hello

Language incompatibility

Programming language

01101000 01101111
01101100 01100001

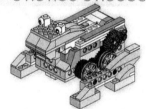

Hello

Hello = 010111010

01101000 01101111
01101100 01100001

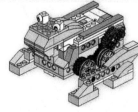

WeDo programming

- The WeDo program uses an **iconographic** programming language.
- A specific task is represented as a **"block."**
- By **"dragging and dropping"** blocks, you can build a program.
- In a **WeDo project**, you can create your program and document your results.

WeDo programming environment

Project box

- You can **create** new projects, check some **building instructions**, and take pictures and notes to **document** your projects.

Connection box

- Indicates when a Hub, sensor, or motor is **connected** to the computer.

Navigation box

- You can zoom in and zoom out the workspace, **navigating** through it by dragging the mouse cursor.

Stop button

- **Stops** any running program in the workspace.

Palette

- Lists all the **programming blocks**.

Drag and drop

- To start a program, you **"drag"** the blocks in the palette and **"drop"** them in the workspace.
- To delete a block from your workspace, simply **"drag"** it and **"drop"** it back in the palette.

Flow blocks

- Are the **yellow** blocks and control the flow of your program.

Display and sound blocks

- Are the **red** blocks and allow you to reproduce **sounds** and **pictures** on the screen.
- You can also perform some mathematical calculations such as **addition**, **subtraction**, **multiplication**, and **division**.

Numeric and text inputs

- These blocks need to work together with the **flow blocks** or the **display and sound blocks**. They allow you to **enter** data in your program. The data can be a random number, a fix number, a text, or the sound level of a microphone.

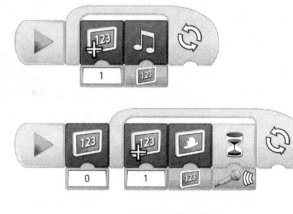

Time to play a little bit with all the blocks you know so far. Here are some examples, but you can try many other block combinations!

Electronics

- Electronics allows you to add **"senses"** to your prototype, making it able to "see" or "hear," thanks to the use of **sensors**.
- Also, your prototype can perform tasks such as moving around or picking up objects using **actuators** such as the **electric motor**.

Hub

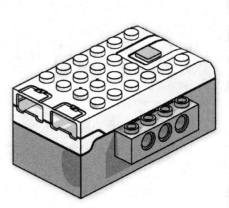

- It allows **communication** between the **computer** and other **electronic devices** such as sensors and motors.
- It communicates with a computer, smartphone, or tablet through **Bluetooth**.
- It is the **power source** for all the other electronic devices. It requires **two AA batteries**.
- It comes with an **LED (actuator)** that you can program to **set the color**.

Electric motor

- An **actuator** that **transforms electrical energy** into **mechanical energy**.
- The electrical energy comes from the batteries inside the Hub.
- It produces **rotational motion**.
- Five programming blocks allow us to control the electric motor: motor power, wait for, stop motor, turn anti-clockwise, turn clockwise.

Tilt sensor

· It detects **six different states**. For each state, there is a programming block: shake, tilt down, tilt up, tilt that way, tilt this way, and tilt sensor no tilt.

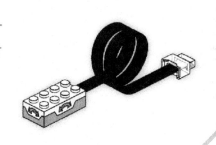

Distance sensor

· It **detects** when an object is in front of it. The distance sensor would be equivalent to the **human eyes** for a robot.
· Four programming blocks can be used with the distance sensor: any distance change, distance change closer, distance change further, and distance sensor input.

Robot

· It is an **electronic** and **mechanical** machine, capable of **movement and action**, that **perceives its environment**, performs tasks **automatically**, has **computational intelligence**, and is **programmable**.

How does a robot work?

A robot **processes** the information and based on its **programming** takes decisions: if there is an obstacle, it moves to avoid it.

Process "Think"

A robot **perceives** the environment around it: **detects** if there are obstacles in front of it.

Sensing "Perceive"

Action "Perform"

A robot uses its **actuator** to perform an **action**: moves or turns on a light.

Robot characteristics

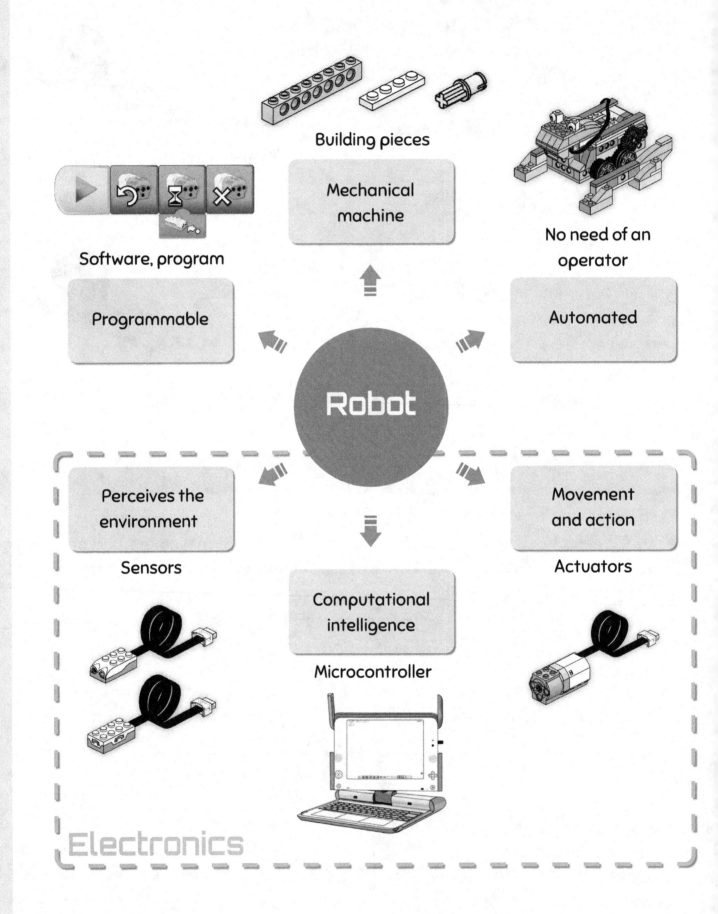

Building pieces

Mechanical machine

No need of an operator

Software, program

Programmable

Automated

Robot

Perceives the environment

Sensors

Movement and action

Actuators

Computational intelligence

Microcontroller

Electronics

Is it a robot?

Only if the answer to all the six questions is YES, we are in front of a robot:

Let's practice the definition of a robot and see if you can identify which are robots and which are not!

1. Is it a mechanical machine?

2. Does it have movement and action?

3. Is it programmable?

4. Does it have computational intelligence?

5. Is it automated?

6. Does it perceive the environment?

Bike

1. YES!
2. YES!
3. NO!
4. NO!
5. NO!
6. NO!

Camera

1. YES!
2. NO!
3. YES!
4. YES!
5. NO!
6. YES!

Smartphone

1. YES!
2. NO!
3. YES!
4. YES!
5. NO!
6. YES!

WeDo

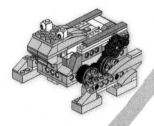

1. YES!
2. YES!
3. YES!
4. YES!
5. YES!
6. YES!

Three-dimensional projections

· Before you start building the several prototypes shown in the book, you can test your skills by **building** some **basic ones**.
· A **three-dimensional object** has length, width, and height; therefore, it has **volume**.
· Let's explore the different methods that are used to represent a **three-dimensional** object on a piece of paper (**two dimensions**).

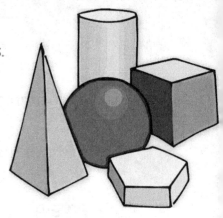

Isometric projection

· It is a graphical representation of a **three-dimensional** object on a **plane** (two dimensions).
· All the building instructions are given in an **isometric projection**.
· **Example:** By only using the following images, can you count how many bricks are in each image?

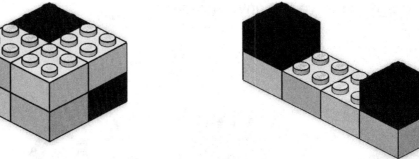

Orthogonal projection

· Similarly to an isometric projection, it is a **graphical representation** of a three-dimensional object but using several plane views:

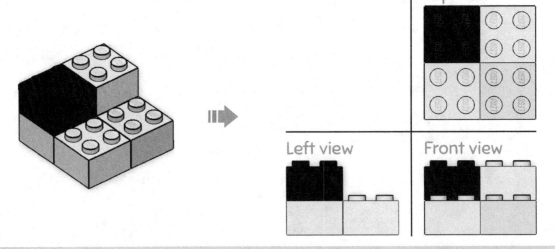

Top view

Left view   Front view

Frog

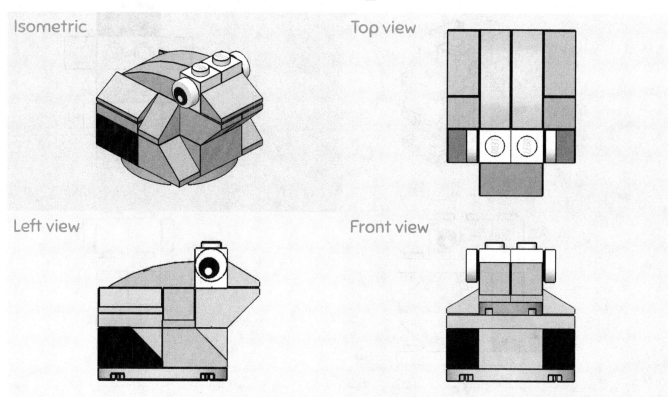

Isometric   Top view

Left view   Front view

Turtle

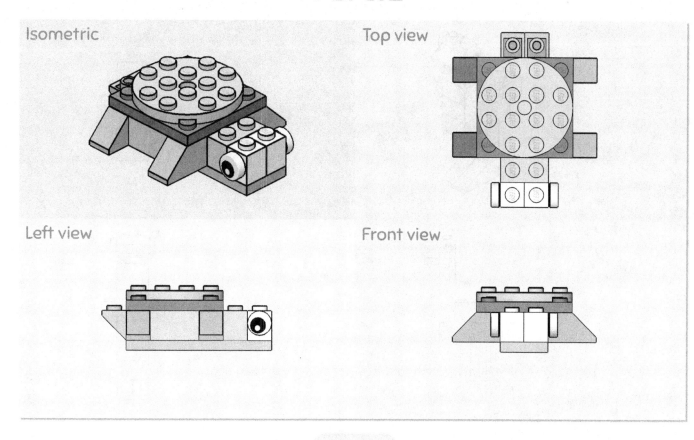

Isometric   Top view

Left view   Front view

Penguin

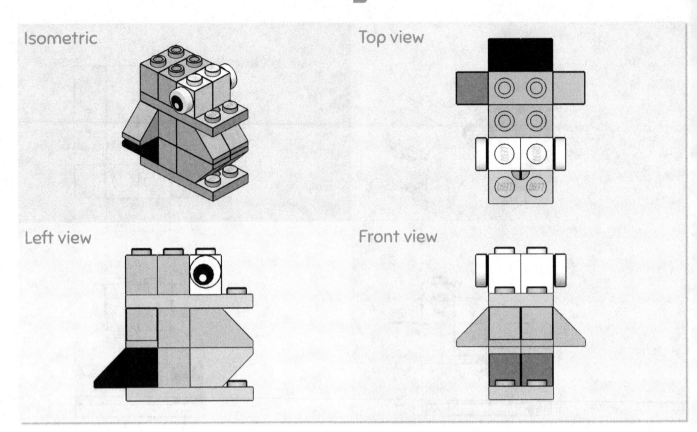

Isometric

Top view

Left view

Front view

American rhea

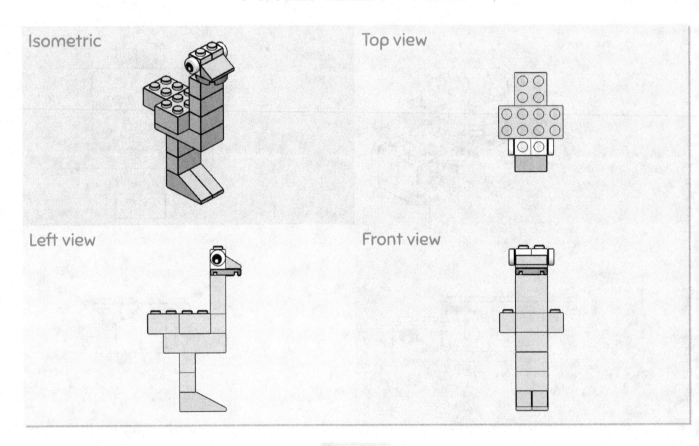

Isometric

Top view

Left view

Front view

Caiman

Isometric

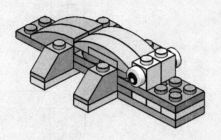

Top view

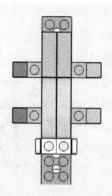

Left view

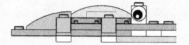

Front view

Sea lion

Isometric

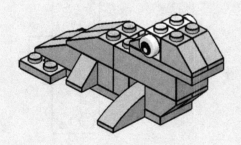

Top view

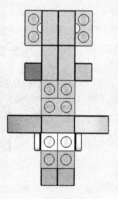

Left view

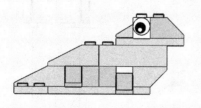

Front view

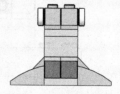

21

Plesiosaurus

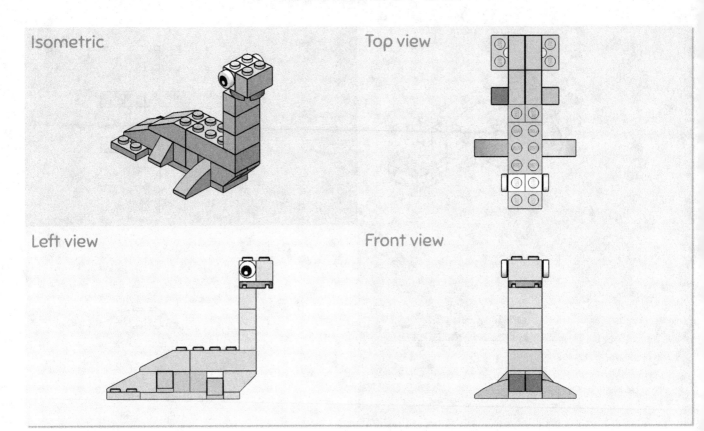

Isometric

Top view

Left view

Front view

Dog

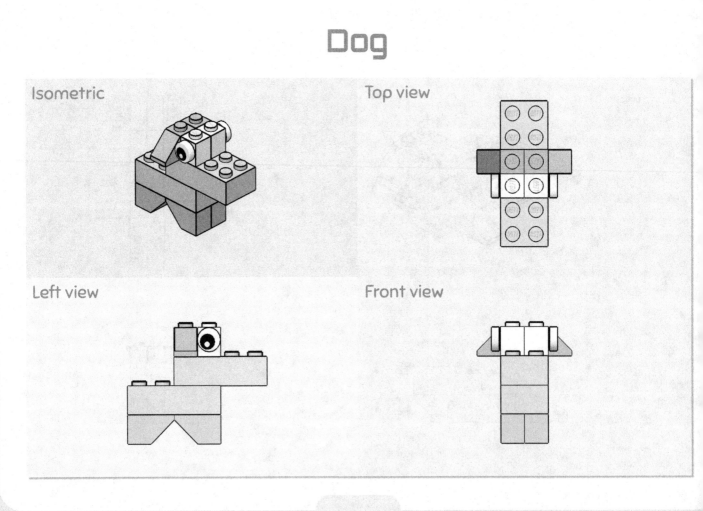

Isometric

Top view

Left view

Front view

Skier

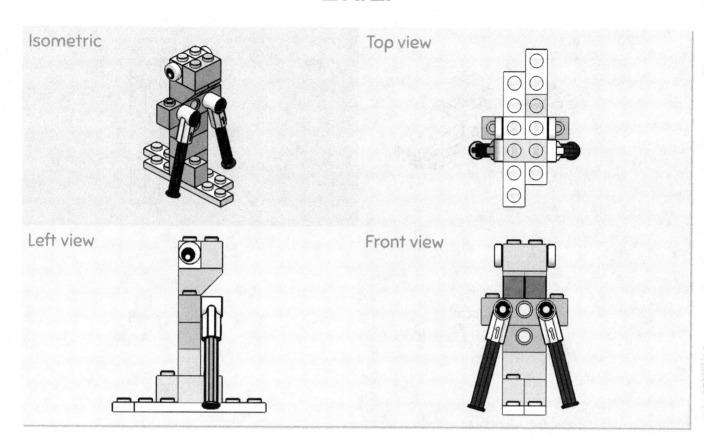

Isometric

Top view

Left view

Front view

Astronaut

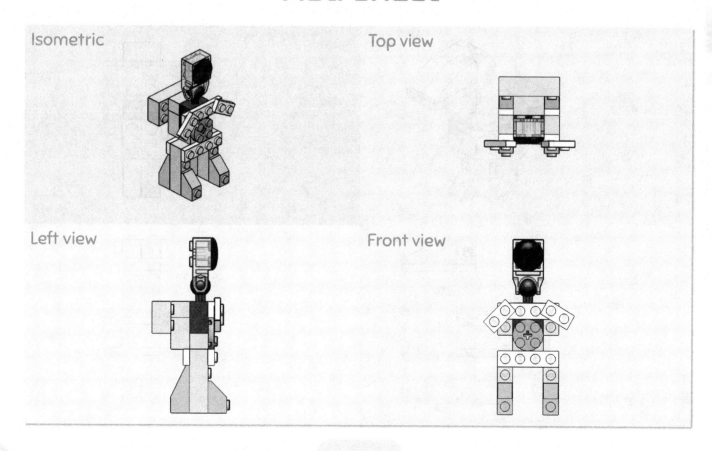

Isometric

Top view

Left view

Front view

Dolphin

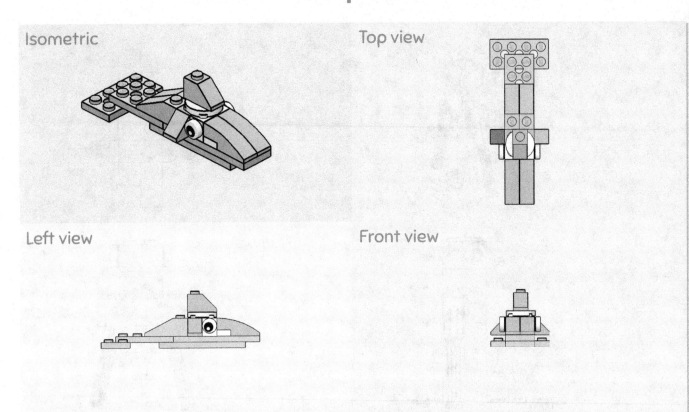

Isometric

Top view

Left view

Front view

Pelican

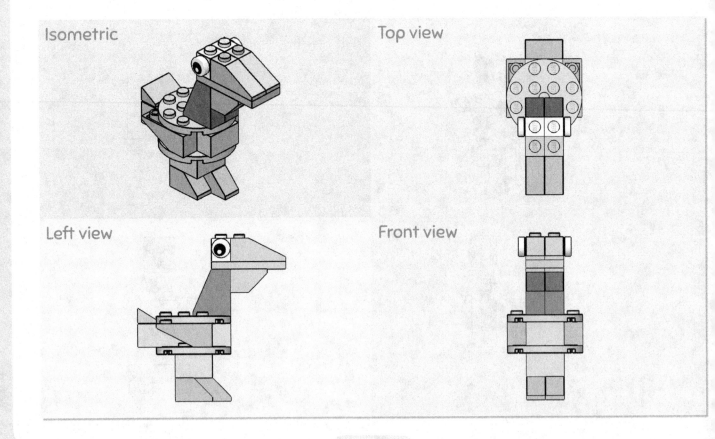

Isometric

Top view

Left view

Front view

Now you are ready to start building robots inspired by wildlife!

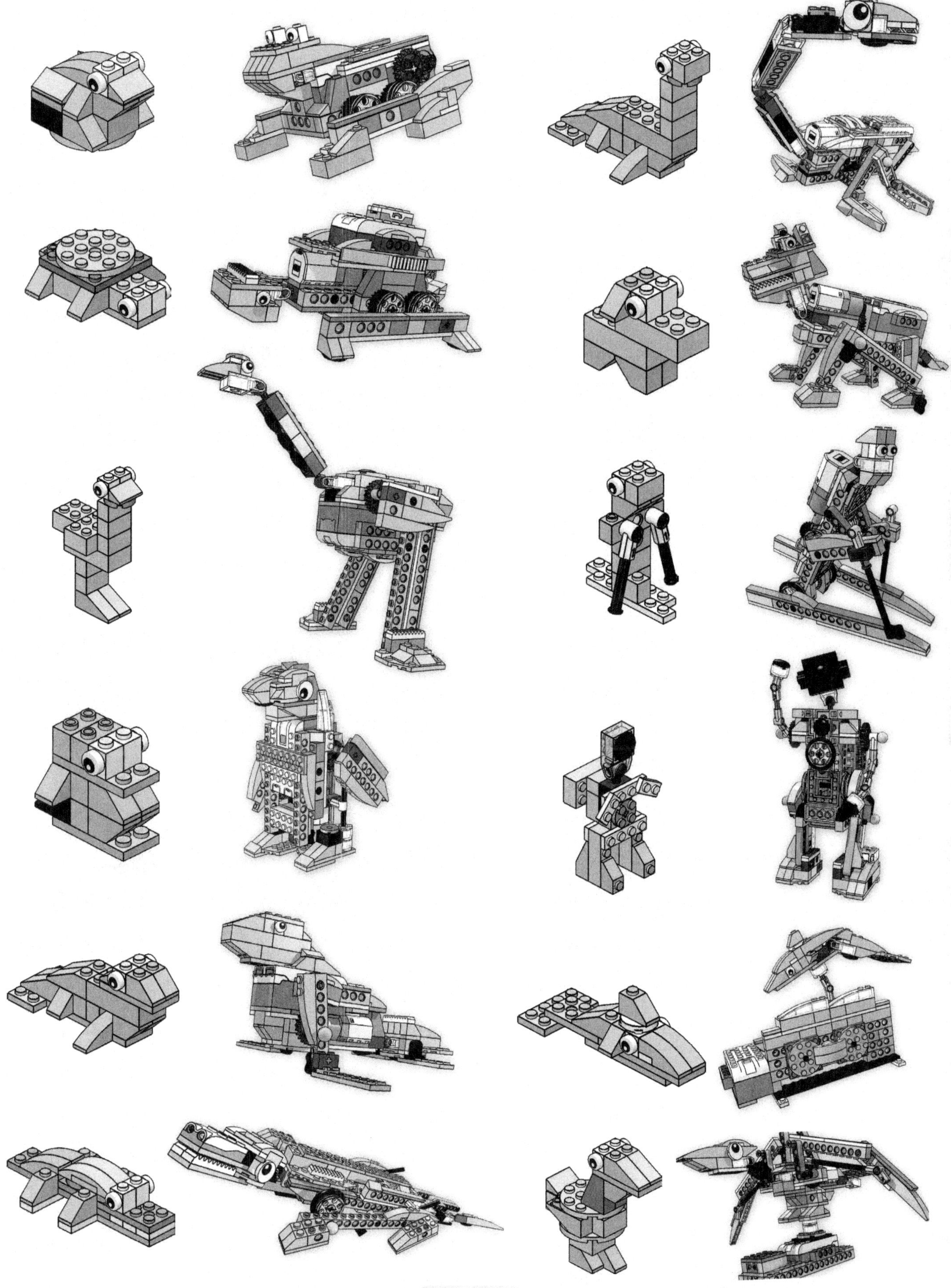

IN-PHASE ROBOTS

Contents

FROG

· In this phase, you can use a **white paper** and a **pencil** to start drawing your ideas!

Looking for inspiration

· **Frogs** are amphibians that are known for their **jumping abilities**, croaking sounds, bulging eyes, and slimy skin.
· Frogs use quick **jumps** to escape from predators.
· A jumping frog can leap away from danger in an instant and hide safely in the water.

How can I replicate the frog jumping motion?

· On a piece of paper, you can sketch some **ideas** to replicate the frog jumping motion!

Parallel motion

· The **parallel motion** is a four-bar linkage in which two bars rotate while the other two bars keep its position.
· The mechanism consists of a bar moving straight up and down from a transmitted motion generated by **two rotating bars**.
· Used to convert the **rotational** motion into a **parallel** motion.

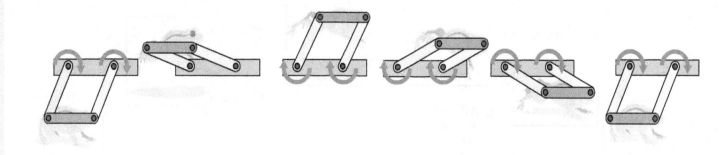

· Given the following building instructions, you can build your own parallel motion linkage.

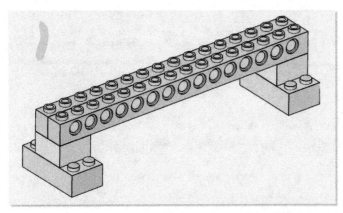

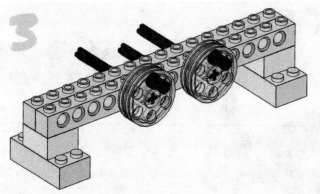

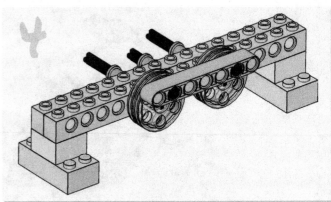

Extra views

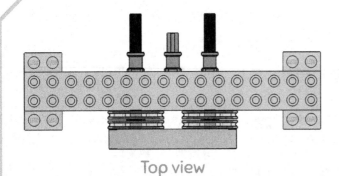

Top view

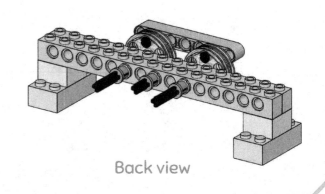

Back view

Test the parallel motion linkage by rotating both axles at the same time!

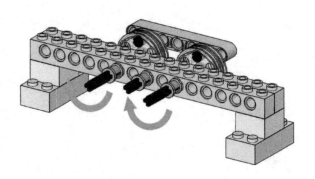

Gear transmission

- Gears have one main purpose: **transmit** mechanical energy.
- **Gear teeth** are designed to avoid **slipping** and provide a **smooth transmission** of rotation between two gears.
- A **gear train** is formed by mounting several gears on a frame so the teeth of the gears engage to transmit **rotational motion**.
- In a gear train, the first gear is the **driver gear**, the last gear is the **follower gear**, and all the gears in between are called **idler gears**.
- **Gearing down**: If a large gear is driven with a small gear, the **torque** (force) increases, but the **speed decreases**.
- **Gearing up**: If a small gear is driven with a large gear, the **speed increases**, but the **torque** (force) **decreases**.

Follower

Driver

Gearing down

Driver

Follower

Gearing up

Driver

Idler

Follower

Gear train

Gear train + parallel motion

- You can add a **gear train** to the parallel motion linkage.

- With the addition of a gear train, you only need to rotate one axle, and the **rotational motion** is **transmitted** to the other axle.

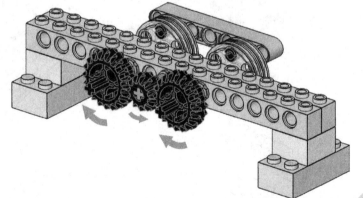

- Now you are ready to build your WeDo frog prototype!
- Before you start building, prepare a **suitable workspace**.
- Keep in mind that the WeDo set has small pieces, so prepare a table with enough space to easily identify all the pieces and prevent them from getting lost.

1

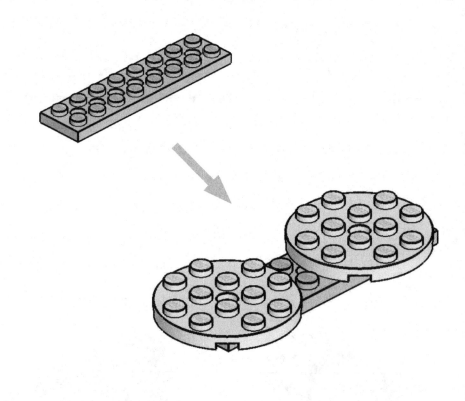

2

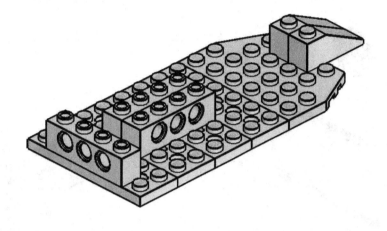

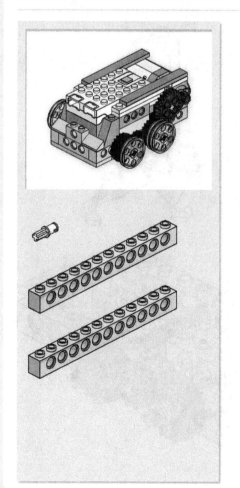

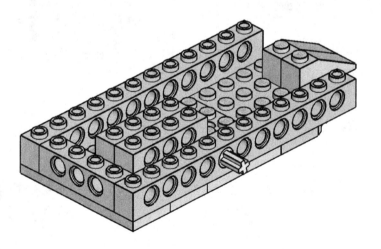

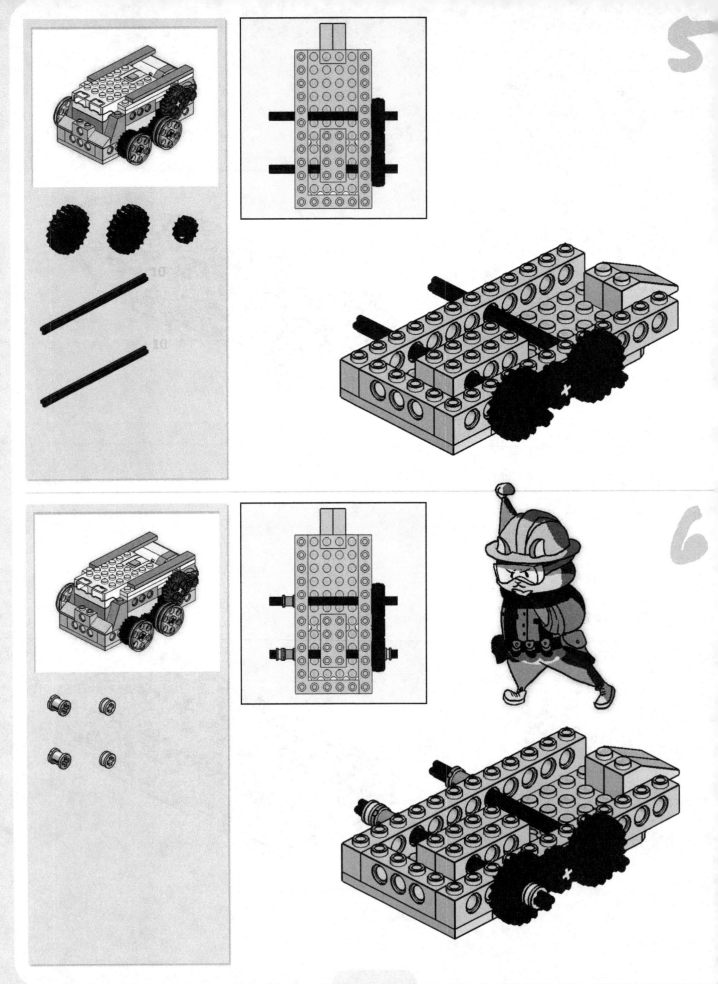

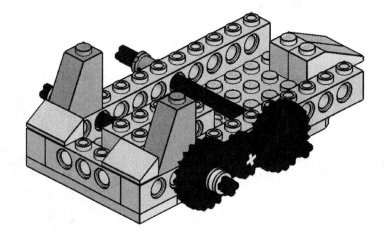

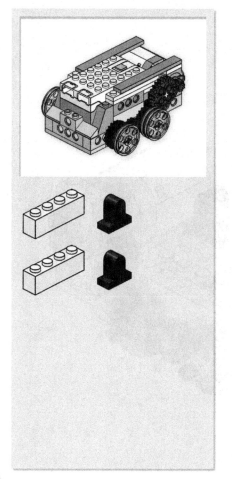

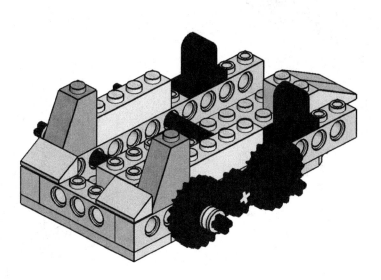

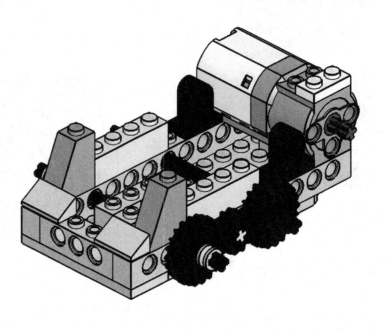

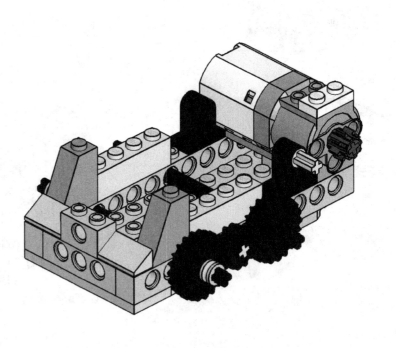

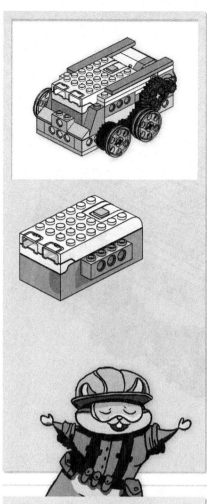

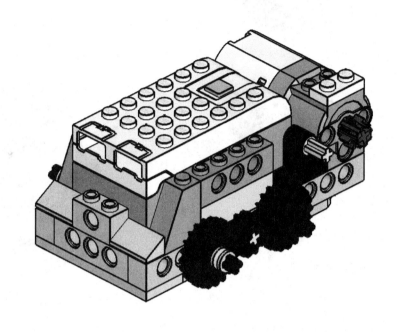

11

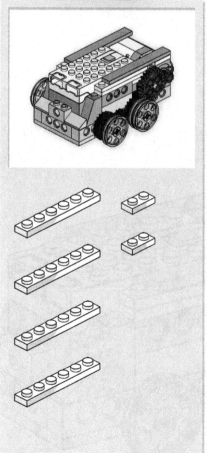

12

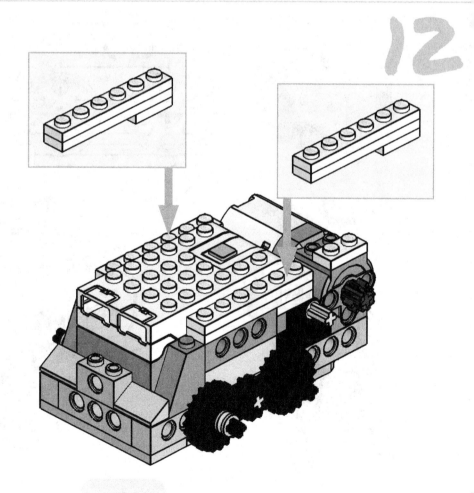

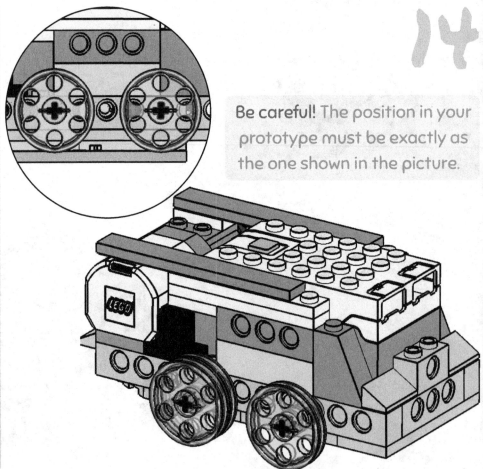

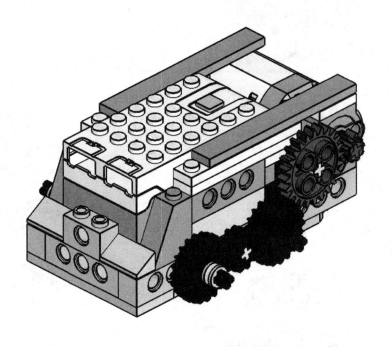

Be careful! The position in your prototype must be exactly as the one shown in the picture.

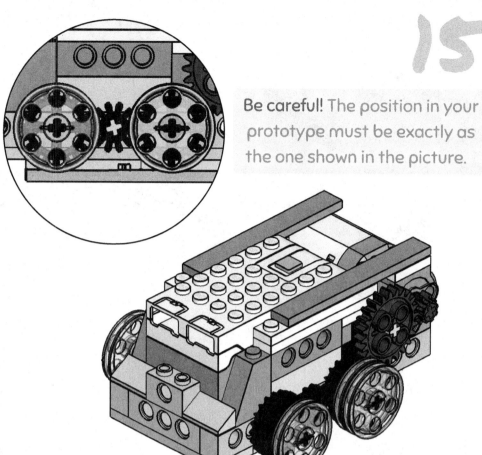

Be careful! The position in your prototype must be exactly as the one shown in the picture.

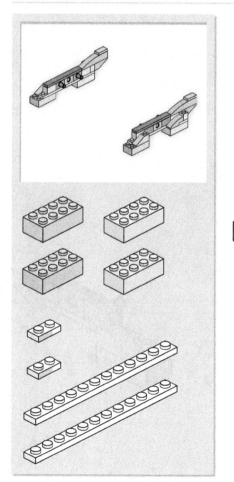

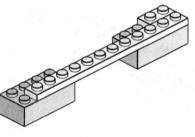

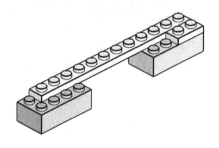

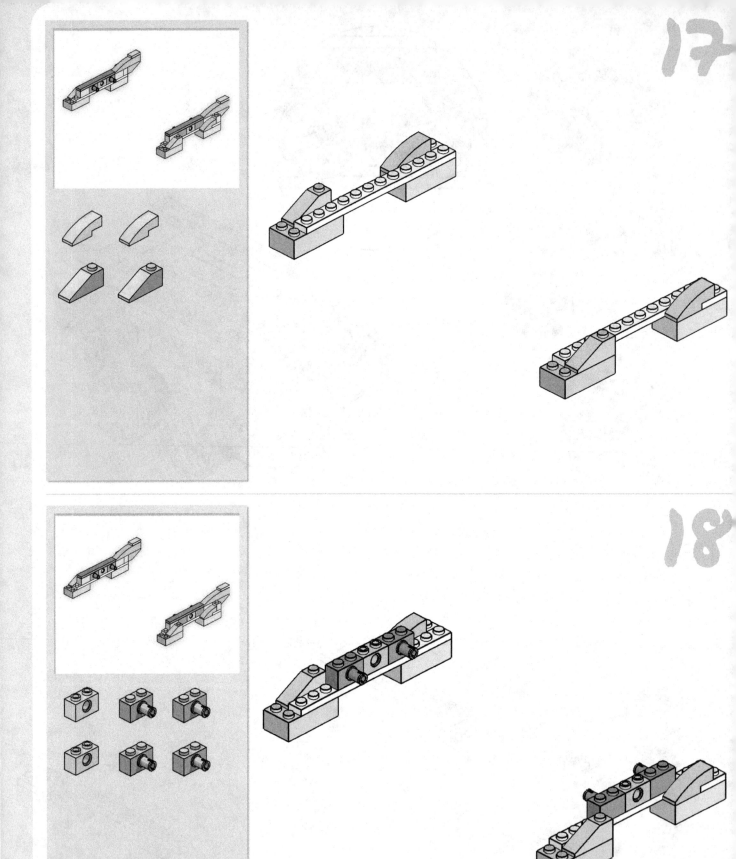

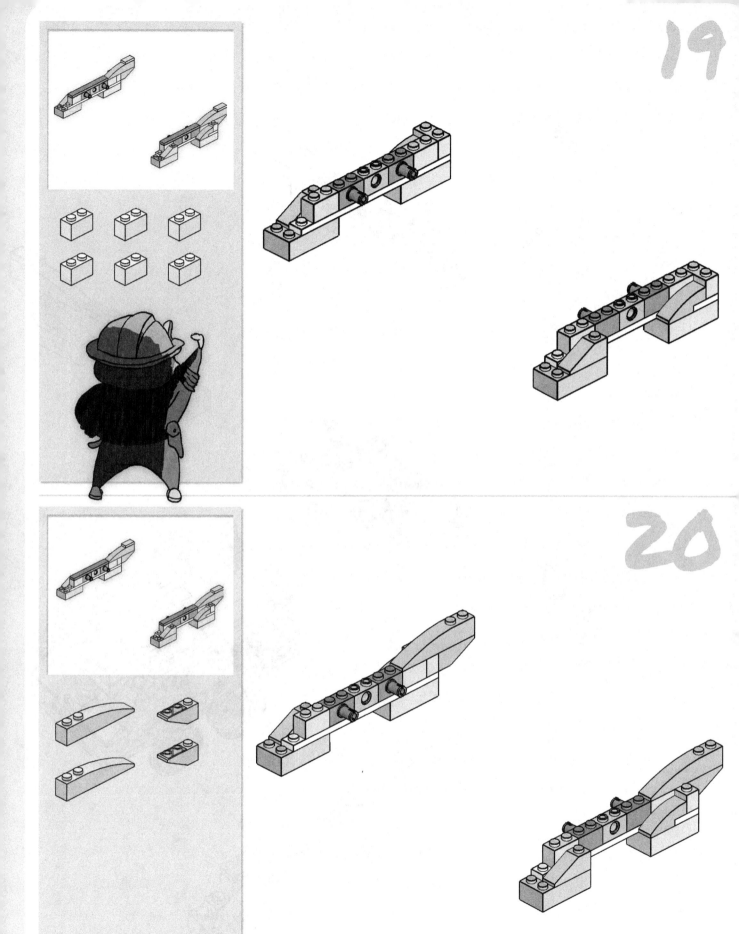

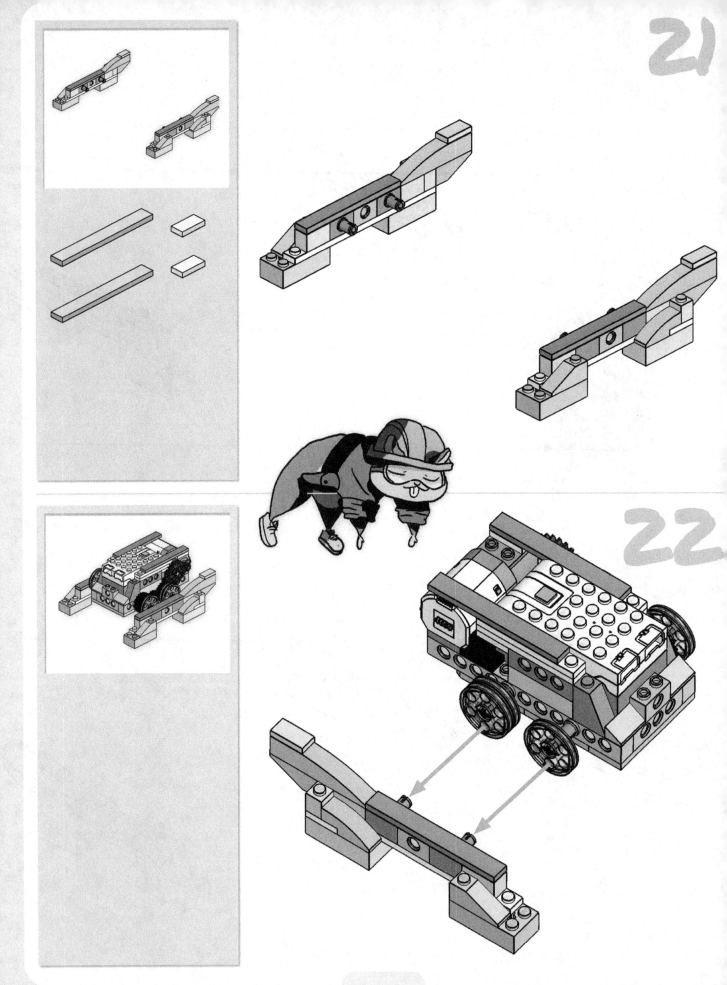

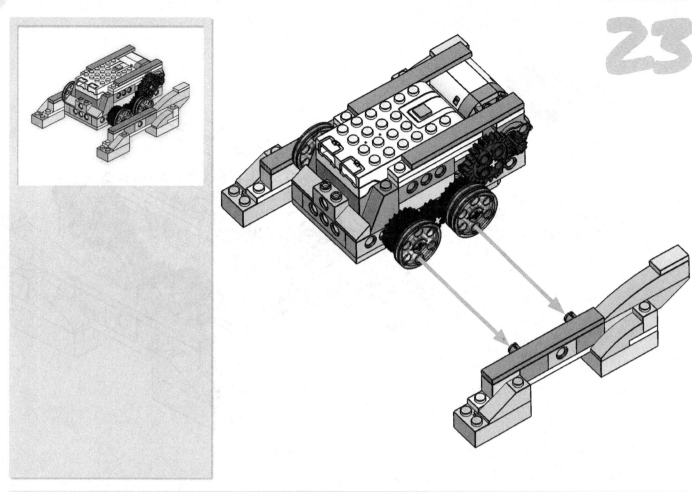

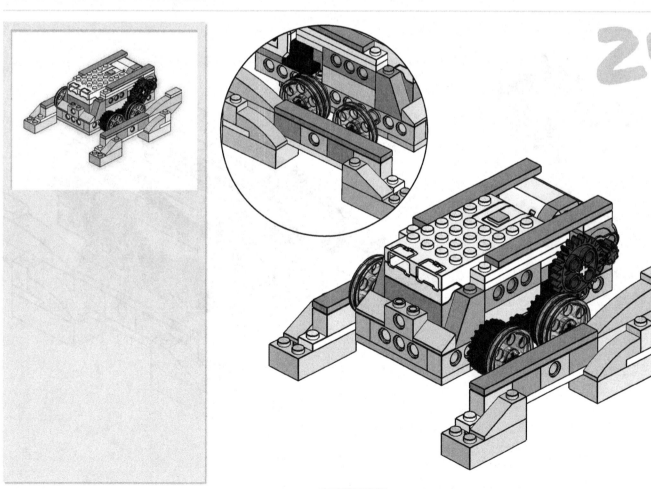

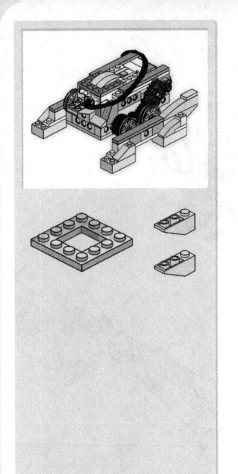

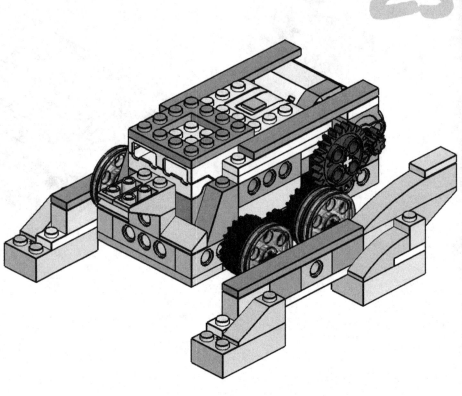

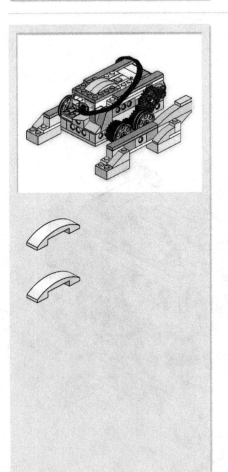

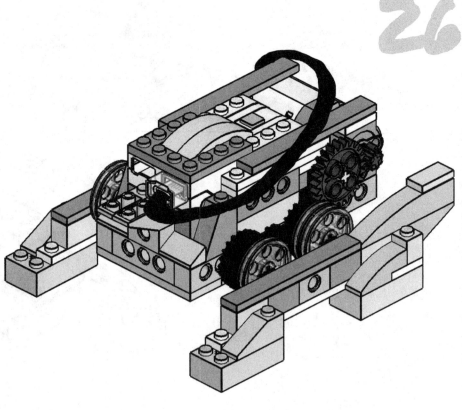

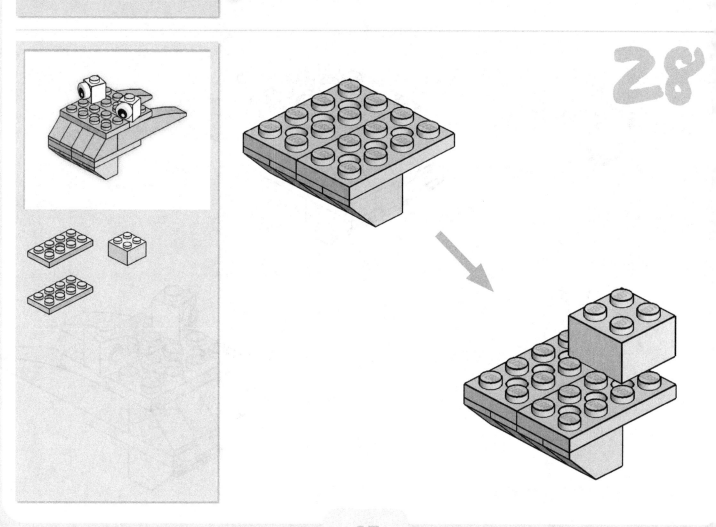

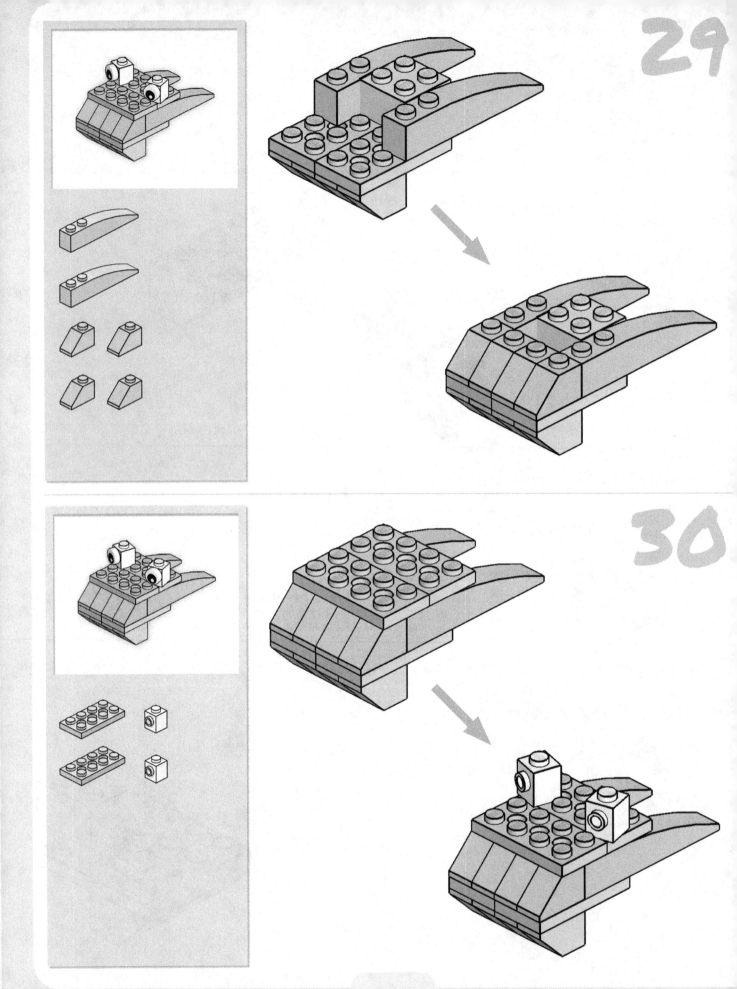

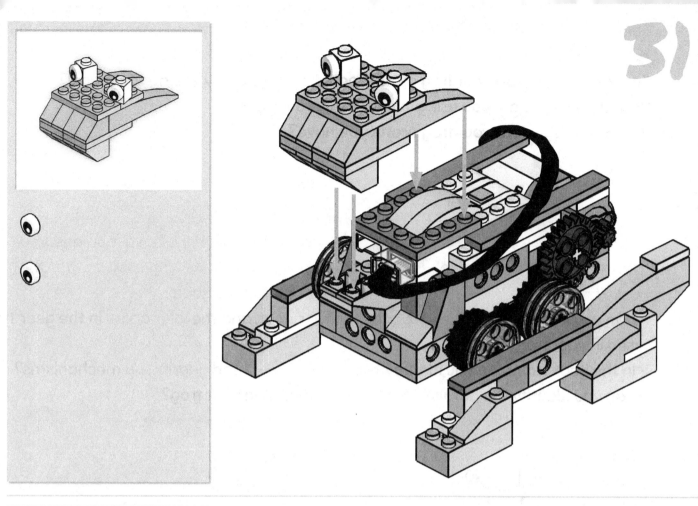

31

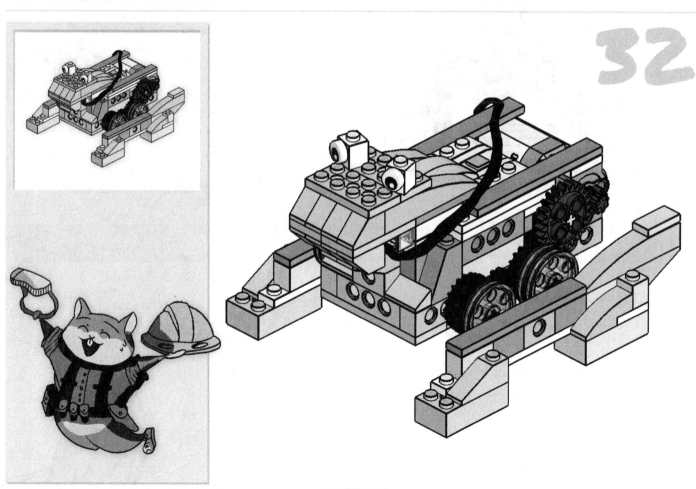

32

- Before going to the next phase, you can identify the mechanisms you are using in your frog prototype.
- Can you predict how your frog prototype will move by only seeing the model?
- How many gears are you using in your frog prototype?
- How many legs does your frog prototype have?

Design features

- Your frog uses the motor to drive two legs.
- Wait... What? Two legs? Don't panic; even though a frog should have four legs, your frog prototype has only two legs. However, these two legs can be disguised so that they can look like four legs. You can use this trick in your future projects!
- Can you identify the driver gear, the follower gear, and the idler gears in the gear train used in your frog?
- In the gear train, can you identify the gearing down and gearing up mechanisms?
- Can you identify the parallel motion linkage used in your frog?

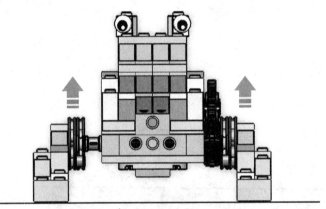

In-phase motion

Gear train mechanism

Program phase: Motor blocks

- In this section, you will explore some of the basics about programming to control the motor rotation.

- The program idea consists of moving your frog for a period of time and then it stops.

- In a more detailed way, your frog will move forward for 10 seconds, and then it will stop.

Thanks to programming, you can make your frog prototype come to life!

Once you have a clear idea of what you want your prototype to do, you can elaborate an algorithm by using a flowchart. This way, the programming will be easier!

Flowchart

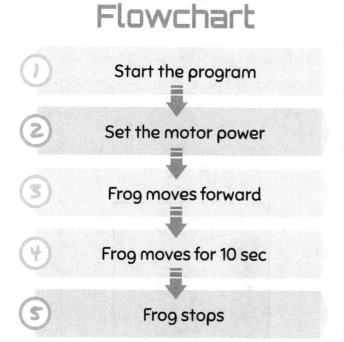

① Start the program

② Set the motor power

③ Frog moves forward

④ Frog moves for 10 sec

⑤ Frog stops

· The flowchart indicates **five tasks**. Therefore, we can assign a **programming block** for each task:

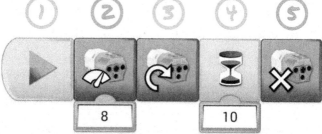

Block equivalences

· The **number of tasks** is not always equal to the **number of blocks**. For example, in the preceding program, **tasks 4** and **5** can be programmed using only **one motor block**:

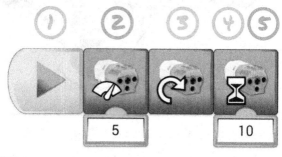

· **Task 3** indicates that your frog should go forward. Which of **these blocks** will make your frog go forward?

· You will find out the answer to this question on the **test phase**!

· Before testing your prototype, verify the **communication** between your WeDo softwar and your WeDo Hub (Smart Hub).

1 · Turn on your Smart Hub and pair it with the software.

2 · Once your Smart Hub is listed, the communication is ready.

3 · In the lower-right corner, you will see all the connected devices.

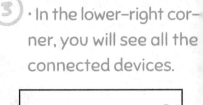

· Now you are ready to test your frog. Execute the programs developed in the **program phase** by clicking the "**Start**" block.

TEST 1: Finding the right motor direction

Now you can find which of these two programs make your frog go forward and backward.

TEST 2: Finding the minimum motor power to move the frog

· Start changing the motor power value to 1 and execute the program.

· Now increase the motor power by 1 and execute the program. Repeat the process unt reaching 10. If you increase the motor power to more than 10, nothing happens, meanin that the maximum power is 10.

TEST 3: 4-block program vs. 5-block program

· Do you find any difference between the program using four programming blocks and th program using five programming blocks?

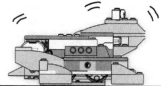

· Your frog walks following an "in–phase" motion, meaning that at any time both legs are exactly in the same position.

Does it work?

· If your answer is **no**, well, that is what **testing is about**.
· There are several things that you can check if your model is not working the way you wanted. The problem could be on the **mechanics**, on the **program**, or on both.
· You can go back to the **build phase** to check any **mechanical issue** or go back to the **program phase** to check any **programming issue**.
· Also, remember to check the Smart Hub energy, since you might be running out of **battery!**

Document & share phase

· You can document your work in different ways:
· Taking **screen captures** of your programs
· **Recording videos** of your prototype performing the pro-grammed tasks
· Taking **pictures** or **drawing sketches** of any structural modi-fication on your prototype
· Taking **notes** during the test phase to report your results

Enhancing the experience

· **Build:** To enhance your building experience, you can add **decorative elements** to im-prove the look of your model. For example, you can try the other pair of eyes available in your WeDo set to replace the ones used in your frog.
· **Programming:** You can also start creating your **own algorithms** to make your frog per-form a **different set of tasks!** You can try different combinations of the motor blocks.

TURTLE

· Remember to have a **white** paper and a **pencil** to start drawing your ideas!

Looking for inspiration

· Turtles are **reptiles** with a body encased in a **bony shell**.
· Turtles are very **adaptive** and can be found on **every continent**, except Antarctica.
· Turtles are extremely **slow** to walk.

What kind of mechanism should I use to replicate the turtle slow walking motion?

Learning from past experiences

· One way to perform a slow motion is by decreasing the **motor power**.
· However, decreasing the motor power will eventually reach a point in which the **power is not enough** to **move the prototype**, as observed during the **test phase** of the frog prototype.

· Similarly to your frog prototype, a **parallel linkage mechanism** and an **in–phase** motion will be used in your turtle prototype for the **walking motion**.

Worm gear

· It is used when **large speed reductions** and **large power increases** are needed.
· It has a compact design; it does not require too much space.

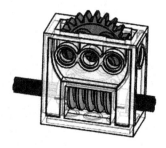

· Given the following building instructions, you can build your own **worm gear mechanism**.

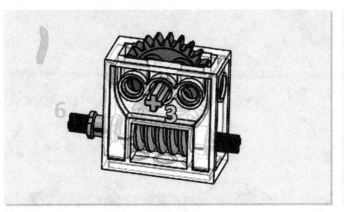

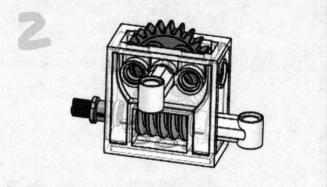

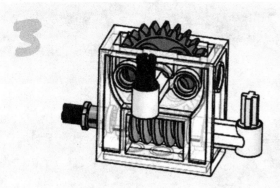

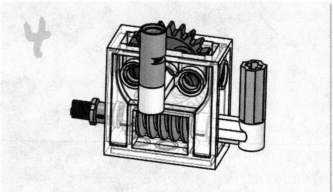

Extra views

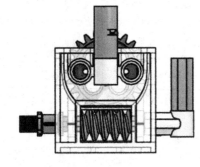

Front view

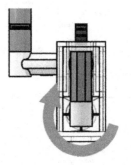

Left view

· You can observe **two cranks**: the green one and the gray one.

· What happens to the **green crank** when you rotate the **gray crank**?

· How many rotations of the **gray crank** must be done to complete **one rotation** of the **green crank**?
· Now try to rotate the **green crank**; you will realize that **you can't.**

Worm gear transmission

· The **worm gear** can be only used as the **driver gear**, never as the **follower gear**.
· The **worm gear** is a **self-lock mechanism**; the follower gear keeps steady, and the only way to make it rotate is by rotating the driver gear.
· The **worm gear transmission** is an extremely **gearing down** mechanism.
· The **follower gear** has **24 teeth**, and the **driver worm gear** is equivalent to **1 tooth**.
· **24 rotations** of the driver gear are needed to complete a full rotation of the follower gear.

1 tooth   24 teeth

Gearing down mechanism

Follower

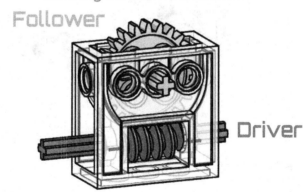

Driver

· Now you are ready to build your WeDo turtle prototype!
· Before you start building, prepare a **suitable workspace**.
· Keep in mind that the WeDo set has small pieces, so prepare a table with enough **space** to easily identify all the pieces and prevent them from getting lost.

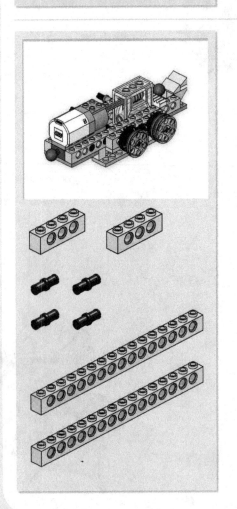

10

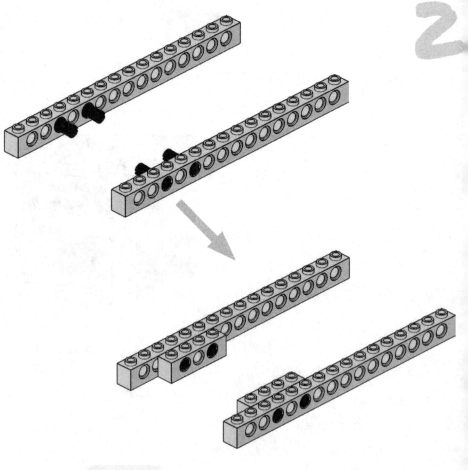

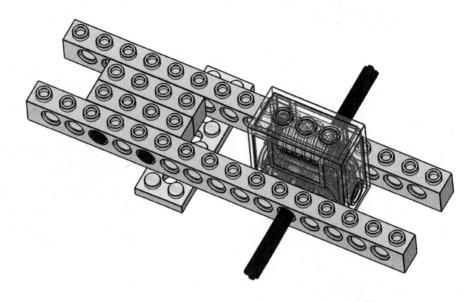

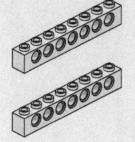

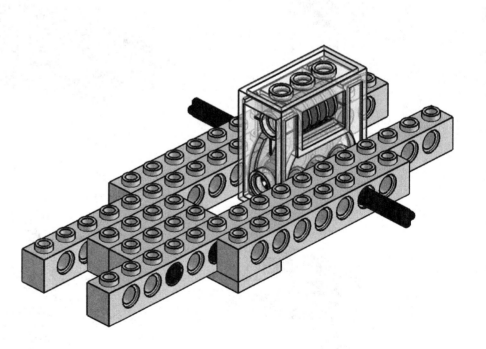

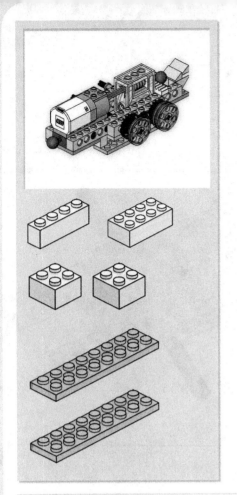

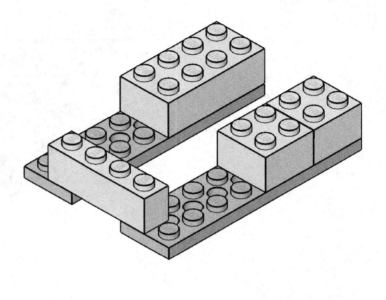

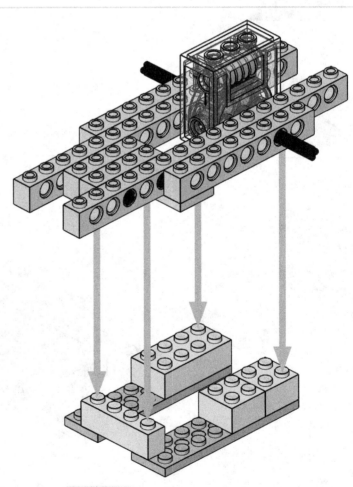

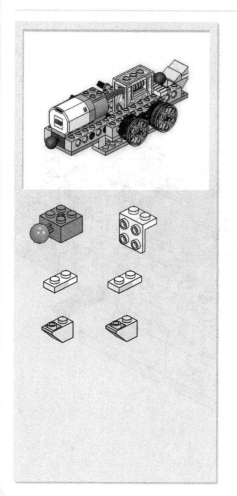

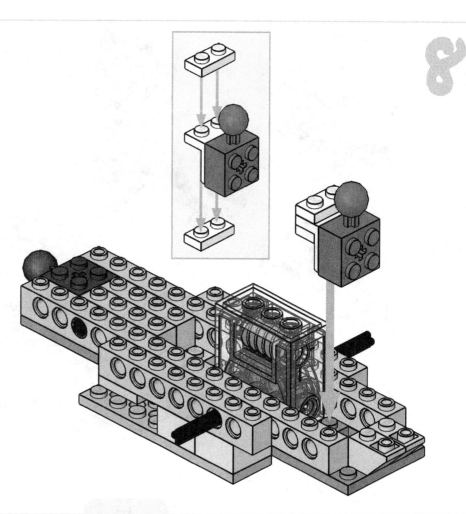

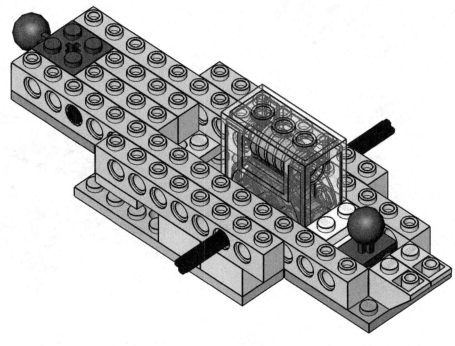

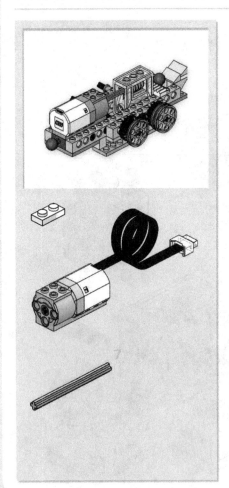

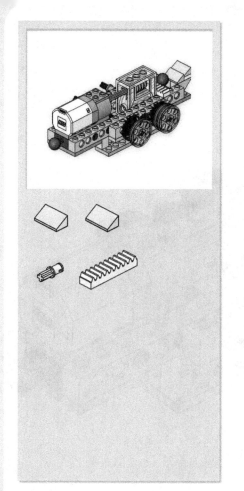

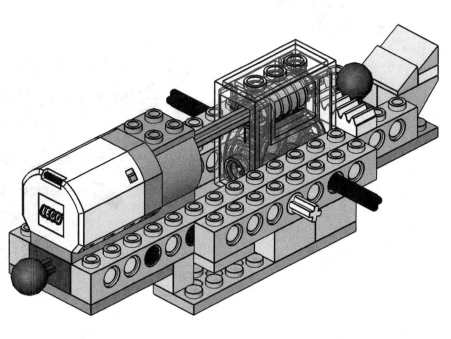

11

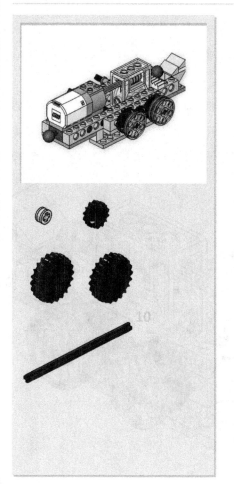

10

12

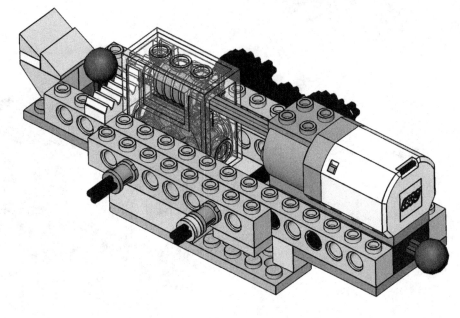

Be careful! The position in your prototype must be exactly as the one shown in the picture.

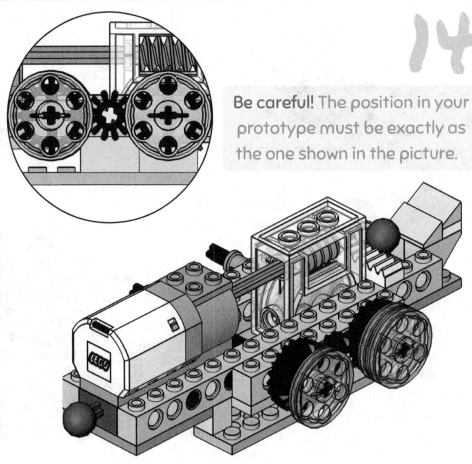

15

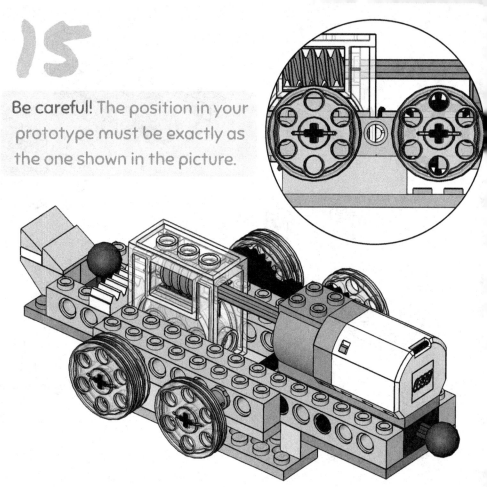

Be careful! The position in your prototype must be exactly as the one shown in the picture.

16

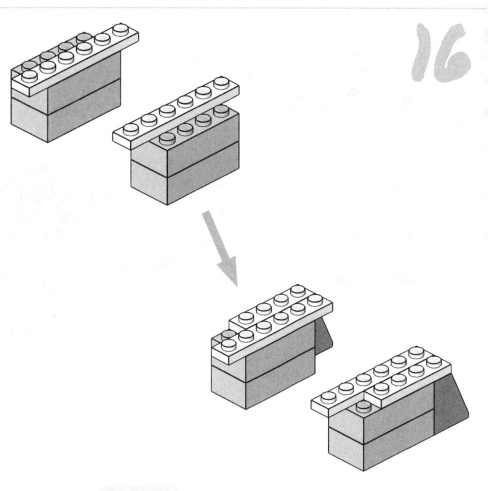

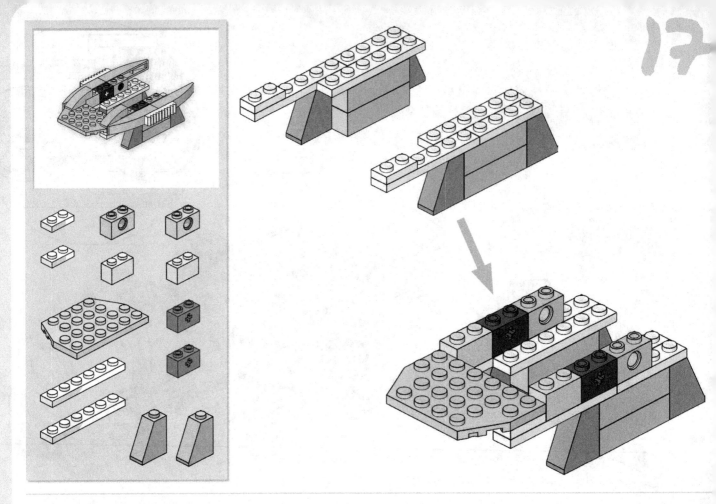

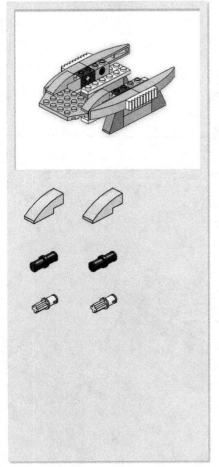

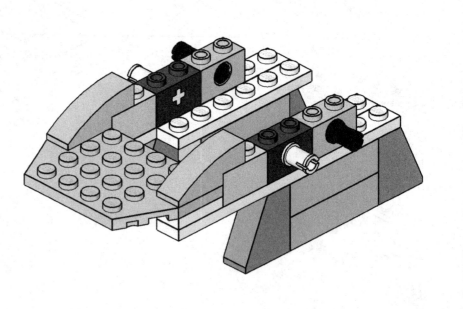

17

18

19

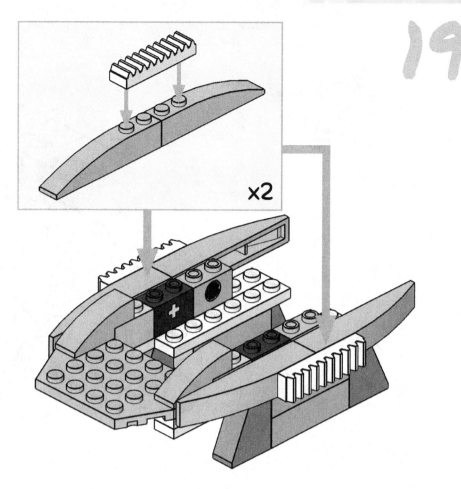

20

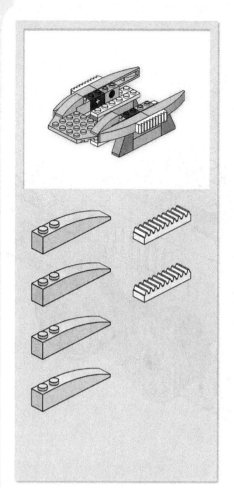

65

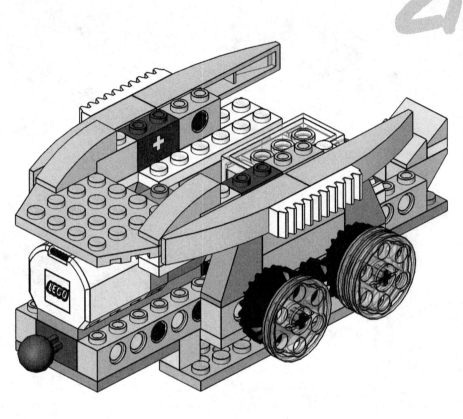

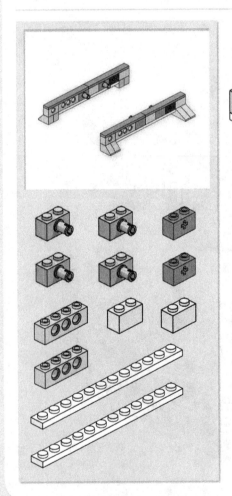

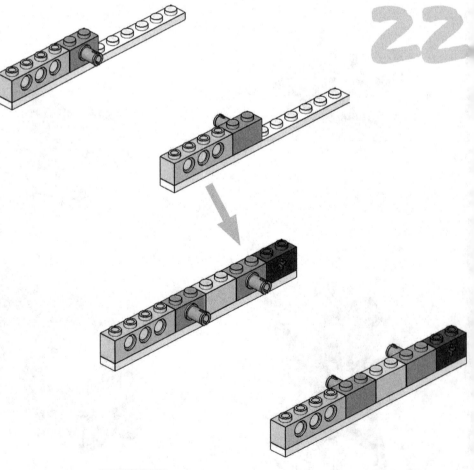

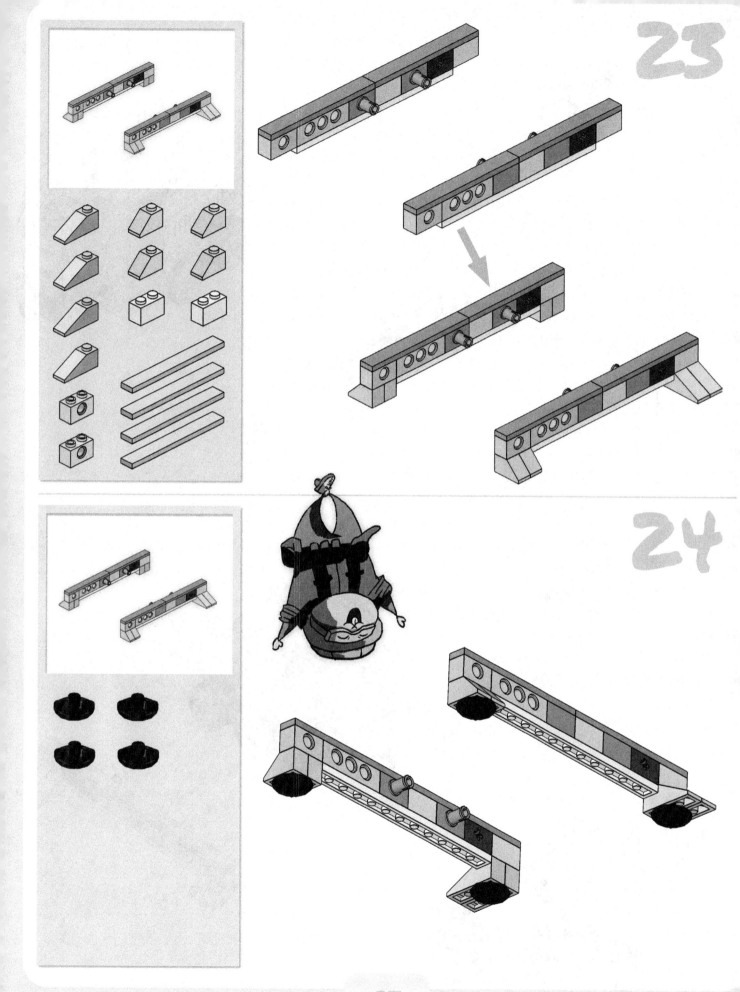

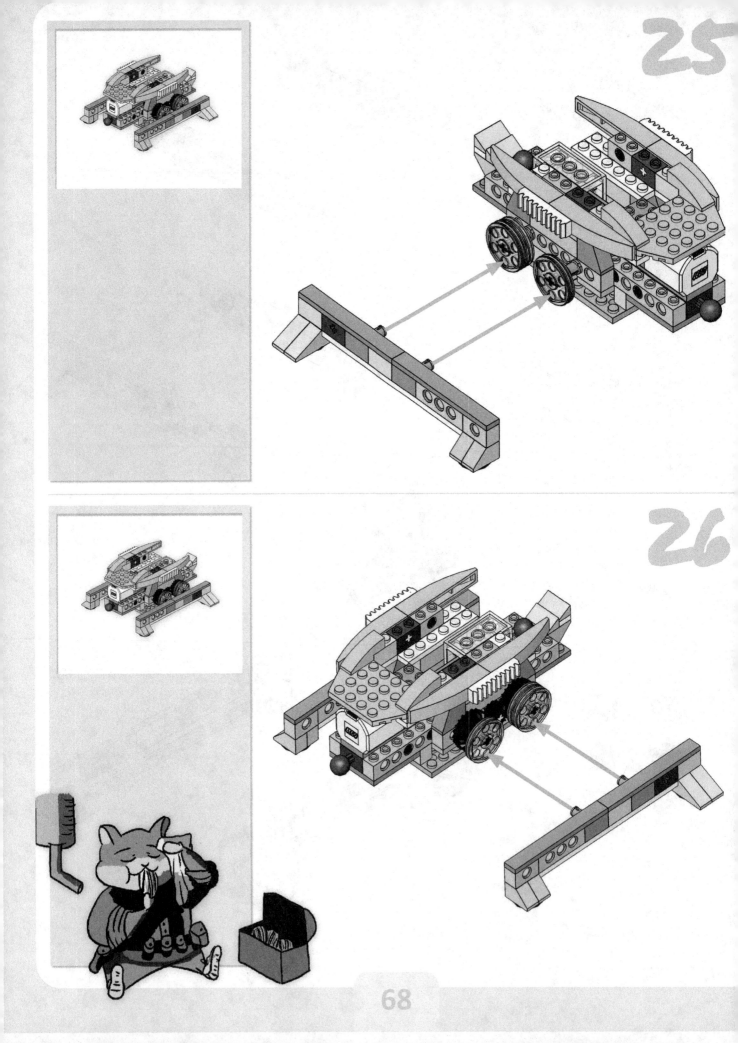

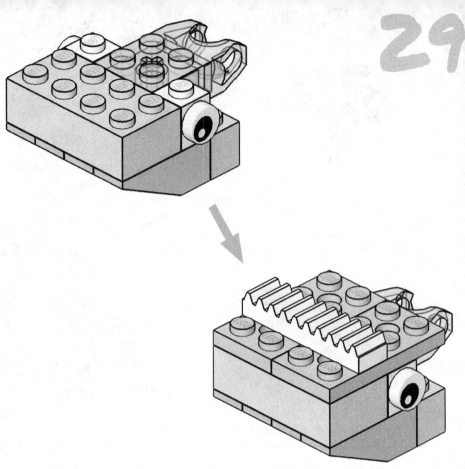

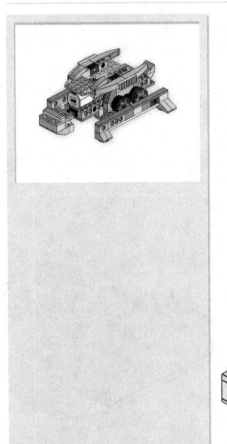

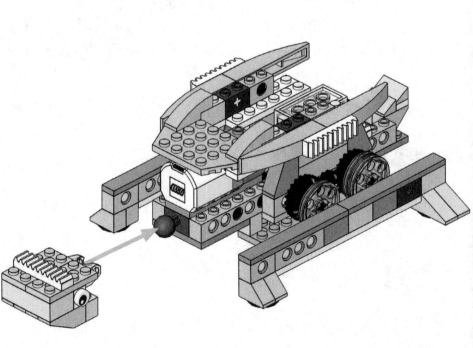

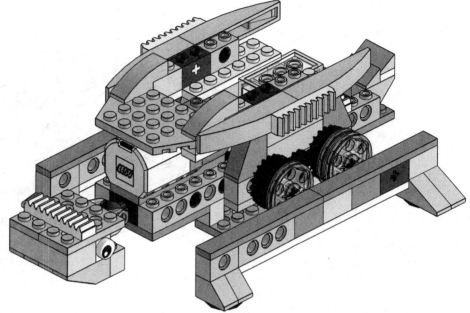

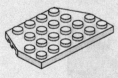

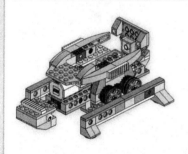

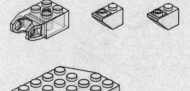

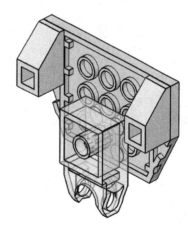

33

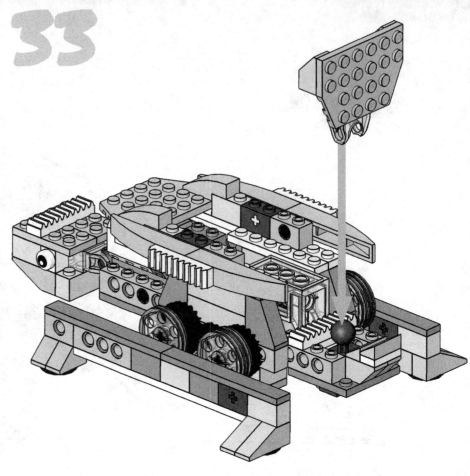

34

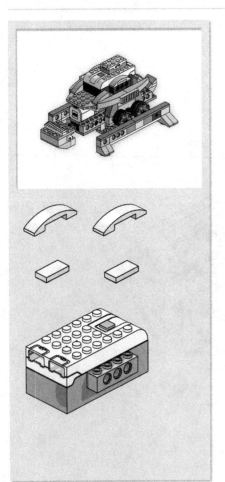

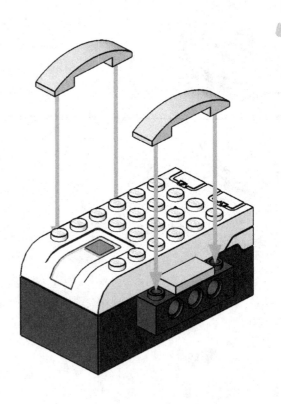

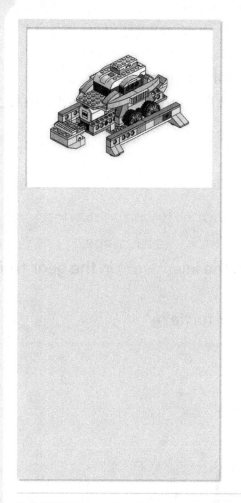

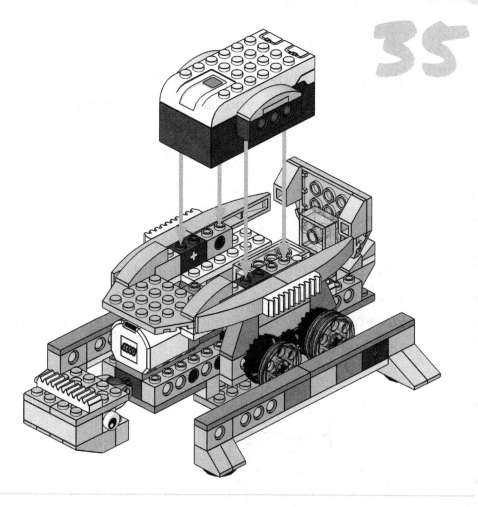

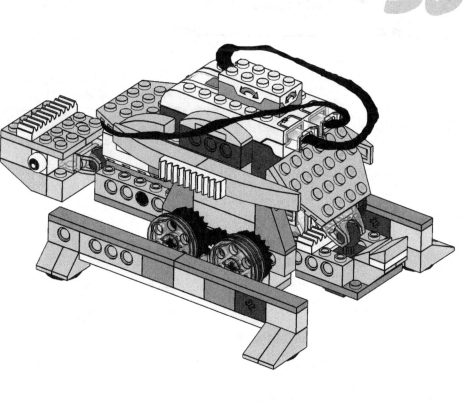

- Before going to the next phase, you can identify the mechanisms you are using in you turtle prototype.
- Can you **predict how your turtle prototype will move by only seeing the model?**
- How many **gears are you using in your turtle prototype? Remember to count the wor gear too!

Design features

- Similarly to your frog prototype, your **turtle** uses the motor to drive the two legs.
- Also, the turtle's **two legs** are disguised so that they can look like **four legs.**
- Can you identify the driver gear, **the** follower gear, **and the** idler gears **in the gear train** used in your turtle?
- Can you identify the parallel motion linkage **used in your turtle?**

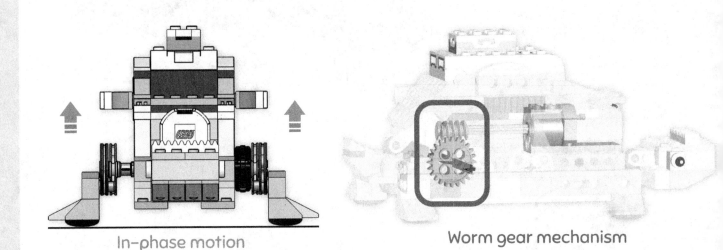

In-phase motion

Worm gear mechanism

Program phase: Tilt sensor and infinite loop

- In this section, you will explore some of the basics about **programming** the tilt sensor.
- Since this is the first time working with a sensor, let's remember the working loop of a ro bot: "**Perceive**" — "**Think**" — "**Perform**."

- Your **program idea** will be about controlling the movement of the turtle by reading the position of the tilt sensor.
- At any time, if the turtle is **standing horizontally,** it must **move forward,** and it must **stop** when it is in another position.

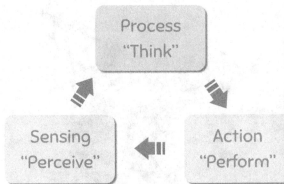

Process "Think"

Sensing "Perceive"

Action "Perform"

The **algorithm** is as follows:

· The turtle waits until it is in the "horizontal position."

· The turtle starts to move.

· The turtle continues moving until it is in "another position" different than the "horizontal position."

· The turtle stops moving.

· Go back to the turtle waiting for the "horizontal position."

Flowchart

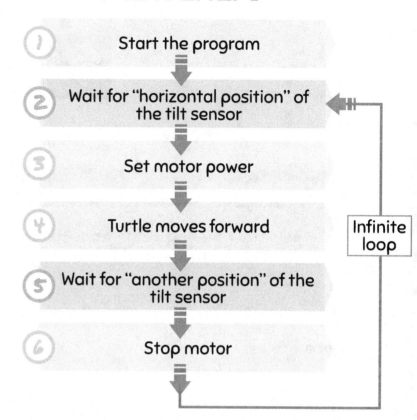

① Start the program

② Wait for "horizontal position" of the tilt sensor

③ Set motor power

④ Turtle moves forward

⑤ Wait for "another position" of the tilt sensor

⑥ Stop motor

Infinite loop

· The flowchart indicates **six tasks** and a **loop**. Therefore, we can assign a **programming block** for **each task** and a **loop block** going from the **sixth task** back to the **second task**:

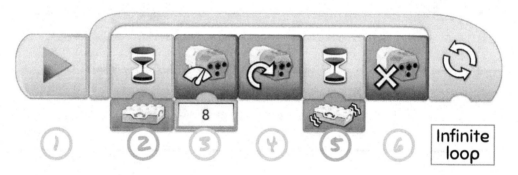

① ② ③ ④ ⑤ ⑥ Infinite loop

Block equivalences

· The **number of tasks** is not always equal to the **number of blocks**. For example, in the preceding program, **tasks 5 and 6** can be programmed using only **one motor block**:

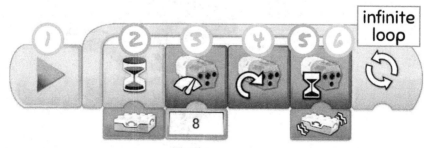

· **Task 4** indicates that your turtle goes forward. Which of **these blocks** will make your turtle go forward?

· You will find out the answer to this question on the **test phase**!

Test phase: Tilt sensor states

· Before you start testing, remember to verify the **communication** between your WeDo software and your WeDo Hub (Smart Hub).

Tilt sensor

· Once you set up the communication, you should see in the **bottom-right corner** all the **devices connected** to your Hub: one tilt sensor and one motor.
· Before running the program, move your turtle to different positions to find out how many **states** have the **tilt sensor**.

 0　 7　 5　 9　 3

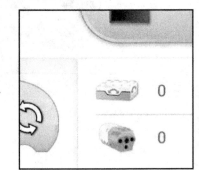

· Now you are ready to test your turtle. Execute your program developed in the **program phase** by clicking the "Start" block.

TEST 1: Finding the right motor direction

Let's find which of these two programs make your turtle move forward and backward.

76

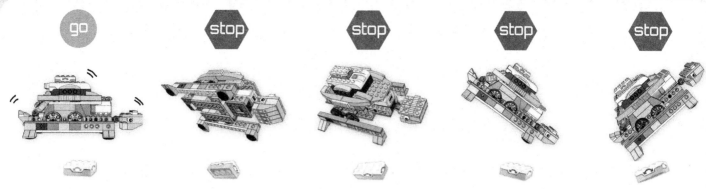

In-phase motion

- Similar to your frog, your turtle walks following an **in-phase** motion.
- In an **in-phase** motion, at any time, both legs are exactly at the same position.

TEST 2: Finding the minimum motor power to move your turtle

- Start changing the motor power value to 1 and execute the program. At what motor power does your turtle start moving? How different is this value with the one calculated for your frog?

TEST 3: 4-block program vs. 5-block program

Do you find any difference between the program using four programming blocks and the program using five programming blocks?

Does it work?

- Remember that if your answer is **no**, you can go back to the **build phase** to check any **mechanical issue** or go back to the **program phase** to check any **programming issue**.
- Also, remember to check the Smart Hub energy, since you might be running out of **battery**!

Document & share phase

- Remember to collect all your **notes**, **videos**, and **photos** to report your **findings and results** from the three tests you performed.

Enhancing the experience

- **Build:** Move the tilt sensor to the top of the head of your turtle.
- **Programming:** If your turtle's head points up, your turtle goes forward, and if the head points down, your turtle goes backward.

In the next chapter, you will explore the
mechanisms and concepts to develop
prototypes that walk using two legs!

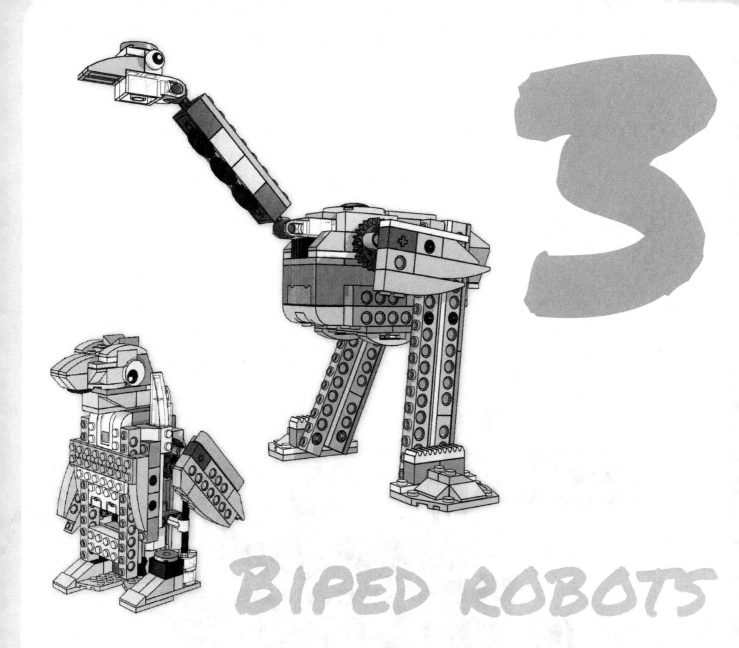

3

BIPED ROBOTS

Contents

HUMBOLDT PENGUIN

Design phase: Out-phase motion

· Remember to have a **white paper** and a **pencil** to start drawing your ideas!

Looking for inspiration

· **Humboldt penguins** are South American penguins that live on the "Ballestas Islands" in the coastal region of Peru.
· They are **medium-sized** penguins, averaging **28 inches tall** and weighing about **9 pounds**.
· Their favorite food is **anchoveta**, a small fish that thrives in the cold waters of the South American coast.

How can I design a robot to replicate the two-leg walking motion of a penguin?

Biped robots

· They are robots that use **two legs** to perform a **walking motion.**
· There are two types of biped robots: **steady biped robots** and **balance shift biped robots**.
· **Balance shift** biped robots **do require** advanced programming using sensors to balance the center of gravity.
· **Steady** biped robots **do not require** the use of sensors or an advanced programming to balance. Given their structure, **steady biped robots** are **always balanced**, avoiding falling while they walk. In this book, we only focus on the development of **steady biped robots**.
· Biped robots **interlace** their legs to walk: one leg in front of another (**walk step**).

Out-phase motion

- An out-phase motion can be used to assure that **one leg is in front of the other** after a walk step.
- An out-phase motion guarantees you that while **one leg** is moving **forward**, the **other leg** is moving **backward**.

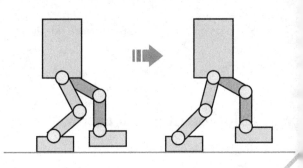

Inverted slider-crank linkage

- It is similar to a gear train; an inverted slider–crank linkage is used to **transmit rotational motion**.
- It consists of two phases: **stance phase** and **swing phase**.

On a piece of paper, you can sketch some **ideas** to replicate the penguin walking motion!

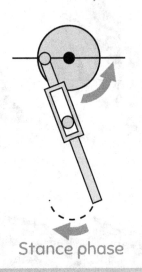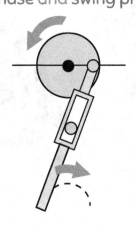

Stance phase   Swing phase

Build phase: Inverted slider-crank linkage

- Given the following building instructions, you can build your own inverted slider–crank linkage.

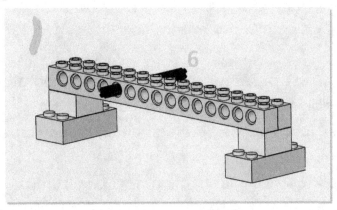

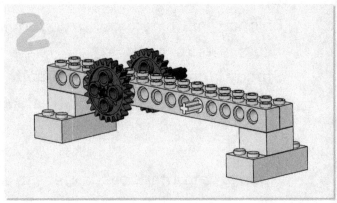

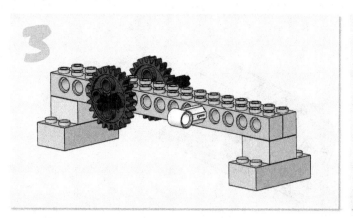 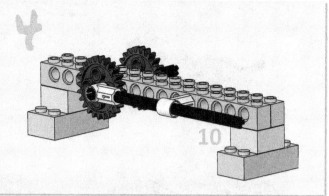

· Turn the gear to see how the axle tip of the opposite side moves.

Swing phase

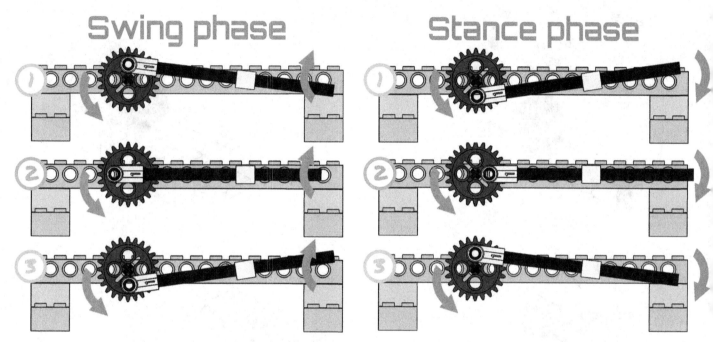

Stance phase

Bevel gears

· Bevel gears operate in **not parallel axles**.

· They can be used as **gearing down** or **gearing up** mechanism when gears of different sizes are used.

· Usually, bevel gears are made for **perpendicular axles** (90 degrees); however, they can be also made for **any other angle**.

Follower   Driver

Gearing down mechanism using bevel gears

· Now you are ready to build your WeDo penguin prototype!

· Before you start building, prepare a **suitable workspace**.

· Keep in mind that the WeDo set has small pieces, so prepare a table with enough space to easily identify all the pieces and prevent them from getting lost.

Building instructions

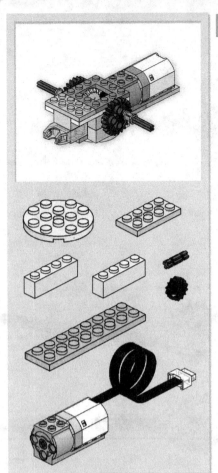

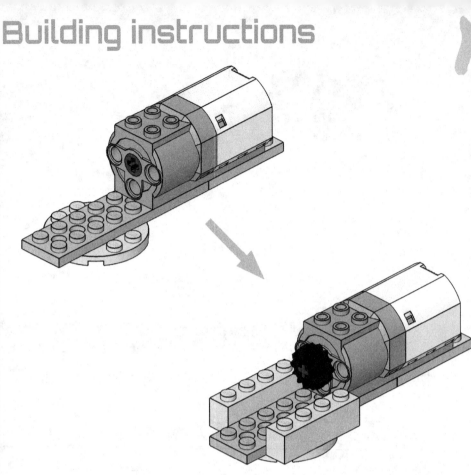

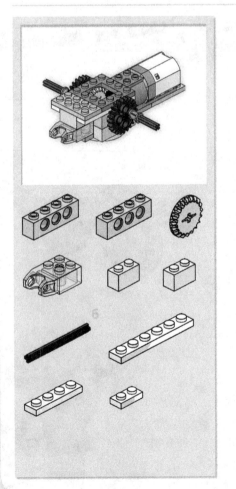

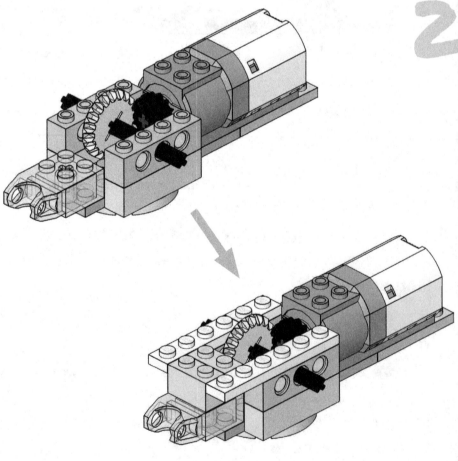

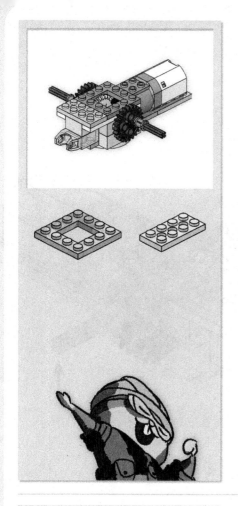

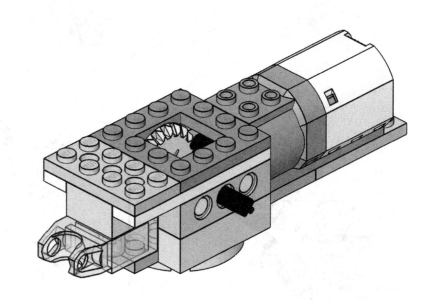

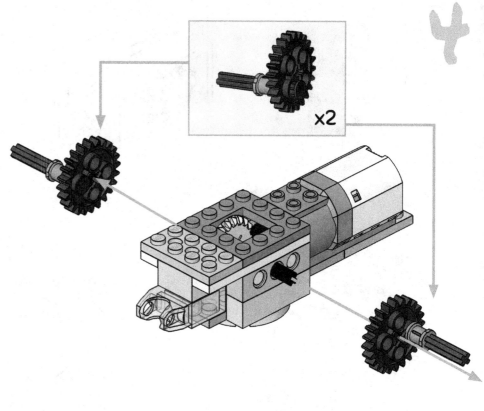

×2

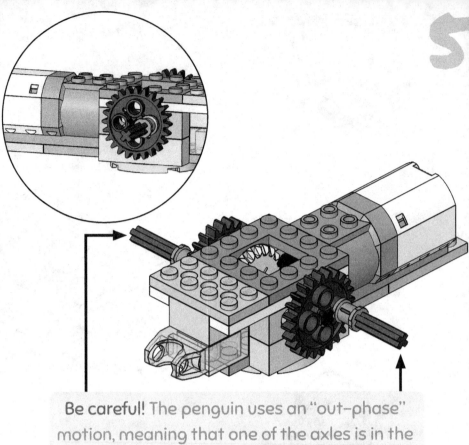

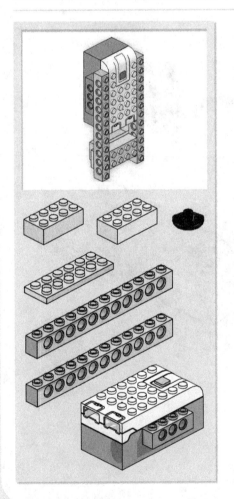

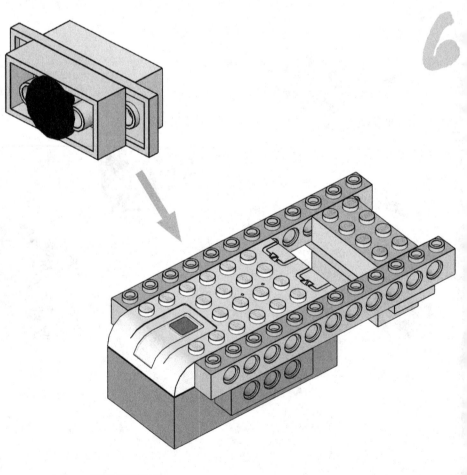

Be careful! The penguin uses an "out-phase" motion, meaning that one of the axles is in the opposite position of the other one.

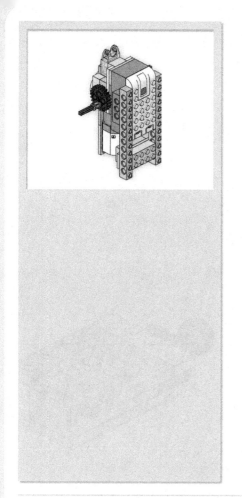

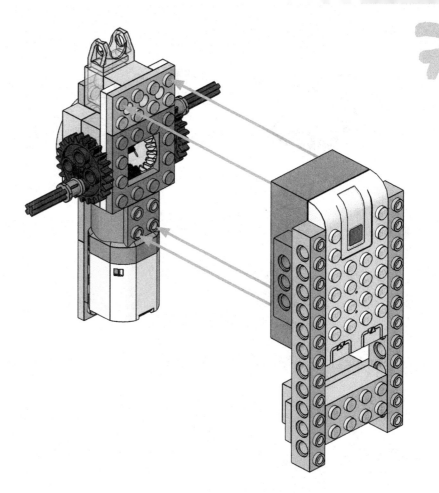

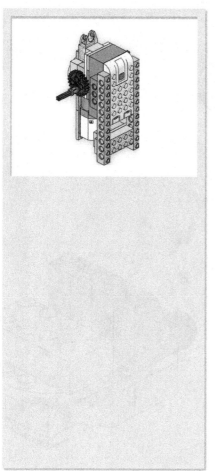

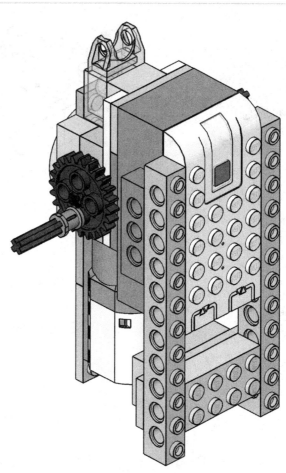

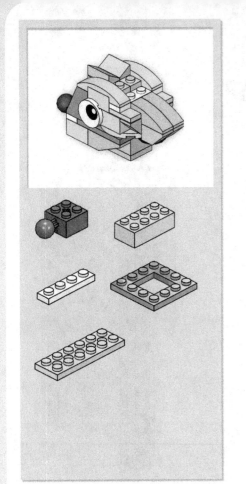

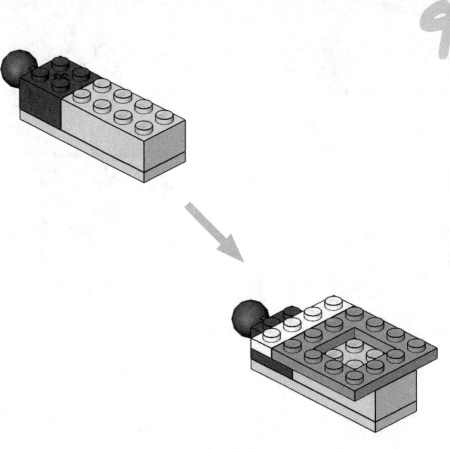

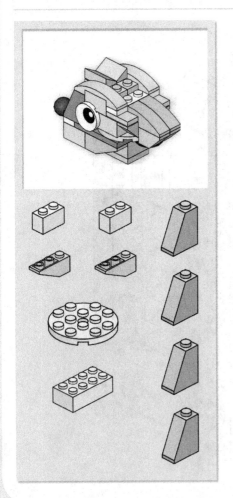

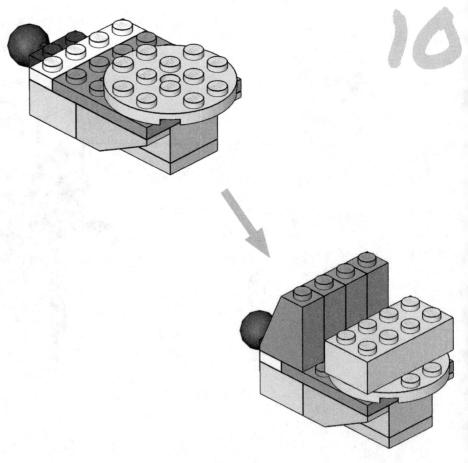

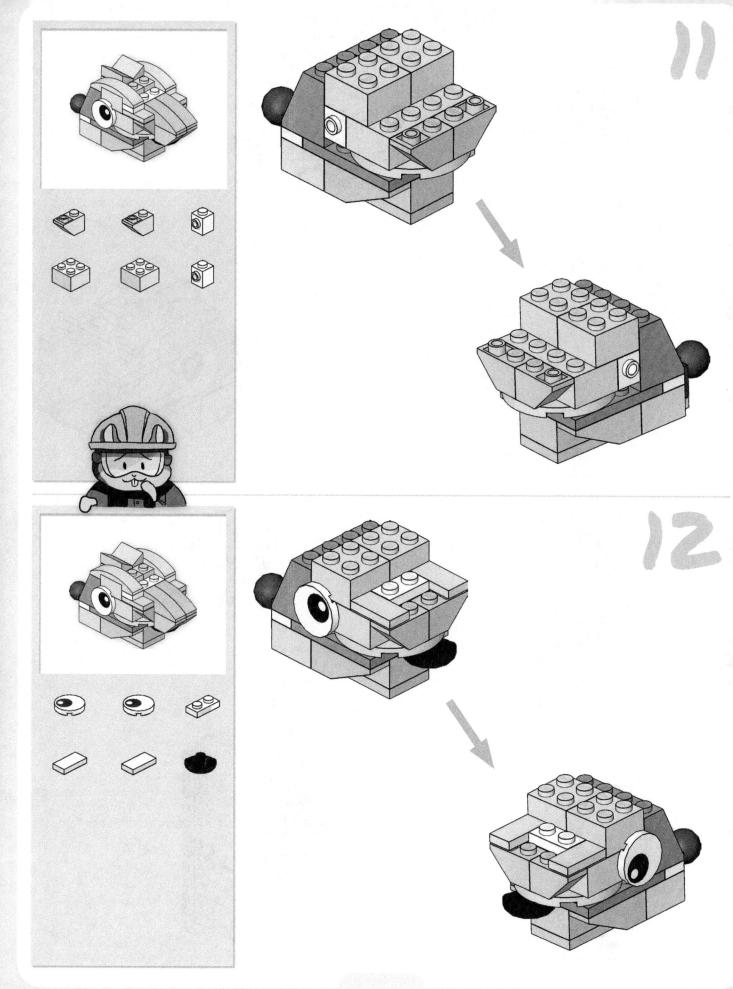

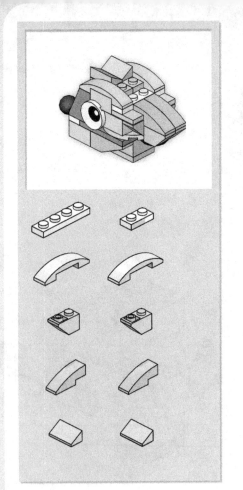

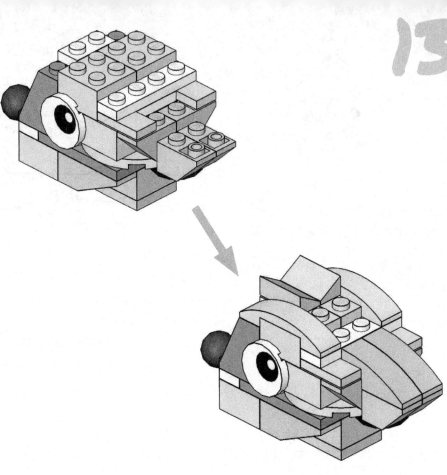

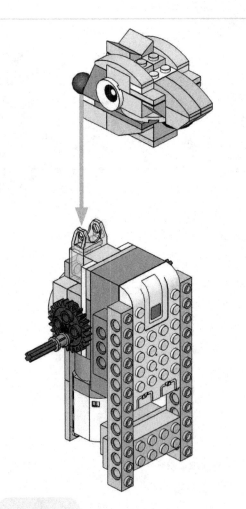

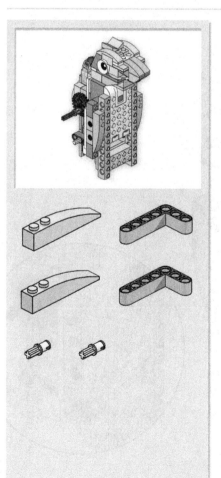

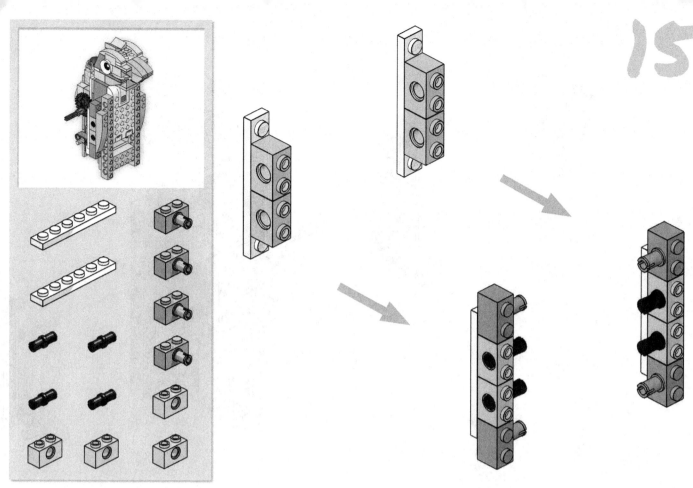

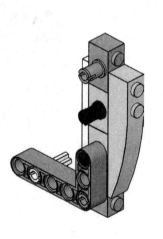

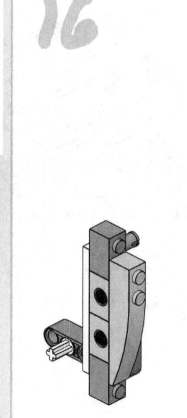

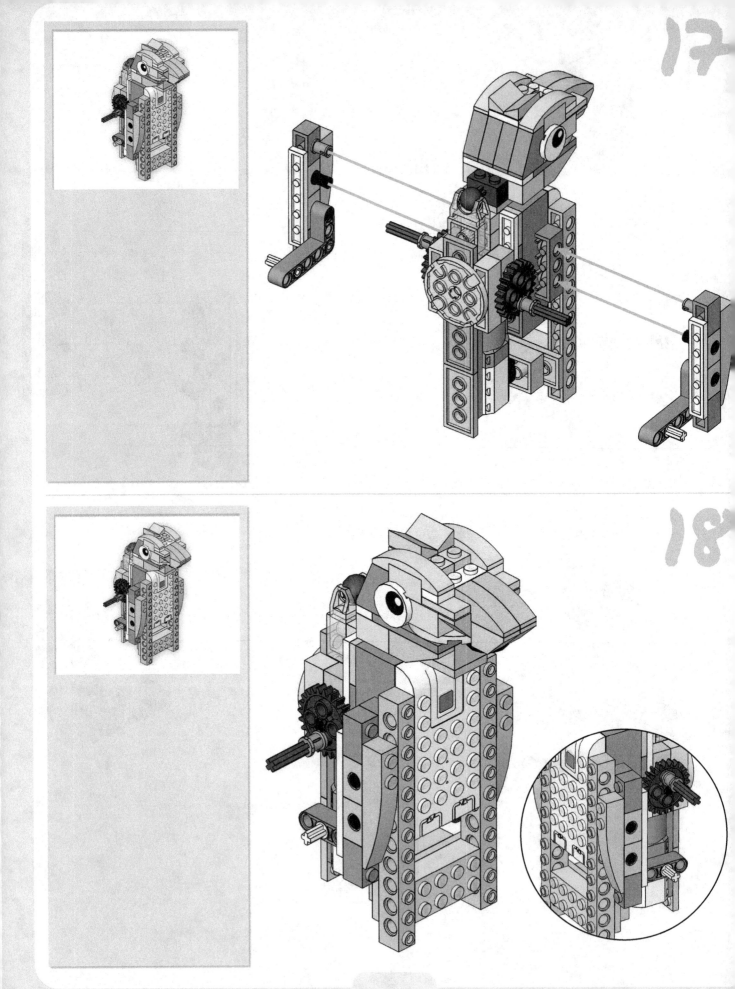

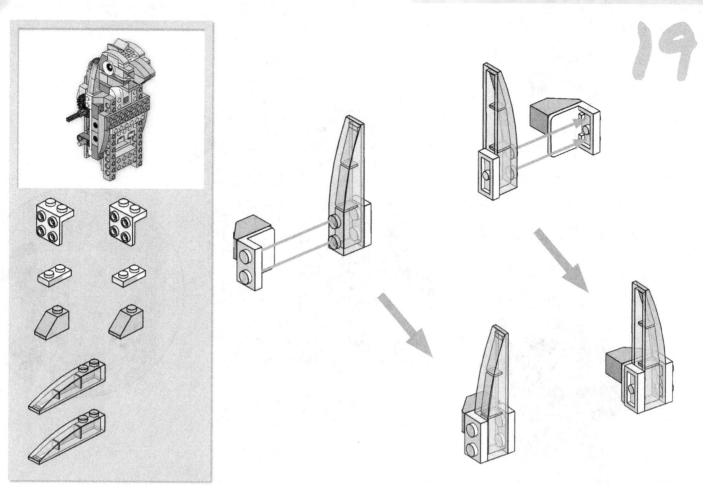

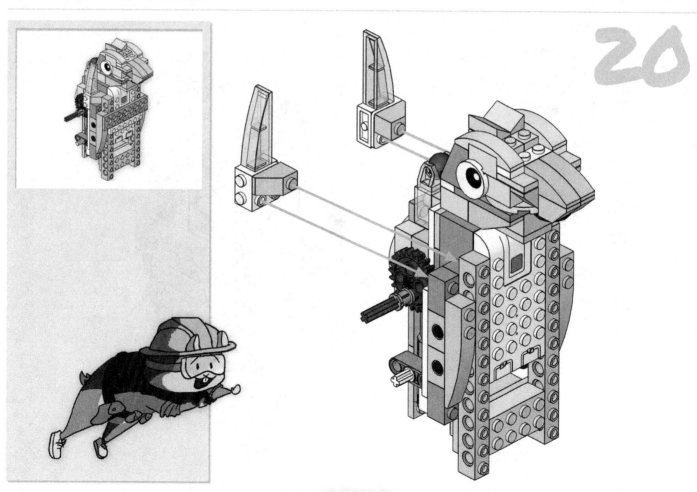

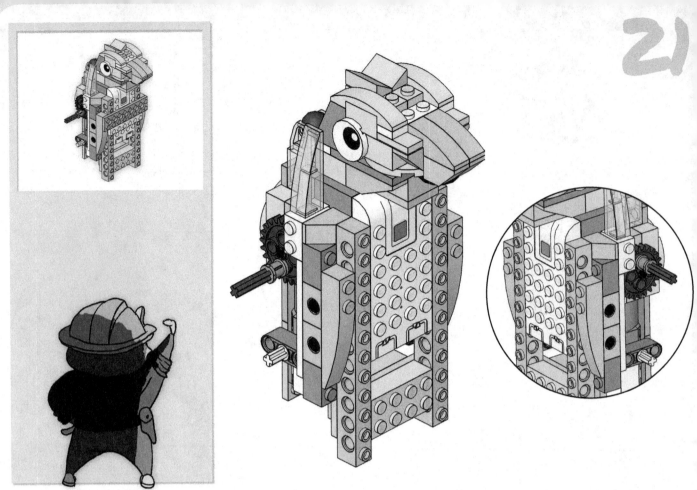

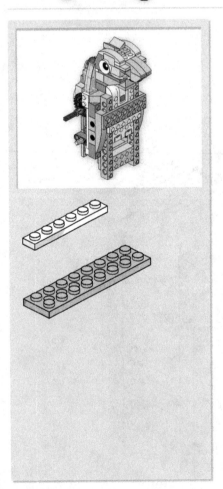

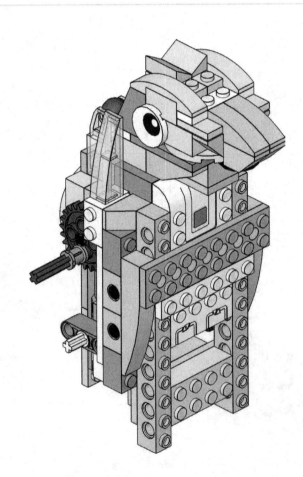

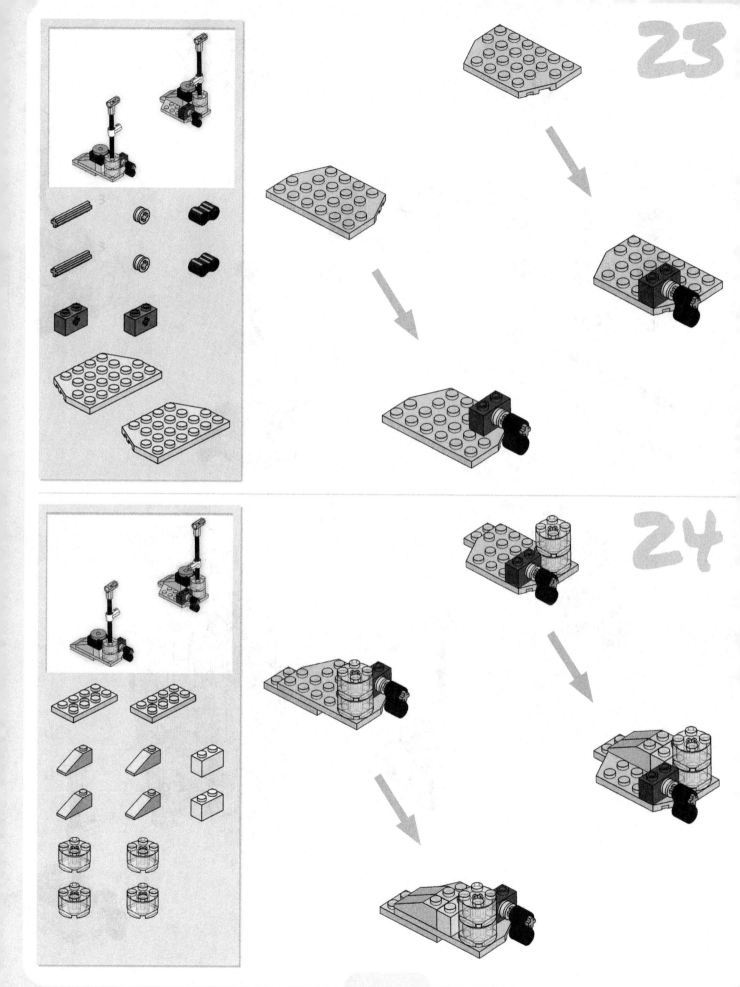

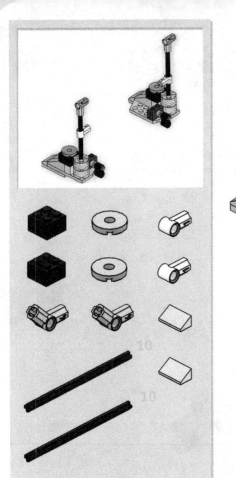

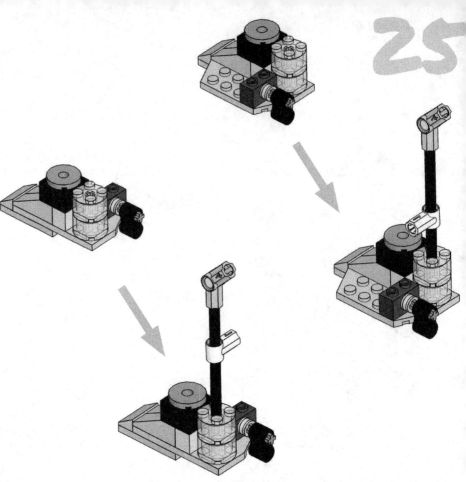

25

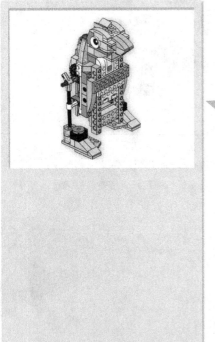

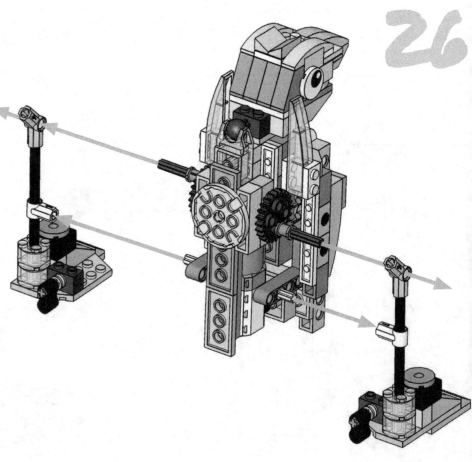

26

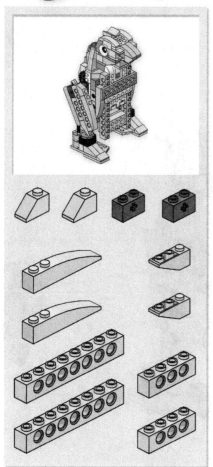

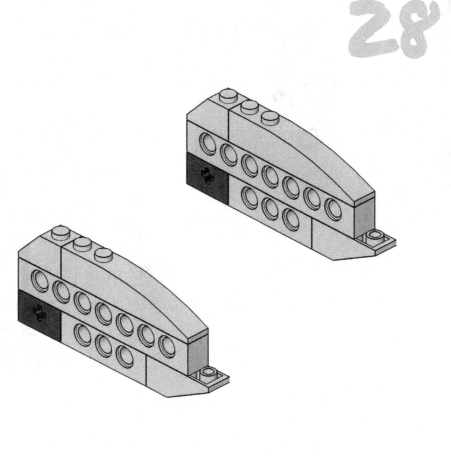

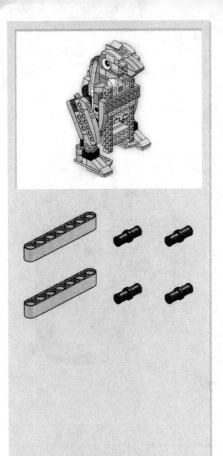

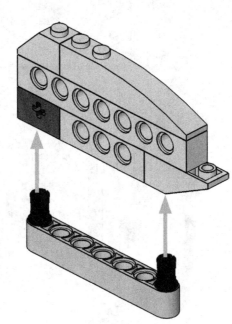

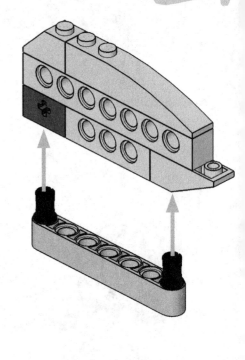

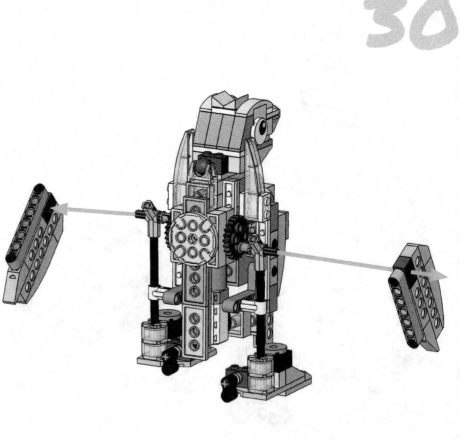

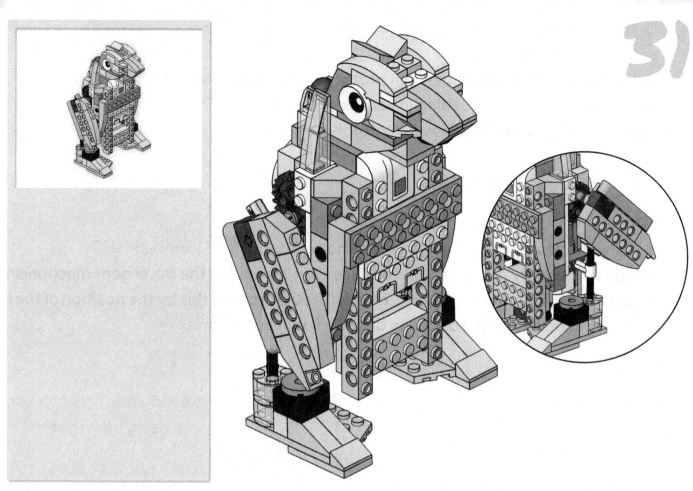

31

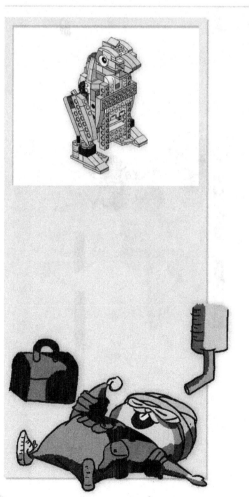

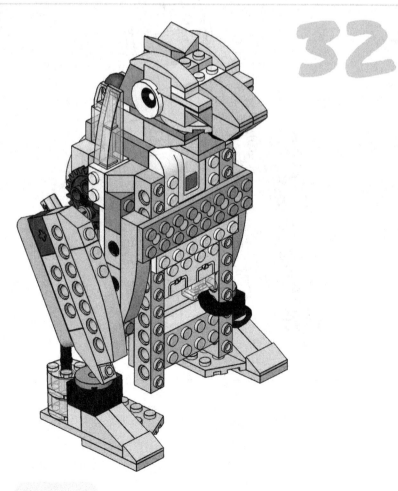

32

· Before going to the next phase, you can identify the mechanisms you are using in you penguin prototype.

· Can you predict how your penguin prototype will move by only seeing the model?

· How many gears are you using in your penguin prototype?

· How many legs does your penguin prototype have?

Design features

· Your penguin uses the motor to drive the two legs.

· Can you identify the bevel gears and the inverted slider–crank linkage?

· Can you identify the driver gear and the follower gear in the bevel gear mechanism?

· Are the two legs in an out-phase motion? You can check this by the position of the legs. One leg should be in the opposite direction of the other one.

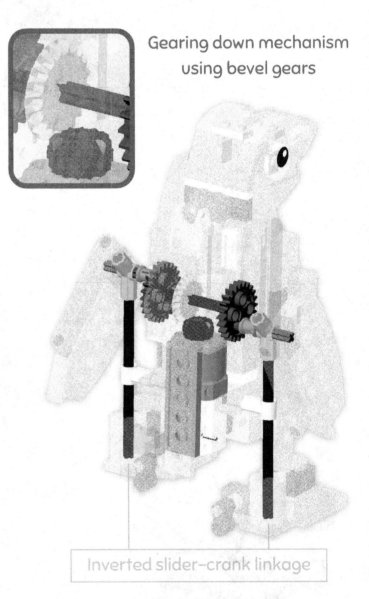

Gearing down mechanism
using bevel gears

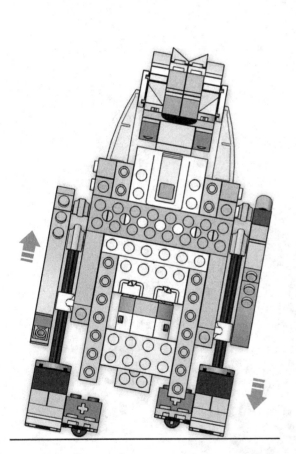

Out–phase motion

Inverted slider–crank linkage

- In this section, you will explore the use of finite loop to perform repetitively tasks.
- The **program idea** consists of moving your penguin back and forth.
- In a more detailed way, your penguin will move forward for 4 seconds, then backward for another 4 seconds, then forward again for 4 seconds, and finally backward for another 4 seconds.

Flowchart

1. Start the program
2. Set motor power
3. Penguin moves forward
4. Wait for 4 seconds
5. Penguin moves backward
6. Wait for 4 seconds
7. Penguin moves forward
8. Wait for 4 seconds
9. Penguin moves backward
10. Wait for 4 seconds
11. Penguin stops

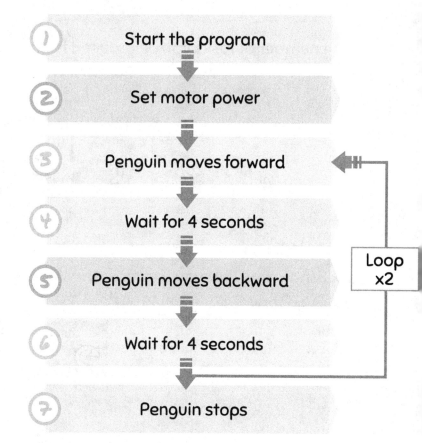

1. Start the program
2. Set motor power
3. Penguin moves forward
4. Wait for 4 seconds
5. Penguin moves backward
6. Wait for 4 seconds
7. Penguin stops

Loop x2

You can use finite loops to avoid repetition of programming blocks! In the example, both flowcharts list the same tasks, but using a finite loop we can reduce the number of tasks from 11 to 7!

· The first flowchart indicates **11 tasks**. Therefore, we can assign a **programming block** for each task:

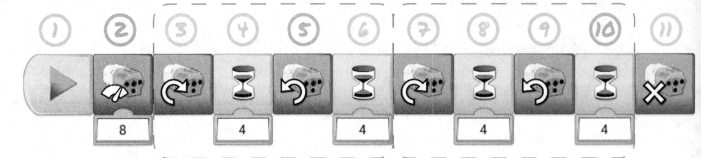

Using a finite loop

· The **number of tasks** can be reduced from 11 to 7 using a finite loop block:

· **Task 3** indicates that your penguin should go forward. Which of **these blocks** will make your penguin **go forward**?

· You will find out the answer to this question on the **test phase**!

Test phase: Controlling motor direction

· Remember to verify the **communication** between your WeDo software and your WeDo Hub before you start testing your prototype.

· Start testing your prototype by executing the program developed in the **program phase** by clicking the "Start" block.

TEST 1: Finding the right motor direction
· Identify in which direction your motor has to rotate to make your penguin move forward and backward.

TEST 2: 11–block program vs. 7–block program

· Do you find any difference between the program using 11 programming blocks and the program using 7 programming blocks?

TEST 3: Friction to walk

· Remove the rubber parts located at the bottom of your penguin legs:

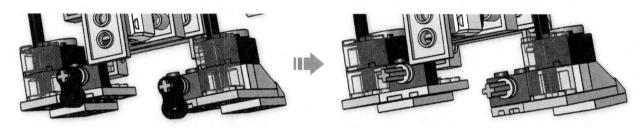

· Execute your program and test how your penguin moves without the rubber parts. Does it walk better or worse?

Friction: Why is it useful?

· **Friction** is the force that resists the sliding of one solid object over another. Thanks to friction, you can walk without slipping.
· **Rubber materials** present higher friction than **plastic materials**, which makes your penguin walk better when it is using a rubber piece.

Document & share phase

· Remember to collect all your **notes**, **videos**, and **photos** to report your **findings and results**.
· Record a video of your penguin moving with and without the rubber parts and make a comparison.
· Write your findings and results obtained from the **three tests** performed in the **test phase**.

Enhancing the experience

· **Build:** You can try to build different legs for your penguin and see if it can walk.
· **Programming:** Program different motor power when your penguin is moving back and forth.

AMERICAN RHEA

Design phase: Stable motion

· Remember to have a **white paper** and a **pencil** to start drawing your ideas!

Looking for inspiration

· **American rheas** are a species of flightless birds native to eastern South America.
· They are the **largest** South American **birds** and are related to **ostriches** and **emus**.
· They use their long, **powerful legs** to outrun trouble.
· Their **wings** are used to **change direction** while running, helping them to keep their balance at any moment.

Wow, American rheas are extremely fast when they run!

· On a piece of paper, you can sketch some **ideas** to replicate the American rhea's running motion!
· There is a concept that you have to keep in mind while designing a walking robot: **center of gravity**.

Center of gravity

· The **center of gravity** of an object is the point at which its **weight** is evenly dispersed and all sides are **in balance**.
· You can **change** your **center of gravity** if you move your body in different positions. For example, try standing using only one leg; is it more difficult to keep the balance than standing using your two legs?
· When you design a walking robot, you have to keep the concept of **center of gravity** in mind, since the legs of your robot will be moving to make it walk. At all times, your robot must keep its balance while walking to avoid falling.

· Let's explore more the concept of the center of gravity.

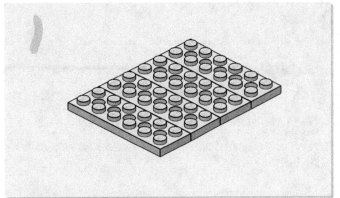

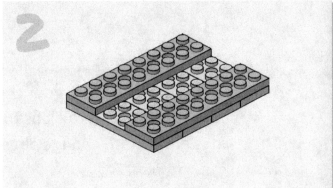

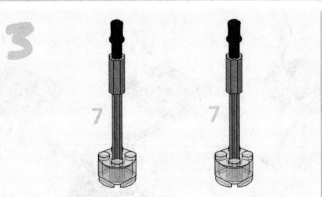

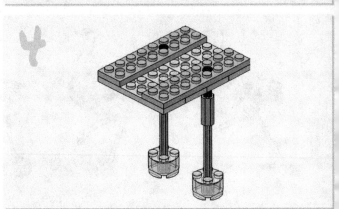

Keeping the balance

· Let's see if your structure can keep its balance for different positions.

· Change the **position of the legs** as shown in the following:

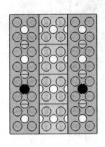 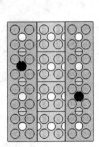 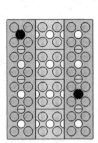 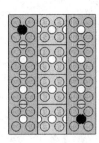 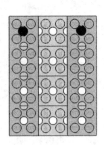 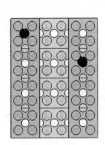

· Does it keep its balance in all **six cases**?

· Why in some cases the structure does not fall and in others it does? The answer is the **location** of the **center of gravity**.

· So, how can you solve this falling issue? Well, there are **two possible solutions**: one is modifying the body, making it smaller, and the other solution is increasing the **contact area** between the legs and the ground.

· Modify the legs to increase the **contact area** with the ground.

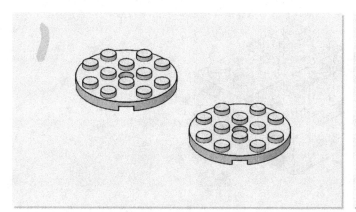

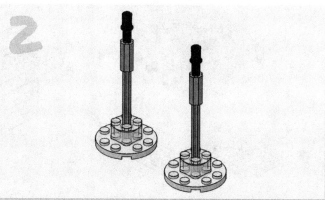

Improving the stability

· Try again testing all the different positions of the legs. Does it keep falling?
· Since we have increased the **contact area** between your structure and the ground, the **center of gravity** is now always located between the legs, **avoiding falling**.

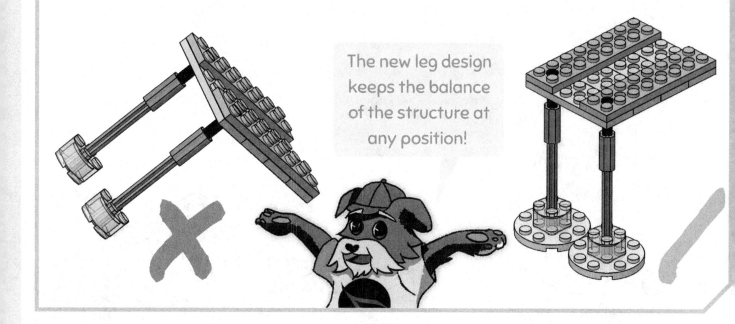

The new leg design keeps the balance of the structure at any position!

· Now you are ready to build your WeDo American rhea prototype!
· Before you start building, be sure to prepare a **suitable workspace**.
· Keep in mind that the WeDo set has small pieces, so prepare a table with enough space to easily identify all the pieces and prevent them from getting lost.

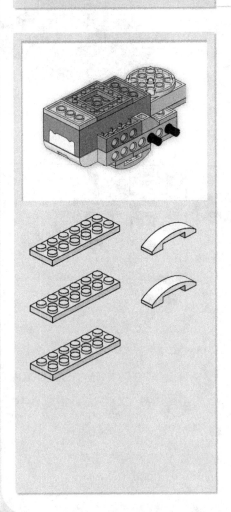

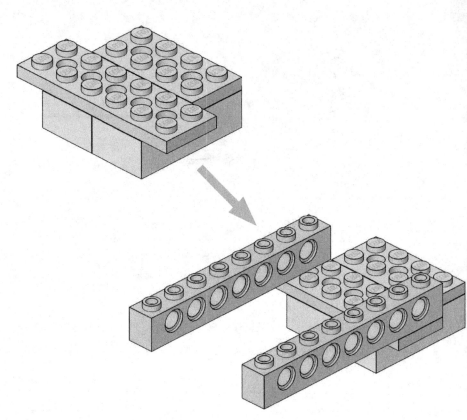

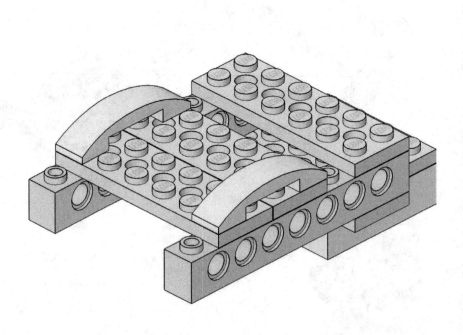

2

Flip your prototype upside down to have the same view.

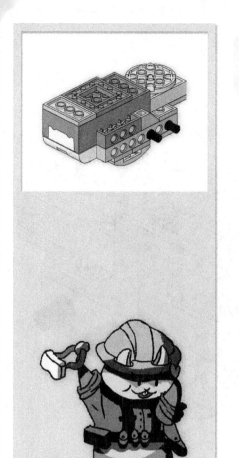

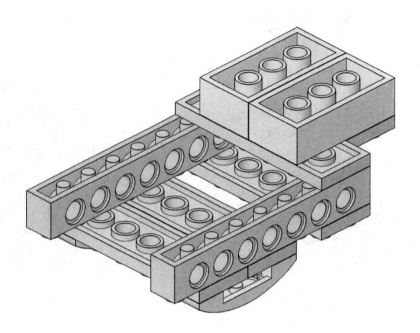

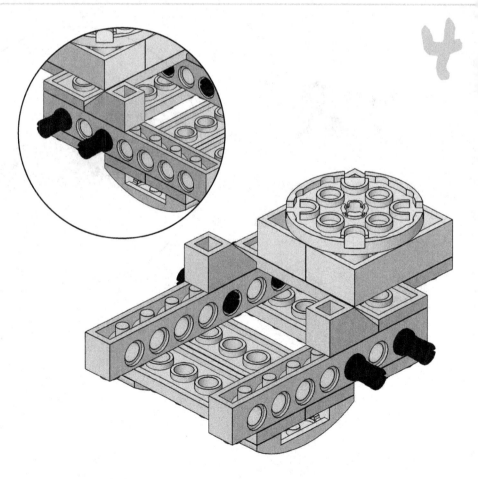

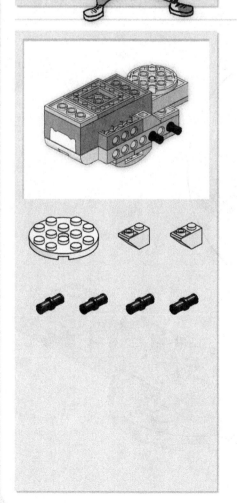

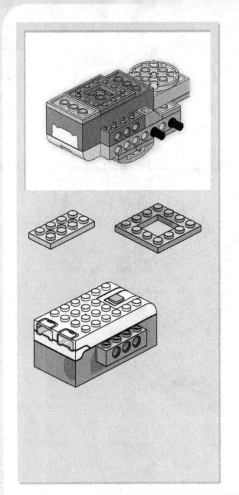

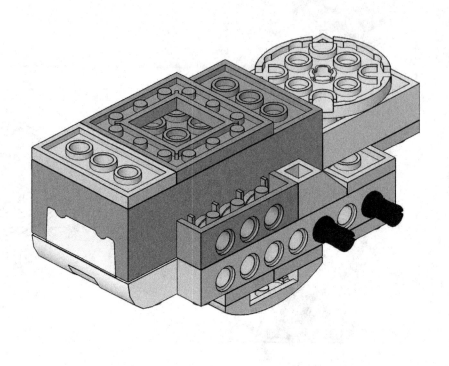

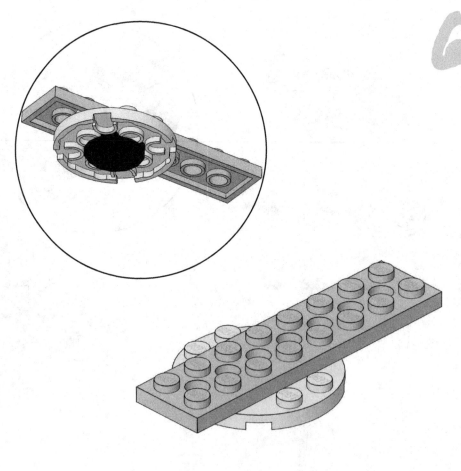

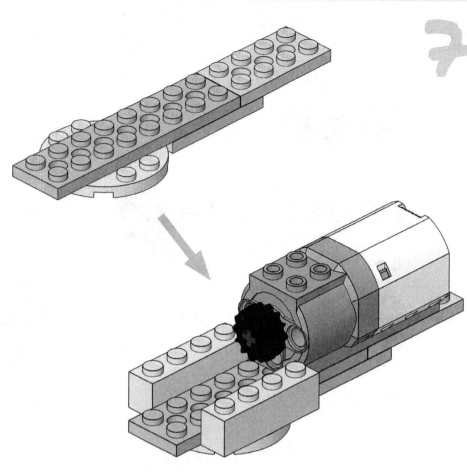

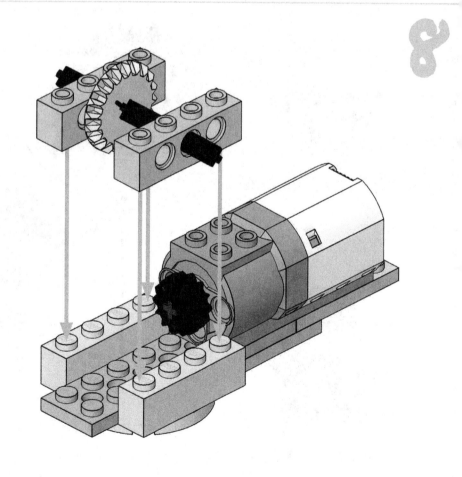

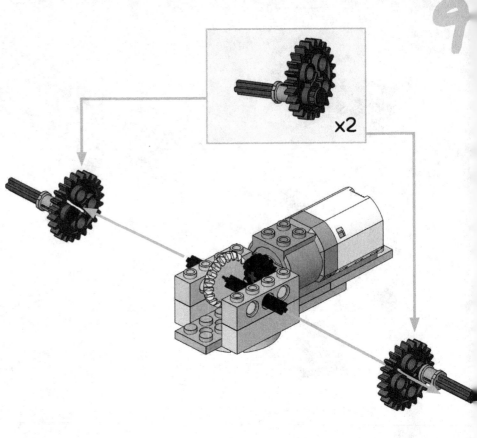

x2

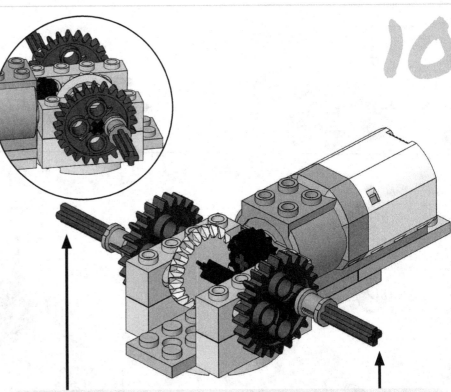

10

STOP

Be careful! The American rhea uses an "out-phase" motion, which means that one of the axles is in the opposite position of the other one.

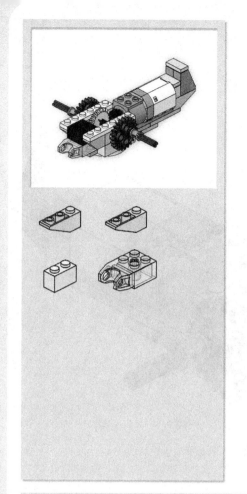

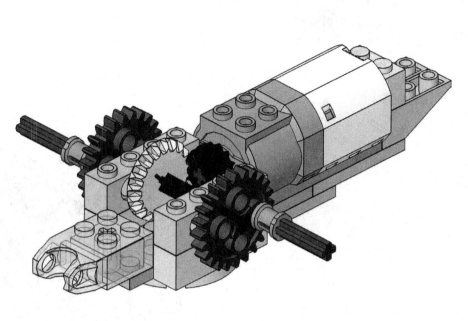

11

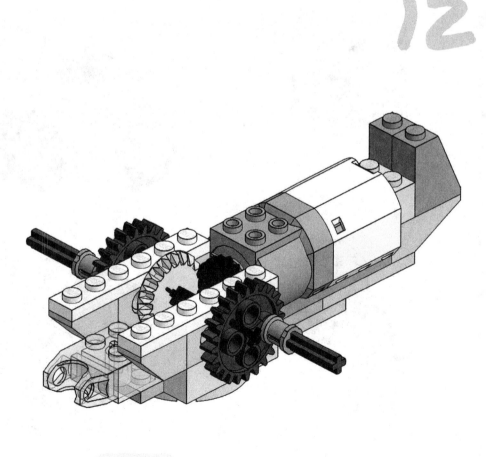

12

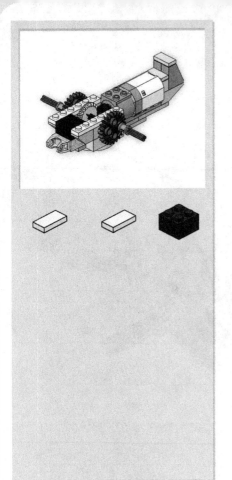

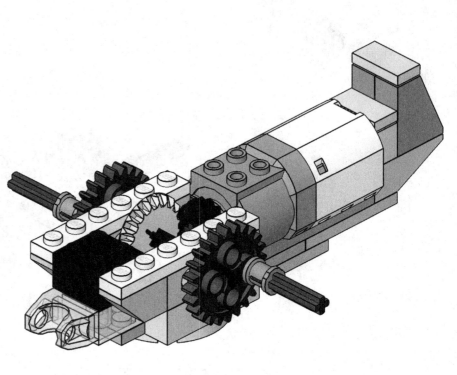

13

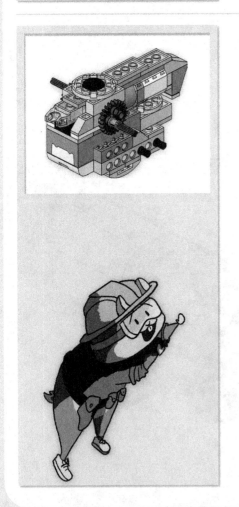

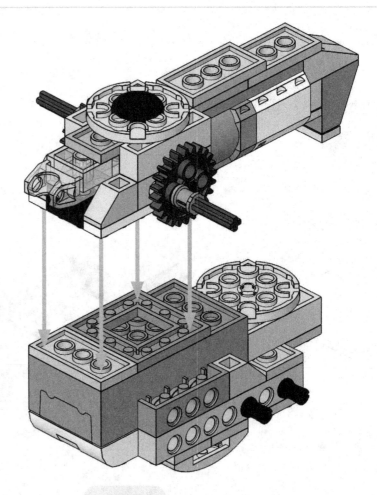

14

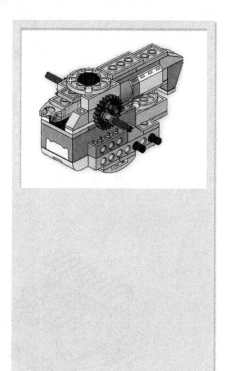

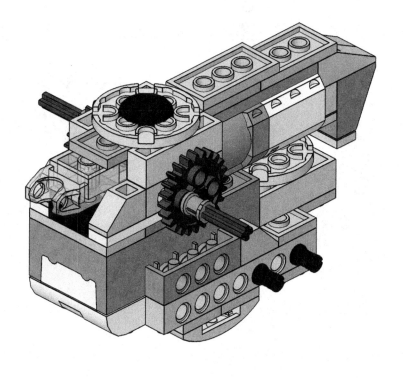

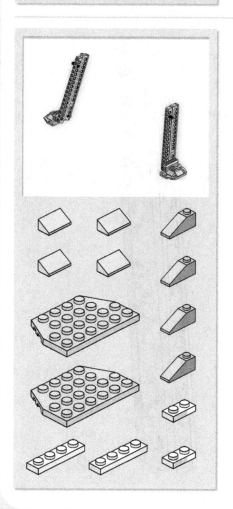

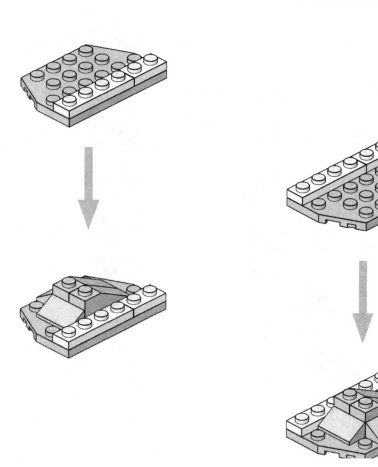

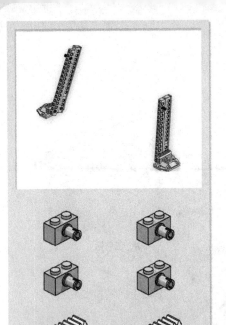

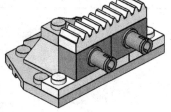

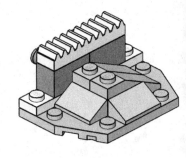

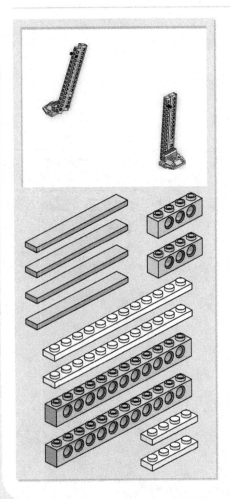

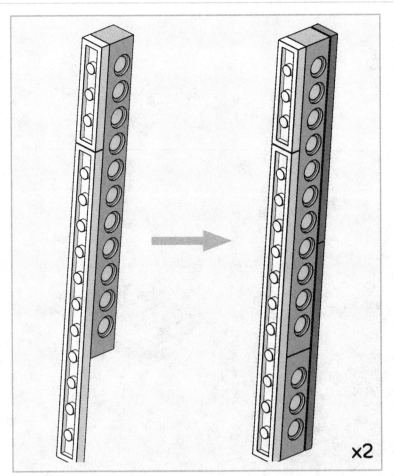

x2

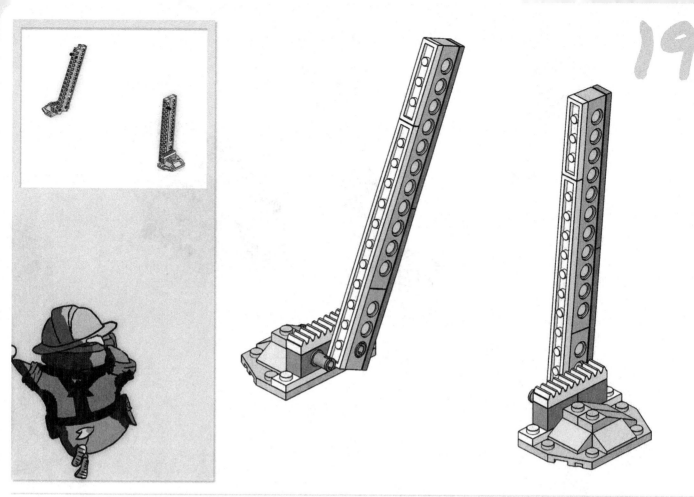

19

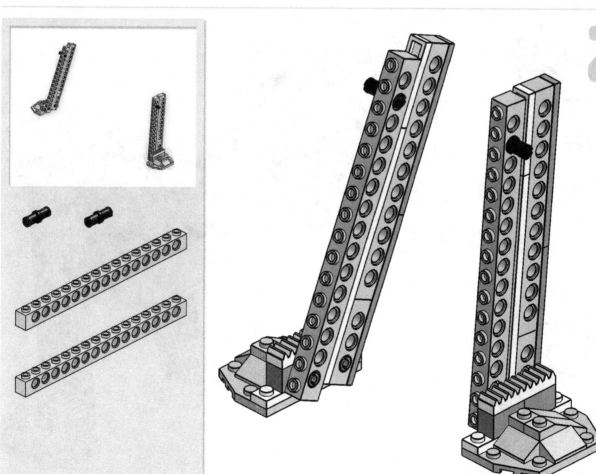

20

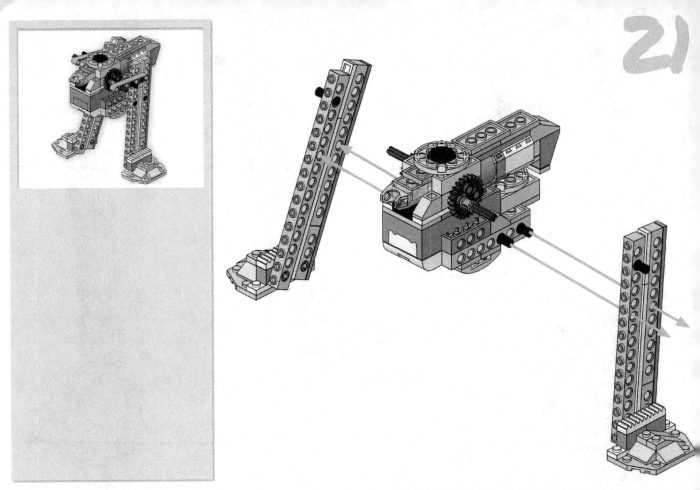

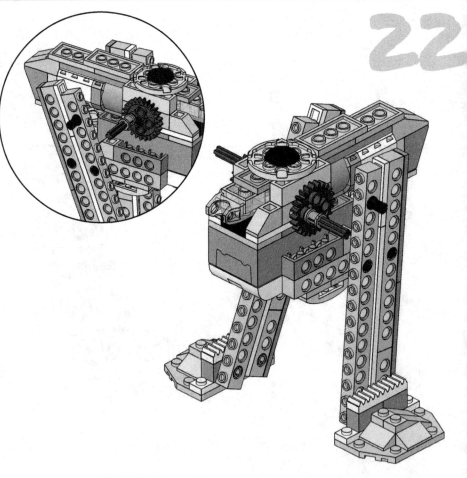

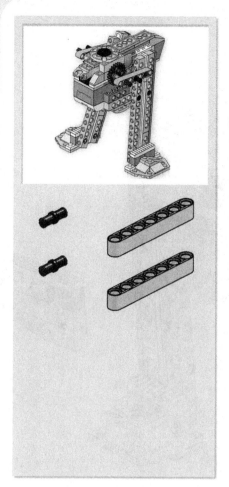

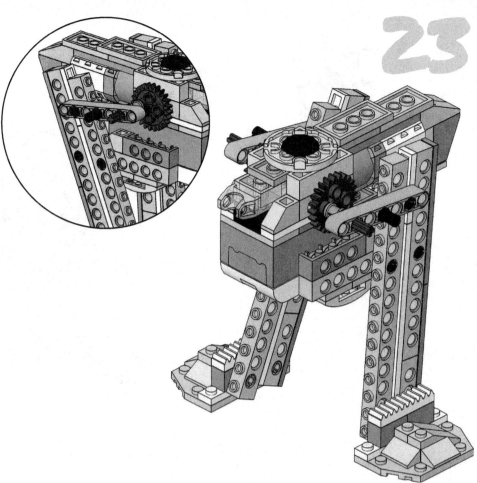

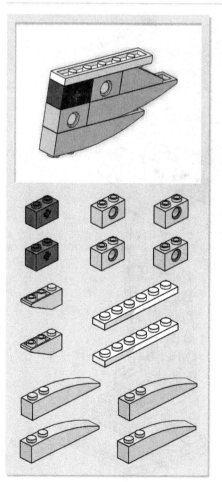

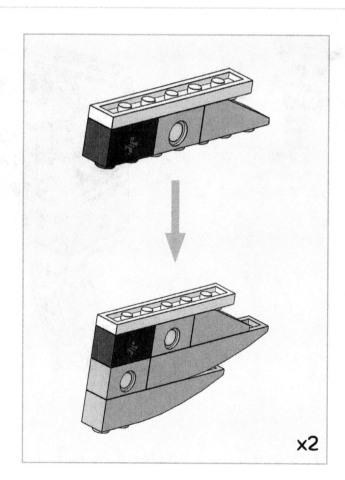

x2

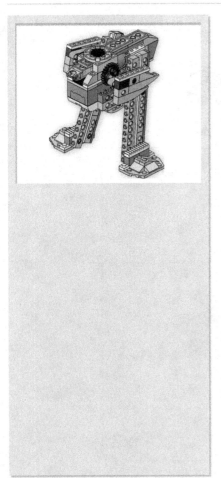

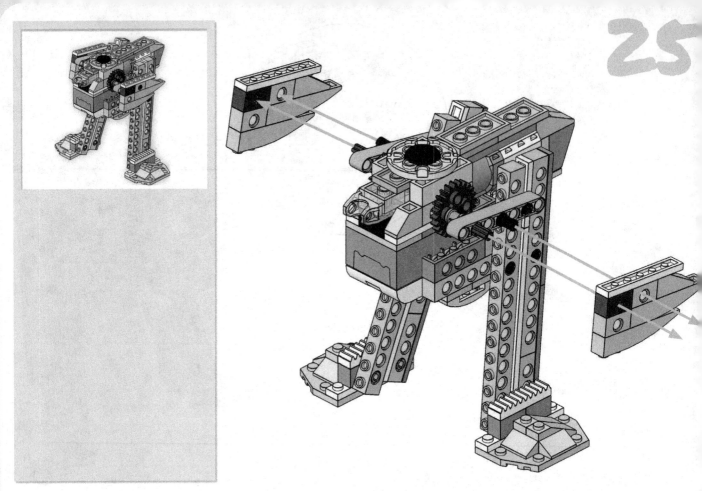

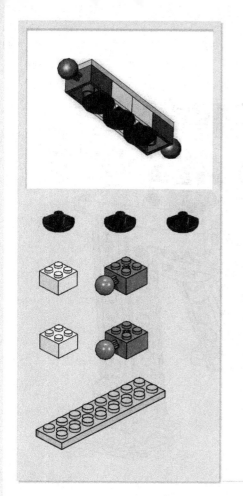

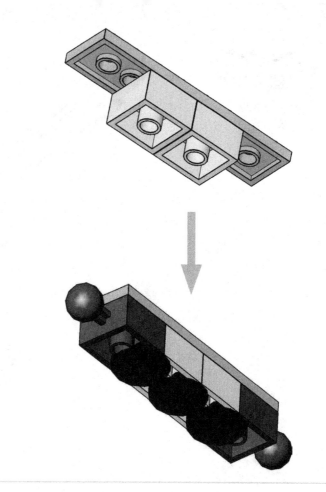

25

27

28

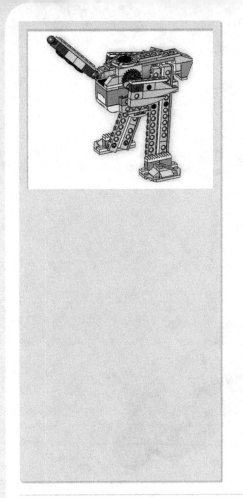

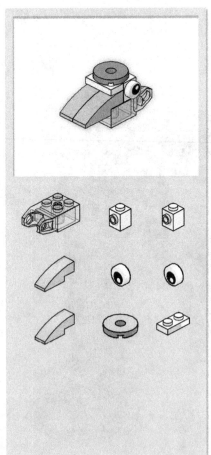

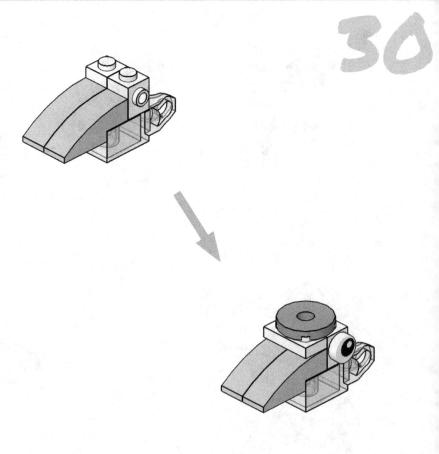

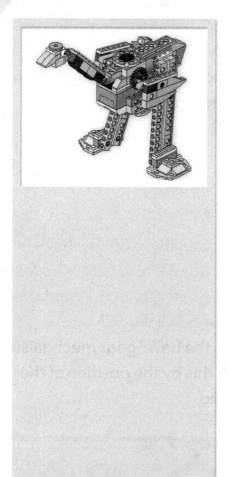

31

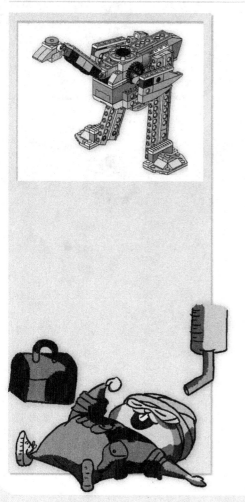

32

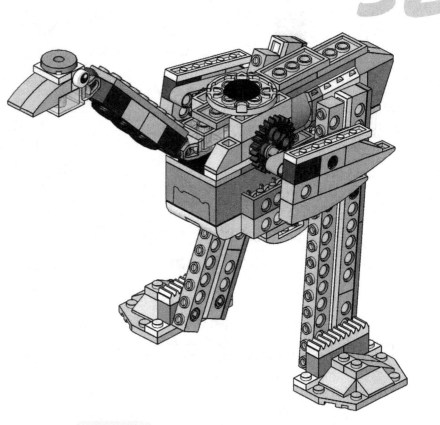

· Before going to the next phase, you can identify the mechanisms you are using in yo[u]
American rhea prototype.

· Can you predict how your American rhea prototype will move by only seeing the model?

· How many gears are you using in your American rhea prototype?

· How many legs does your American rhea prototype have?

Design features

· Your American rhea uses the motor to drive the two legs.

· Similar to the inverted slider–crank linkage used in your penguin, a Chebyshev's lambda linkage allows the walking motion of your prototype. You will see in detail this linkage in the next chapters since you will be using it a lot to make different walking robots.

· Can you identify the bevel gears and the Chebyshev's lambda linkage?

· Can you identify the driver gear and the follower gear in the bevel gear mechanism?

· Are the two legs in an out-phase motion? You can check this by the position of the legs. One leg should be in the opposite direction of the other leg.

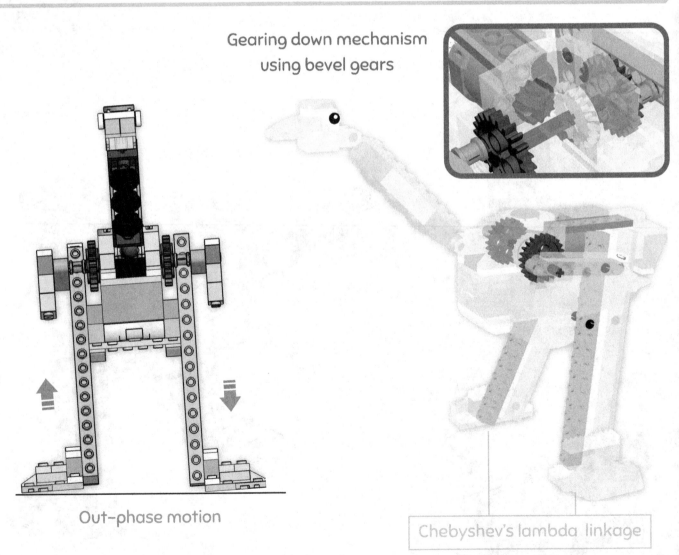

Gearing down mechanism
using bevel gears

Out–phase motion

Chebyshev's lambda linkage

- In this section, you will explore the use of the **keys** from your **keyboard** to make your American rhea move forward and stop.
- The **program idea** consists of moving forward your American rhea when you press the key "F" and stopping it by pressing the key "S."
- In a more detailed way, your American rhea will move forward if you press the key "F," and it will keep moving forward until you press the key "S." If the key "S" is pressed, your American rhea will stop, and it will remain like that until you press again the key "F" to change its state and make it moving forward again.

Flowchart

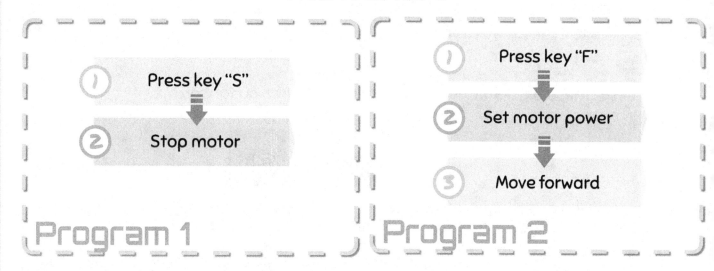

Program 1

1. Press key "S"
2. Stop motor

Program 2

1. Press key "F"
2. Set motor power
3. Move forward

In this case, you have two programs running simultaneously. Since you can press a key at any moment, the two programs must be always ready to execute!

Parallel programming

- Parallel programming refers to when **more than one program** (multiple programs) is **running simultaneously**.
- Since a key can be pressed at any moment, the two programs must run at the same time, and depending on which key is pressed, only **one of them** will be executed at that moment.

· Given the flowchart, you have to develop **two programs**:

Start on key press blocks

· In this opportunity, you are using a different block to start your program: **start on key press block**.

· Be careful when using this block; remember that it is case sensitive, meaning that if you set it up to execute when you press "F," if you press "f," the program will not be executed.

· Which of **these blocks** will make your American rhea **go forward**?

· You will find out the answer to this question on the **test phase**!

Test phase: Condition – action

· Remember to verify the **communication** between your WeDo software and the WeDo Hu before you start testing your prototype.

TEST 1: Finding the right motor direction

· Identify in which direction your motor has to rotate to make your American rhea mov forward and backward. Once you identify which block to use, change your program accord ingly. Can your American rhea walk backward?

TEST 2: Condition — action

· Test your prototype by executing the program developed in the **program phase** by press ing the two different keys: "F" and "S."

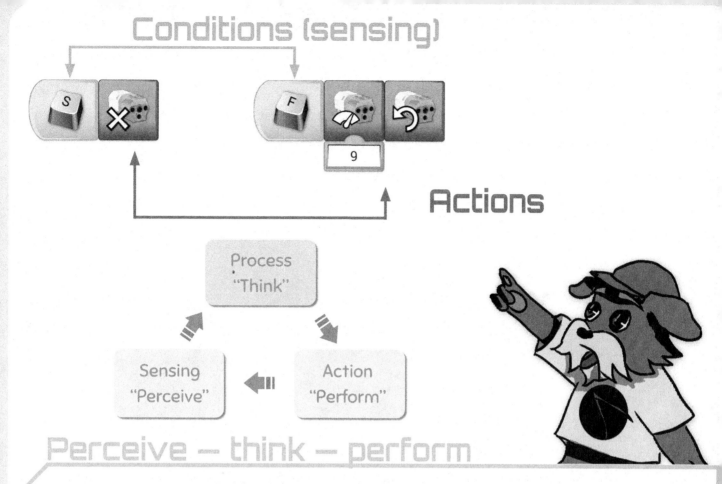

Conditions (sensing)

Actions

Process
"Think"

Sensing
"Perceive"

Action
"Perform"

Perceive – think – perform

• The keys on your keyboard are used as sensors, so your robot will perform an action depending on which key has been pressed (**condition**).

• The "think" process involves the **instructions** (programming blocks) to perform depending on the condition (**sensing**).

• Based on which instruction was sent, your prototype will **perform an action**.

Document & share phase

• Remember to collect all your **notes**, **videos**, and **photos** to report your **findings and results**.

• Record a video of your American rhea performing the three different actions depending on which key you have pressed.

• Report your findings and results from the **two tests** performed in the test phase.

Enhancing the experience

• **Build:** You can try building different legs for your American rhea and see if it can walk.

• **Programming:** Program other actions when other keys from your keyboard are pressed.

In the next chapter, you will explore
another type of motion: crawling!

CRAWLING ROBOTS

Contents

CAIMAN

Design phase: Four-legged crawling motion

• Remember to have a **white paper** and a **pencil** to start drawing your ideas!

Looking for inspiration

• **Caimans** are animals with powerful tails that are used in both **defense** and in **swimming**.

• Caimans are **predators**, and, like **alligators** and **crocodiles**, their diet consists of a great deal of **fish**.

• Caimans can move using two different motions: the "**high walk**" and the "**belly crawl**."

• The **high walk** is when the caiman **lifts** its **entire body** from the ground as it walks.

• The **belly crawl** is when the caiman moves while keeping its **ventral body** in contact with the **ground**.

High walk motion

Belly crawl motion

Crawling motion

• Usually, it is a **slower** motion compared with the walking motion.

• Since the body is in contact with the floor at any moment, the location of the **center of gravity** is **not a problem** as it was for the biped walking motion.

· Given the following building instructions, you can build a simple mechanism to help yo[u] understand the difference between an **in-phase motion** and an **out-phase motion**.

· Let's build both and see the differences:

In-phase motion

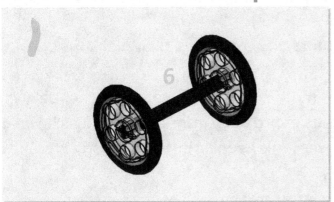

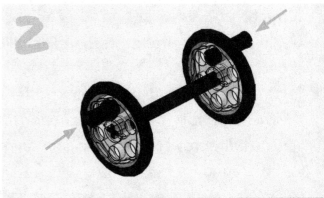

Keep in mind that in an in-phase motion, both connectors must be at the same position.

· Move your in-phase motion mechanism forward and backward.

· What do you observe? Are the positions of the green beams equal or not?

Side view

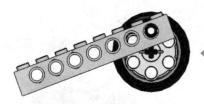

In-phase motion

· The frog and the turtle use an **in-phase motion** mechanism.

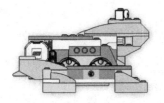
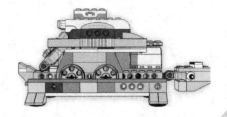

Out-phase motion

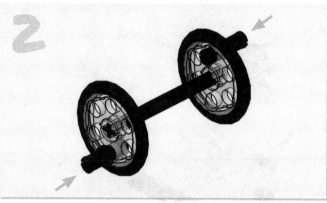

In an out-phase motion, both connectors must be at opposite positions one from the other.

- Move your out-phase motion mechanism forward and backward.
- What do you observe? Is the movement different compared with the in-phase motion?

Side view

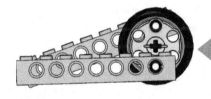

Out-phase motion

- The penguin and the American rhea use an **out-phase motion** mechanism.

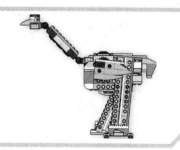

- Now you are ready to build your WeDo caiman prototype!
- Before you start building, prepare a **suitable workspace**.
- Keep in mind that the WeDo set has small pieces, so prepare a table with enough space to easily identify all the pieces and prevent them from getting lost.

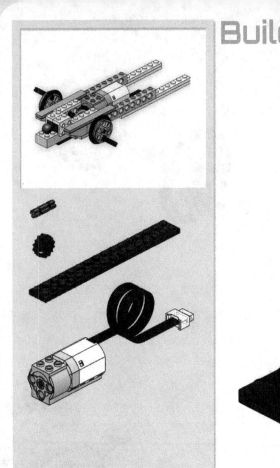

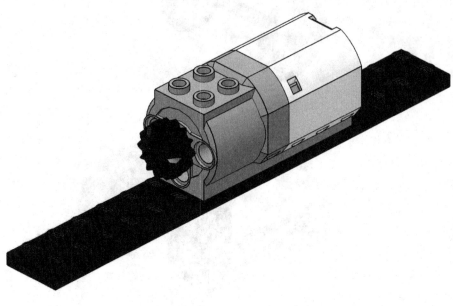

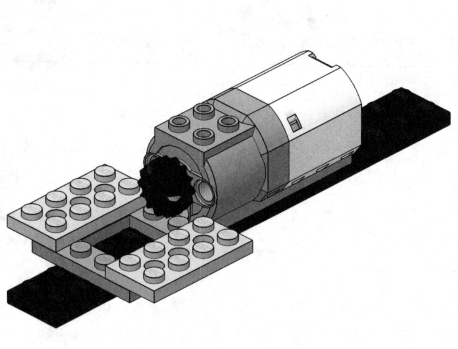

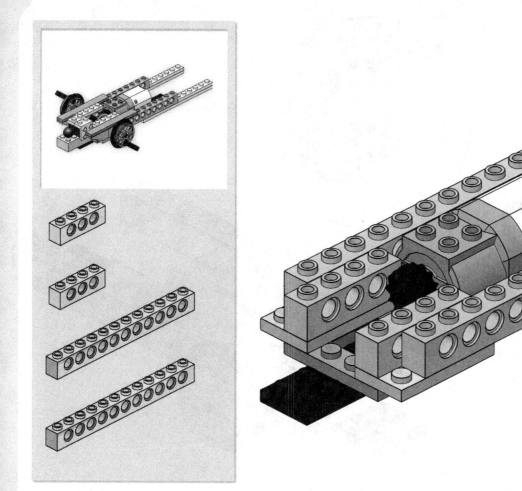

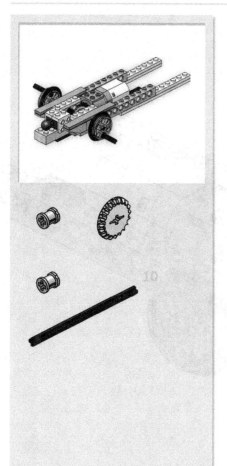

10

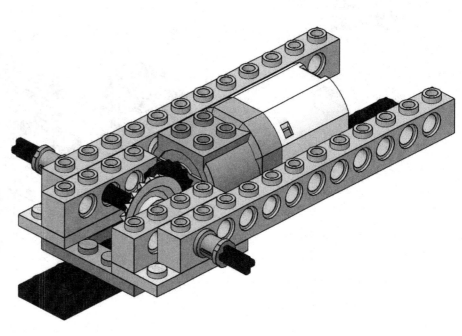

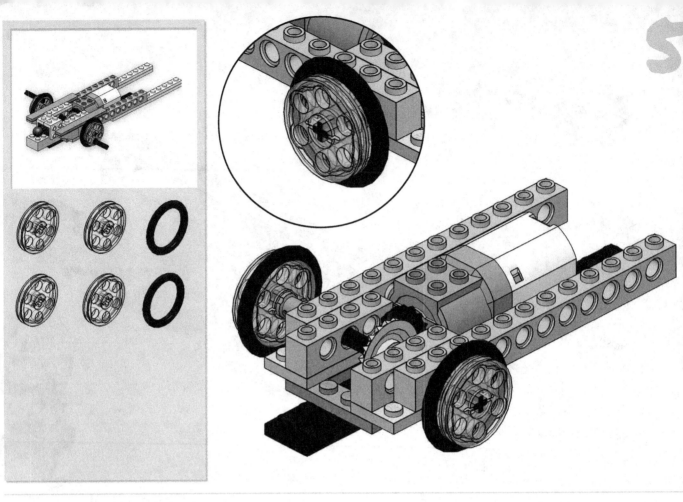

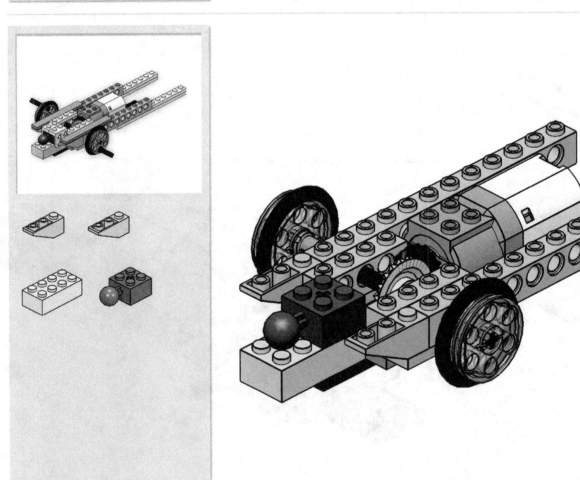

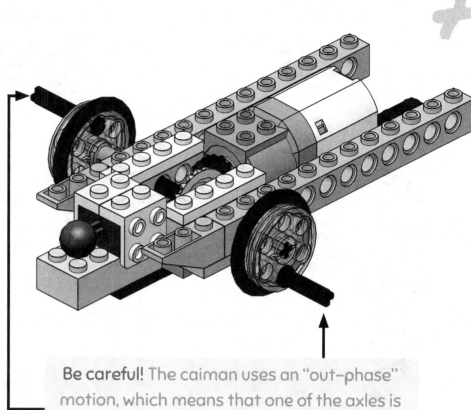

STOP

Be careful! The caiman uses an "out-phase" motion, which means that one of the axles is in the opposite position of the other one.

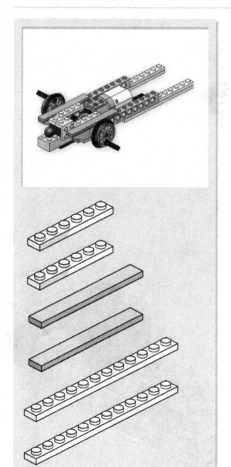

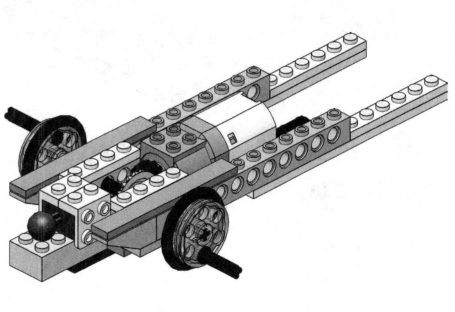

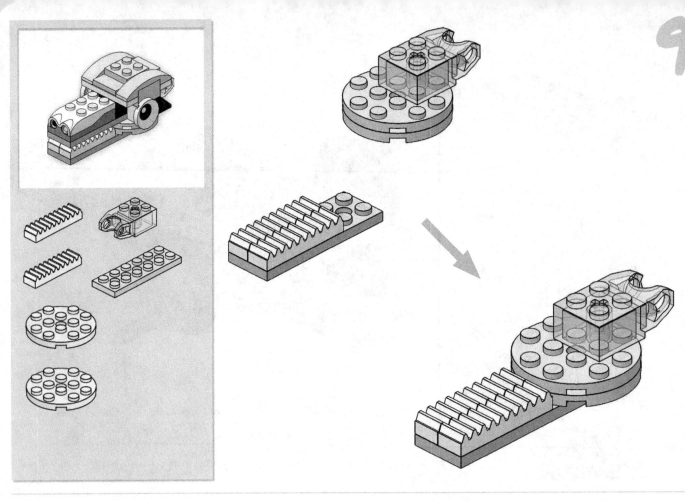

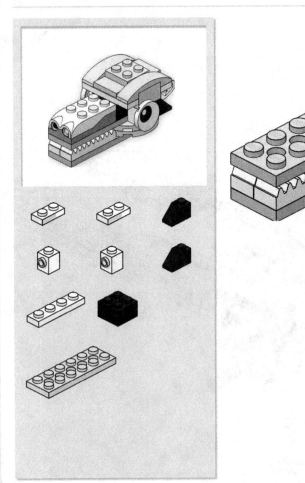

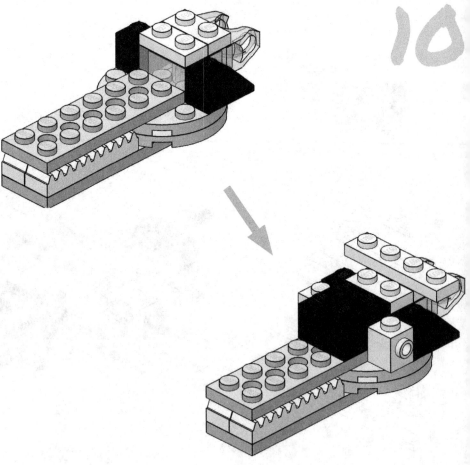

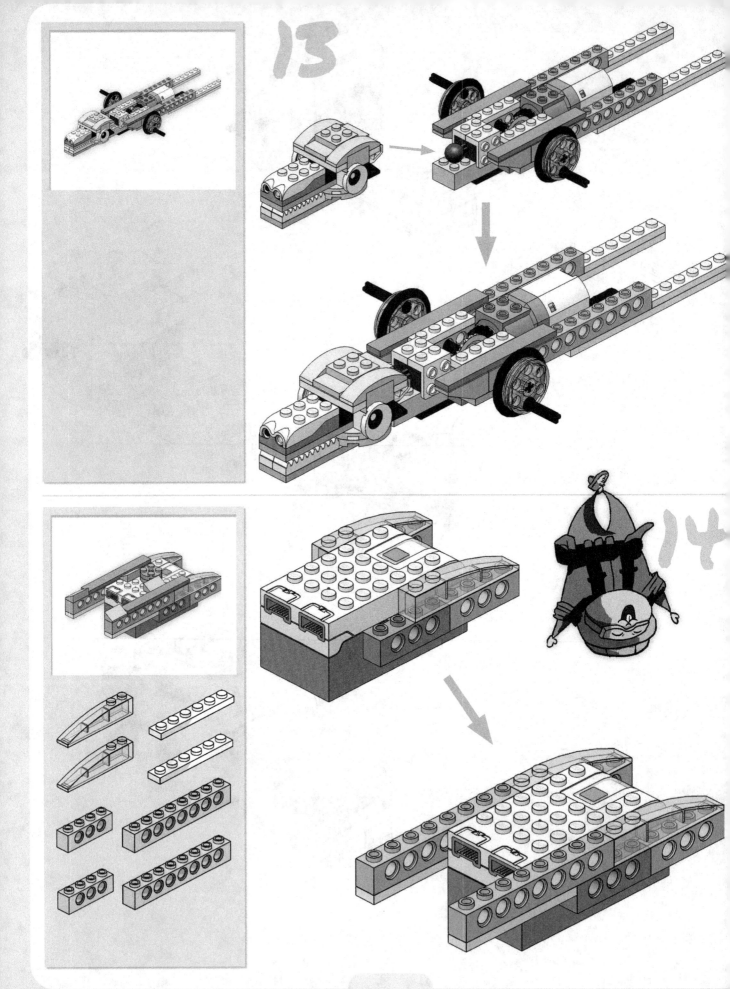

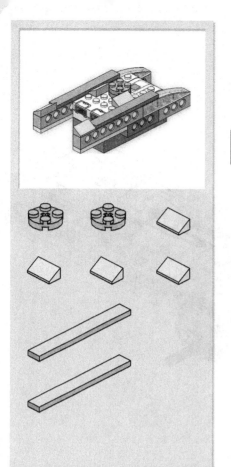

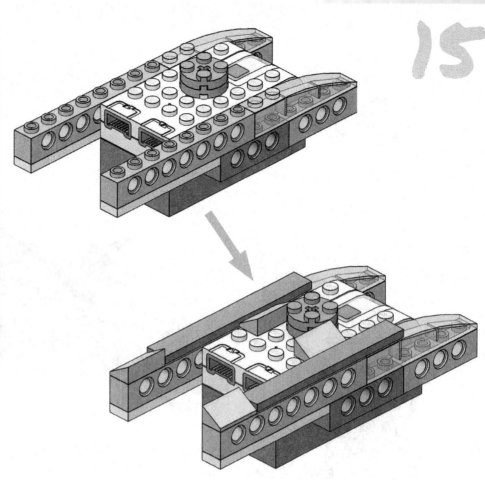

15

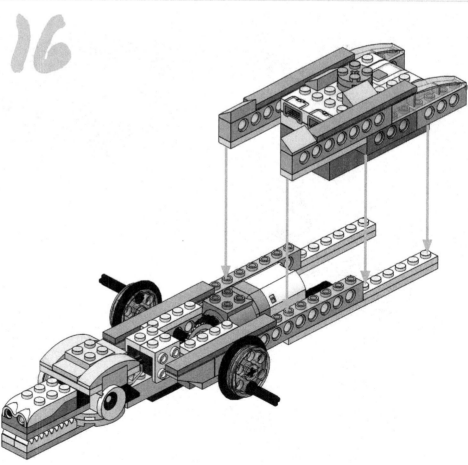

16

In this step, connect the sensor and the motor to the Hub.

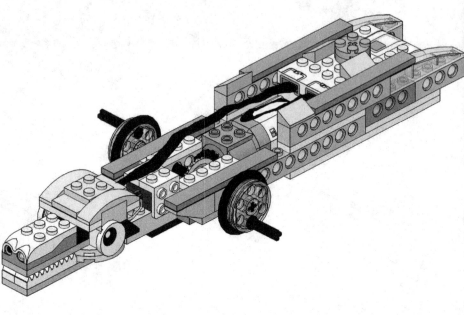

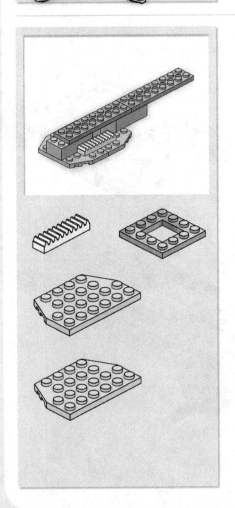

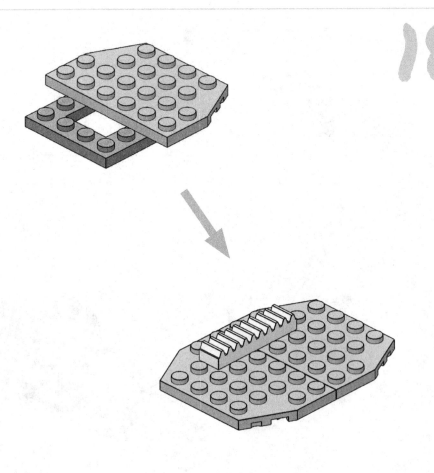

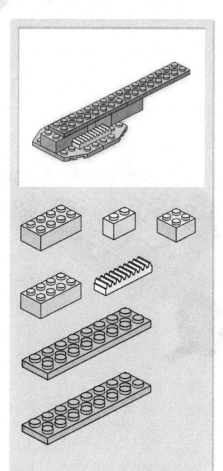

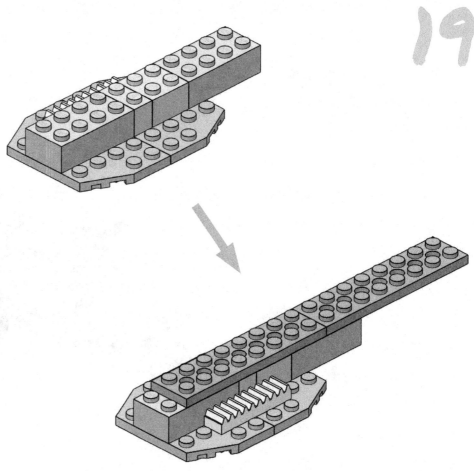

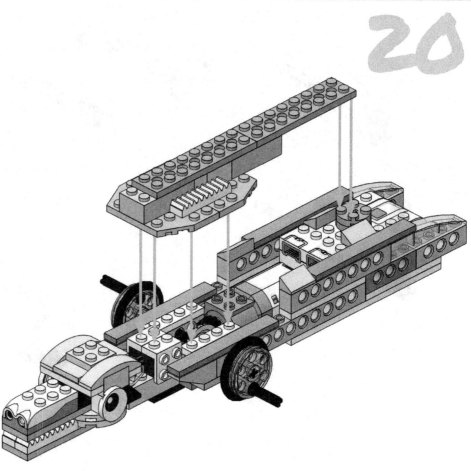

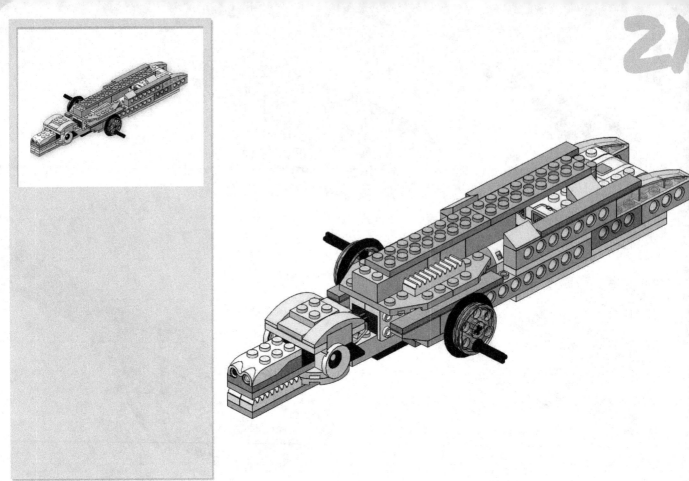

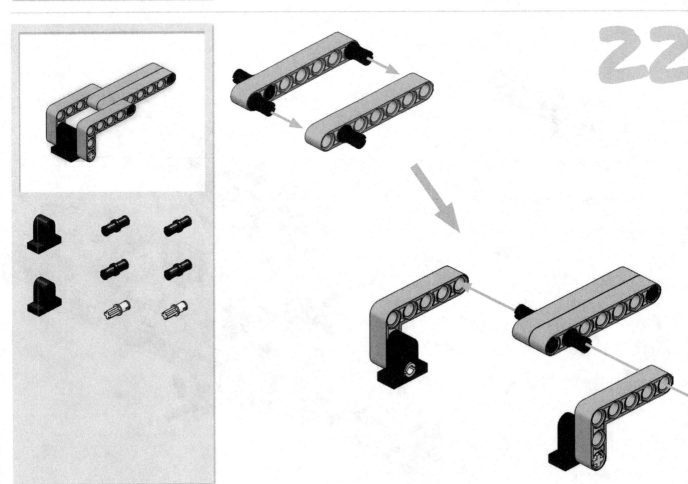

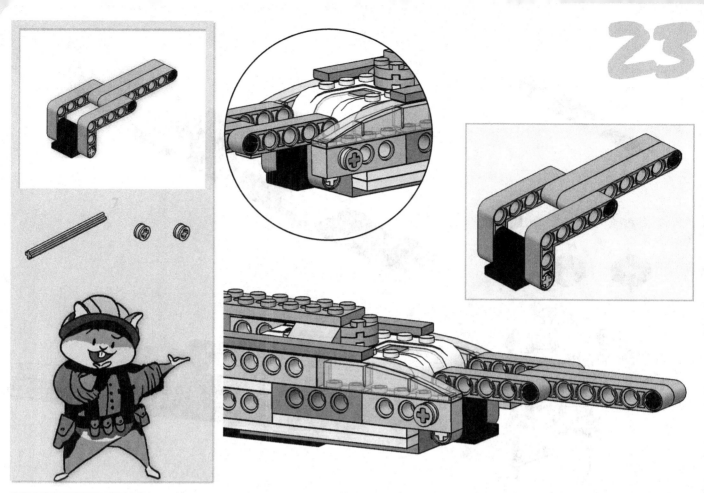

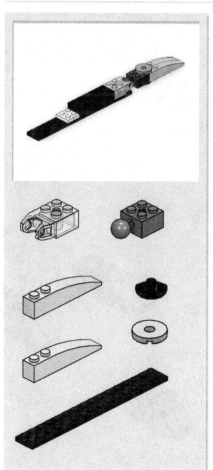

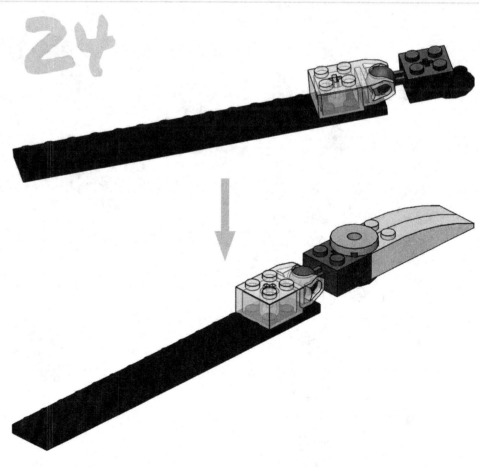

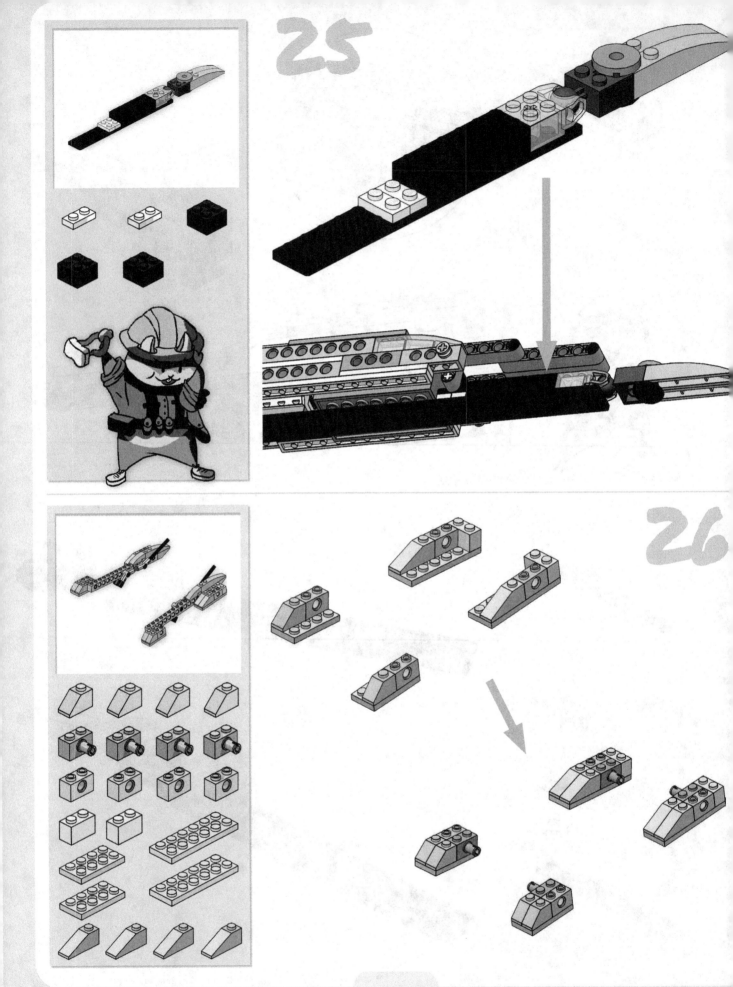

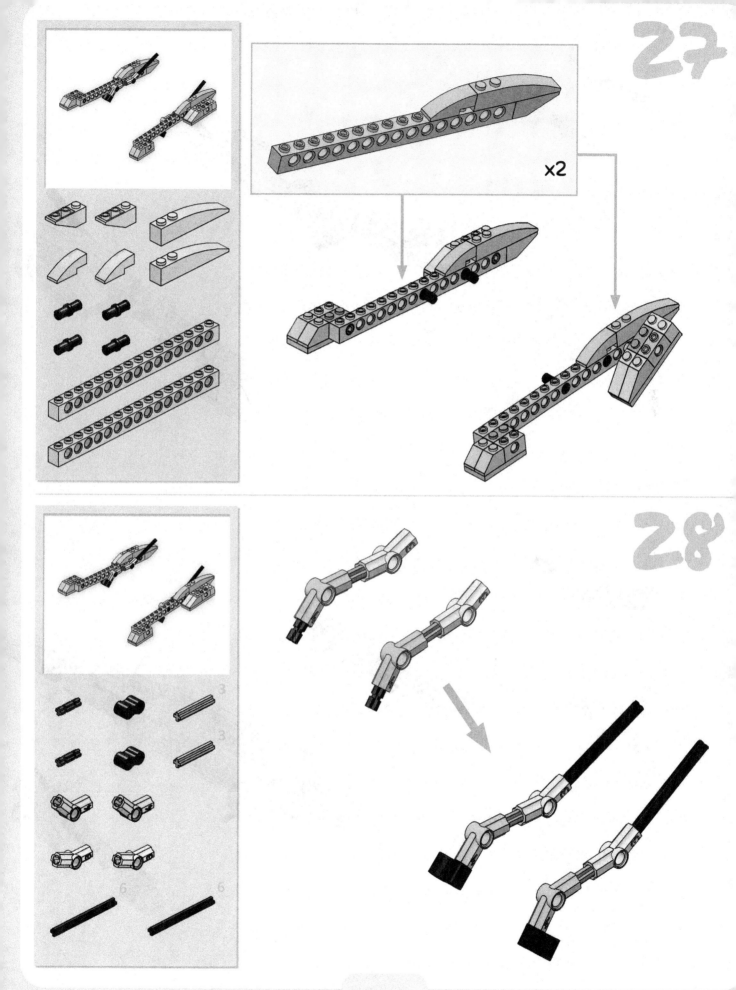

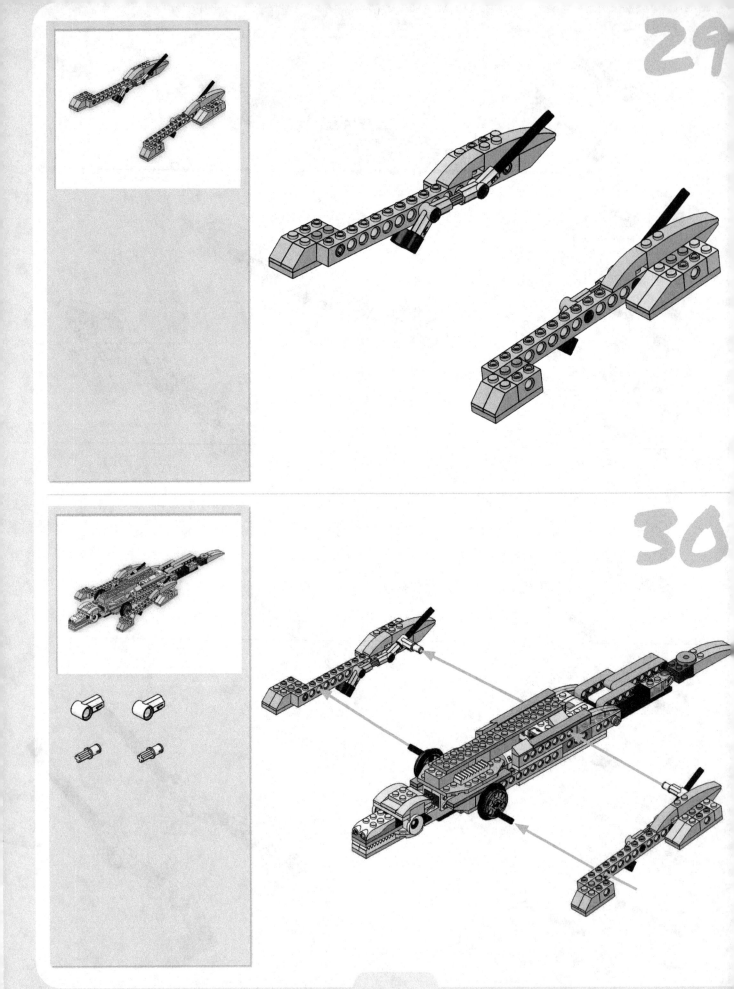

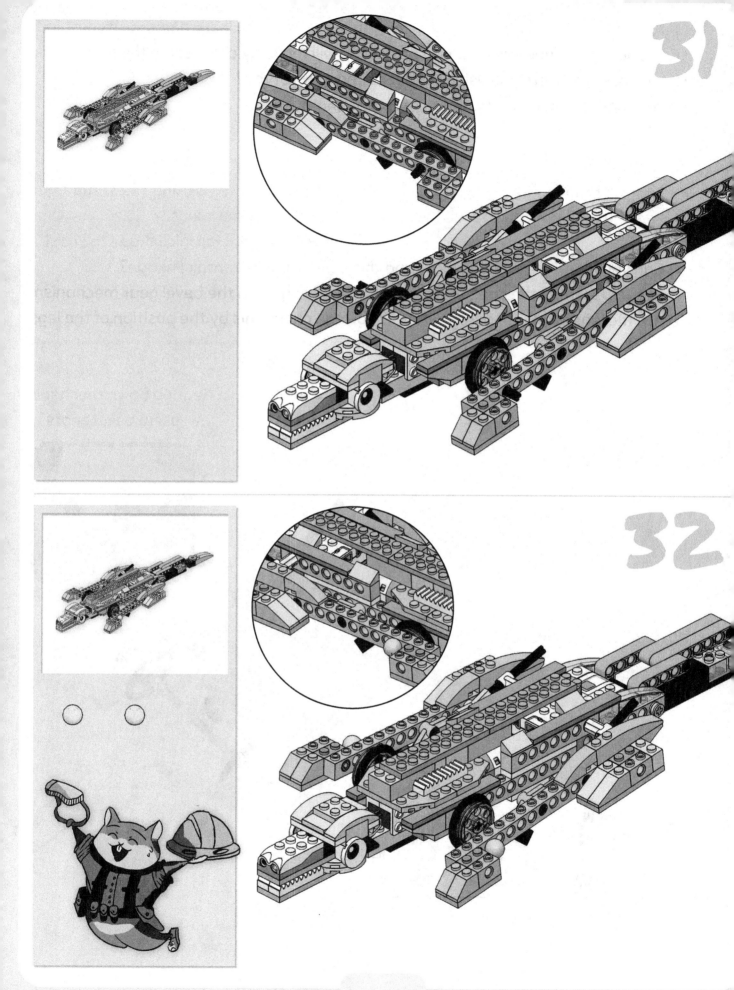

- As usual, let's identify the mechanisms you are using in your caiman prototype.
- Can you predict how your caiman prototype will move by only seeing the model?
- How many gears are you using in your caiman prototype?
- How many legs does your caiman prototype have?

Design features

- Your **caiman** uses the motor to drive its legs. The caiman is using the same trick we used in the frog and the turtle to make two legs look like four legs.
- Similar to the penguin, the caiman uses an **inverted slider–crank linkage** to crawl.
- Can you identify the bevel gears and the inverted slider–crank linkage?
- Can you identify the driver gear and the follower gear in the bevel gear mechanism?
- Are the legs in an out–phase motion? You can check this by the position of the legs.

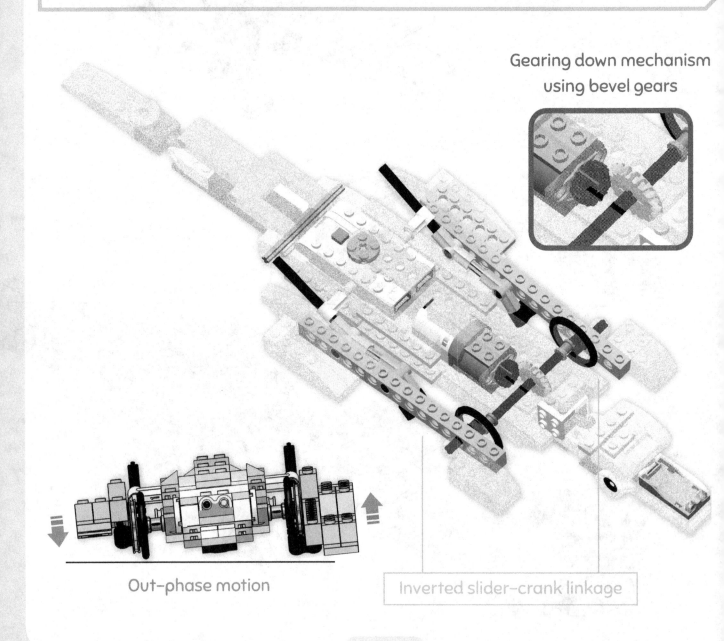

Gearing down mechanism
using bevel gears

Out–phase motion

Inverted slider–crank linkage

- In this section, you will explore the use of the distance sensor.
- The **program idea** consists of making your caiman chase a fish. Therefore, before explaining the program in a detailed way, first you need to build a fish:

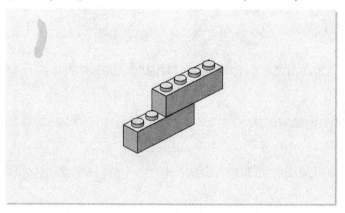

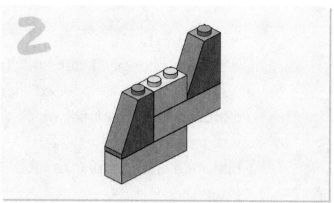

- With your fish ready, now let's focus on the program. The **program idea** is to make your caiman move forward until it finds a fish. Once your caiman finds a fish, it must stop. If you remove the fish, your caiman should start moving forward again.

The **algorithm** is as follows:
- The caiman starts to move **forward**.
- The sensor **detects** if an object is close to it.
- The caiman **stops** moving.
- The sensor detects if there is no longer an object in front of it (**clear path**).
- The caiman starts moving forward again.

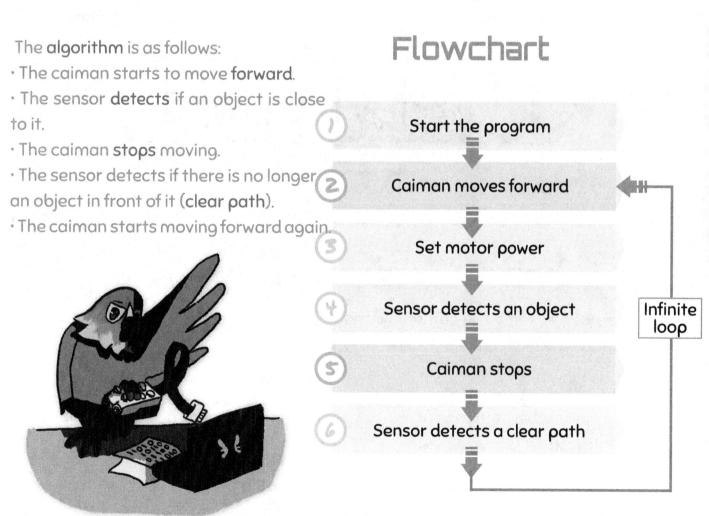

Flowchart

1. Start the program
2. Caiman moves forward
3. Set motor power
4. Sensor detects an object
5. Caiman stops
6. Sensor detects a clear path

Infinite loop

Distance sensor

- The **distance sensor** can be programmed using the **four** different programming blocks available: any distance change, distance change closer, distance change further, and distance sensor input.

- The **distance change closer** and the **distance change further** blocks are suitable to develop the program for your caiman.
- The **distance change closer** block will be used to detect if the fish is close and in front of the caiman.
- The **distance change further** block will be used to detect if the fish is no longer close or has been removed.

- From the flowchart, you have **six tasks** plus an **infinite loop**. Therefore, your program will have six blocks plus the infinite loop block.

- Now, you have everything ready to test your prototype; let's move to the **test phase**!

Test phase: Interacting with environment

- Remember to verify the **communication** between your WeDo software and the WeDo Hub before you start testing your prototype.

TEST 1: Finding the right motor direction
- Identify in which direction your motor has to rotate to make your caiman move forward and backward.

· Before starting your program, locate the fish in front of your caiman in a distance about 10 cm.

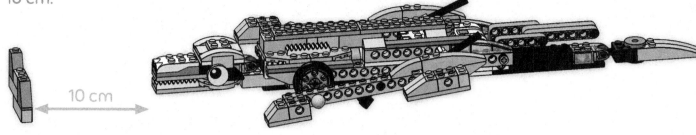

10 cm

· Execute your program by clicking the "Start" block.

go

stop

TEST 2: Friction to walk

· Remove the rubber parts located at the bottom of your caiman legs:

· Execute your program and see how your caiman moves without the rubber parts. Does it crawl better or worse than using the rubber parts?

Document & share phase

· Remember to collect all your **notes**, **videos**, and **photos** to report your **findings and results**.
· Record a **video** of your caiman crawling with and without the rubber parts.
· Describe the importance of the **rubber parts** to develop a stable walking motion.
· Why is the **center of gravity** not a problem in a crawling robot?

Enhancing the experience

· **Build**: Try to modify the out–phase motion of your caiman into an in–phase motion.
· **Programming**: Program different interactions between your caiman and the fish.

SEA LION

· Remember to have a **white paper** and a **pencil** to start drawing your ideas!

Looking for inspiration

· **Sea lions** and seals are **marine mammals**, spending a good part of each day in the ocean to find their food.

· Sea lions are characterized by external **ear flaps**, long **fore–flippers**, and a **big chest** and **belly**.

· They can be found in the **subarctic** and **tropical waters** in both the **Northern** and **Southern Hemispheres**.

· Colonies of sea lions can be seen gathered on **seaside rocks** for **breeding** and **birthing**.

Sea lions use their front flippers and stomach to crawl, roll, or slide while moving on land.

· Before continuing, you can start sketching some **ideas** to replicate the motion of a sea lion!

Chebyshev's lambda linkage

· Chebyshev's lambda linkage is a **three–bar mechanism** that converts rotational motion to approximate straight–line motion.

· Given its output motion (**dotted line**), it is vastly used in walking robots and vehicle suspension mechanisms.

· It was first shown in **1878**.

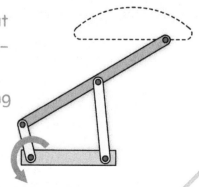

· Given the following building instructions, you can build your own **Chebyshev's lambda lin**age.

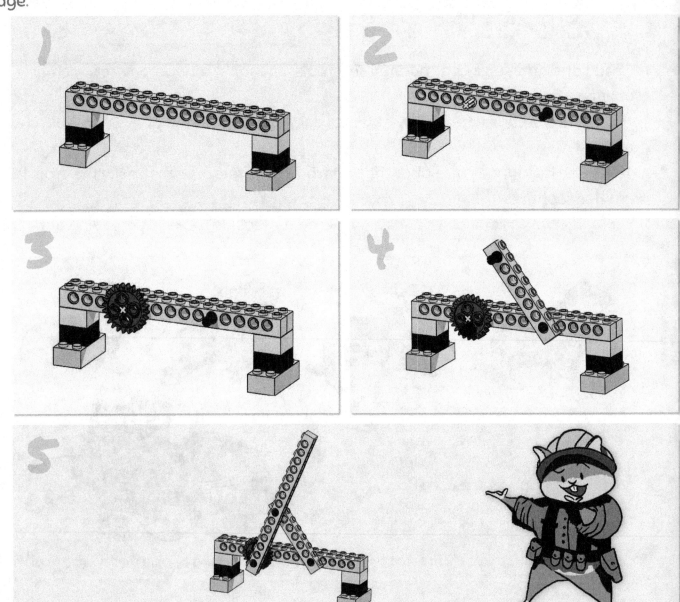

· Can you identify the three bars in the Chebyshev's lambda linkage?
· One of the **bars** is replaced by the **gear**.

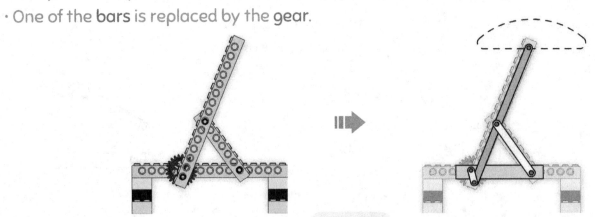

Other output motions

· Let's play a little bit modifying the position of the beams to see what other **kinds of motions** you can get from the **Chebyshev's lambda linkage**.

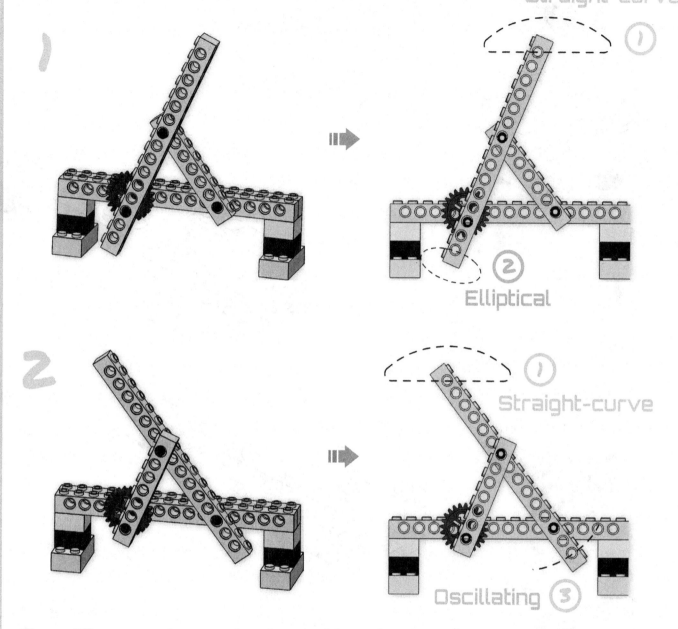

Straight-curve ①

Elliptical ②

Straight-curve ①

Oscillating ③

· Three different motions can be obtained from the **Chebyshev's lambda linkage.** You can use each of them to create different walking robots!

· The **American rhea** prototype uses a Chebyshev's lambda linkage with its **straight-curve** motion.

· Now you are ready to build your WeDo sea lion prototype!

· Before you start building, prepare a **suitable workspace**.

· Keep in mind that the WeDo set has small pieces, so prepare a table with enough space to easily identify all the pieces and prevent them from getting lost.

Building instructions

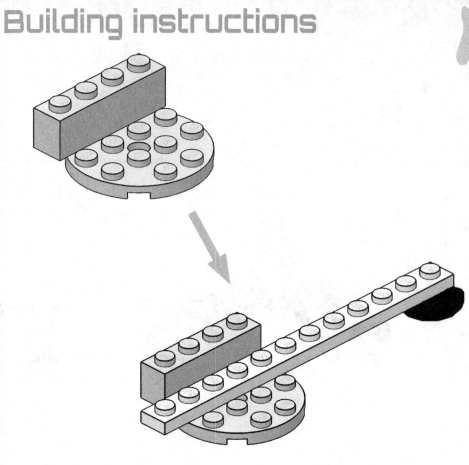

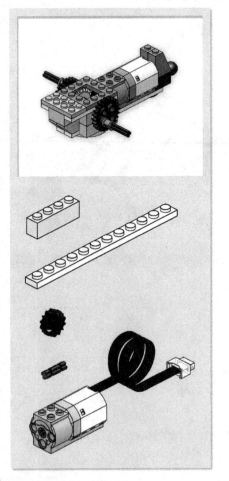

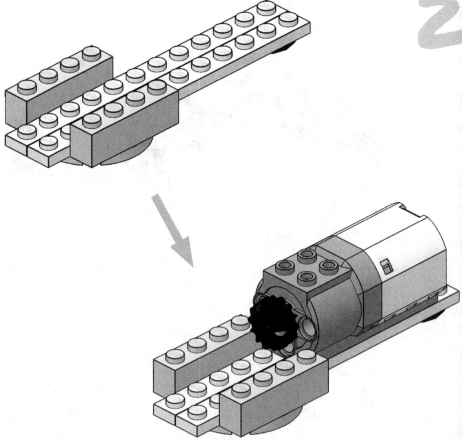

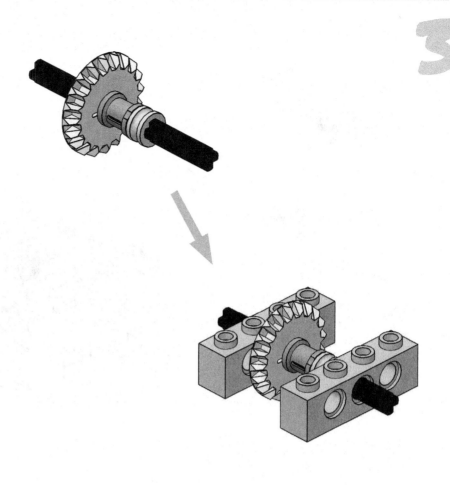

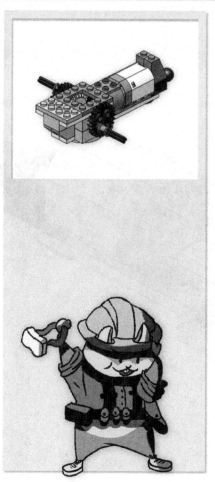

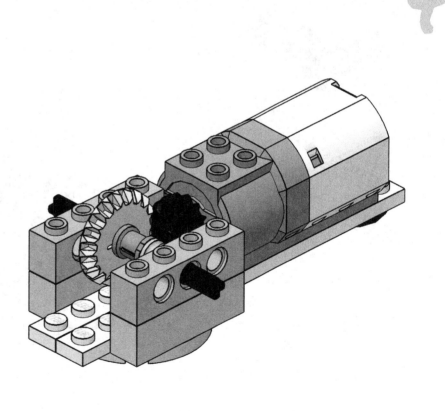

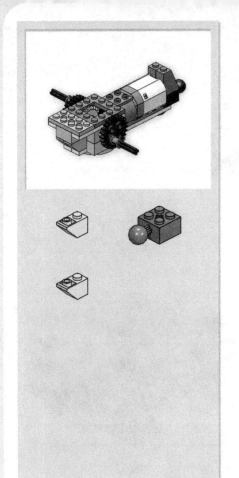

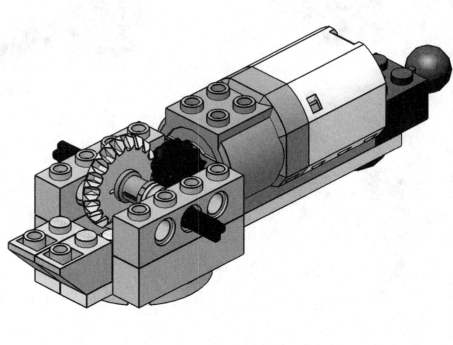

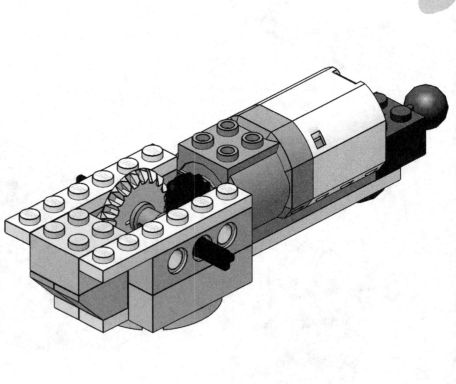

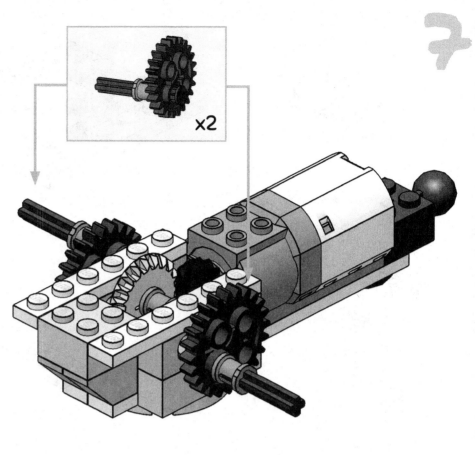

×2

Be careful! The sea lion uses an "out-phase" motion, which means that one of the axles is in the opposite position of the other one.

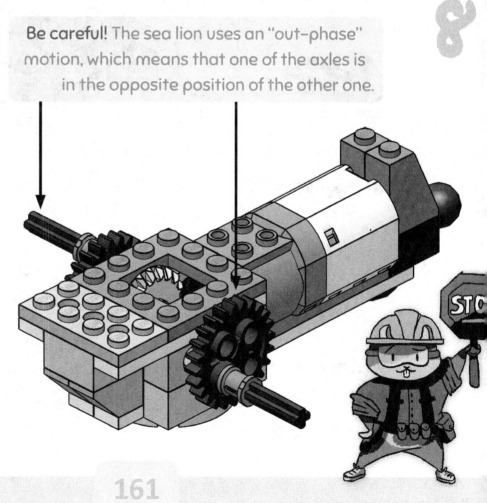

STO

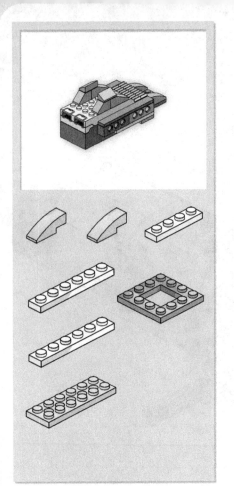

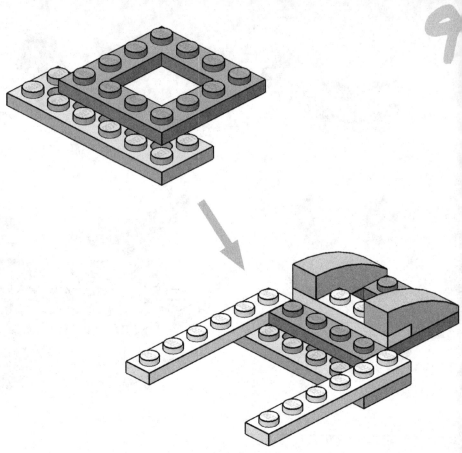

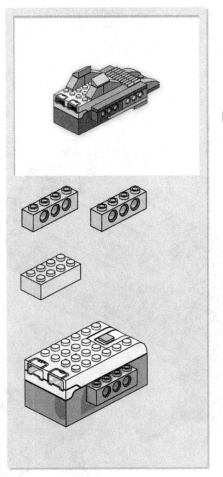

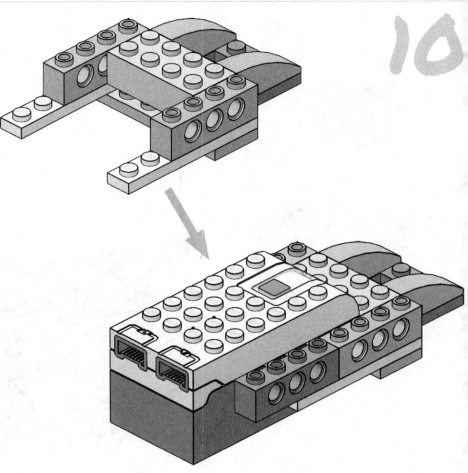

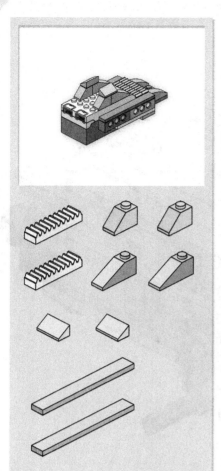

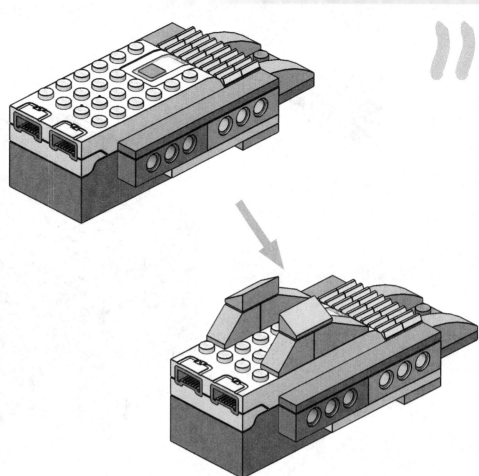

11

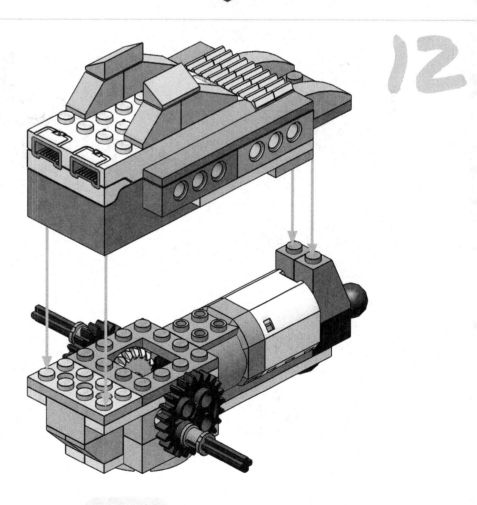

12

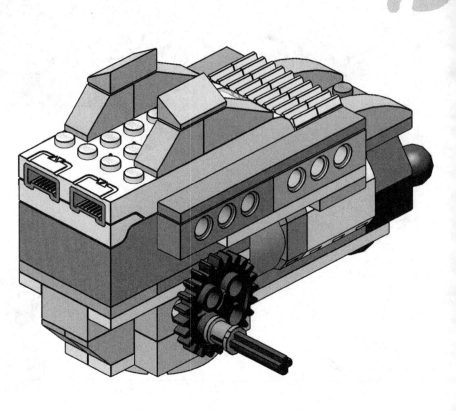

13

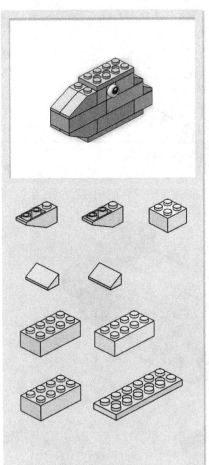

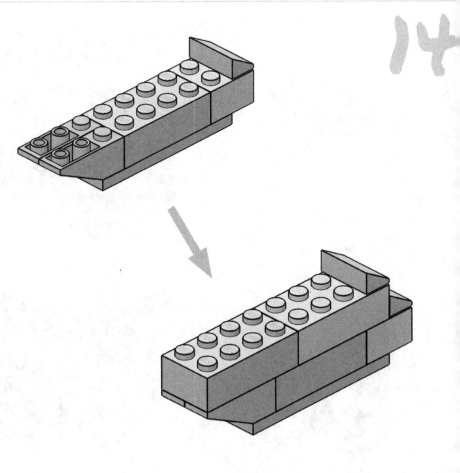

14

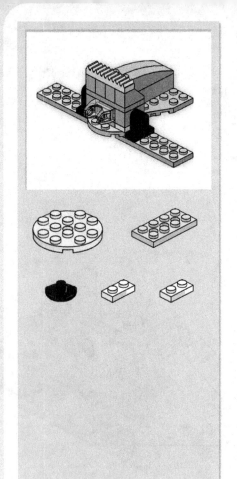

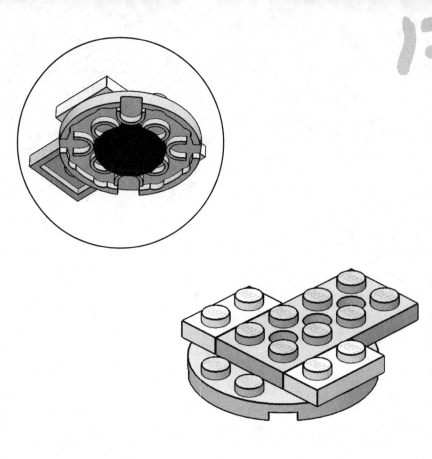

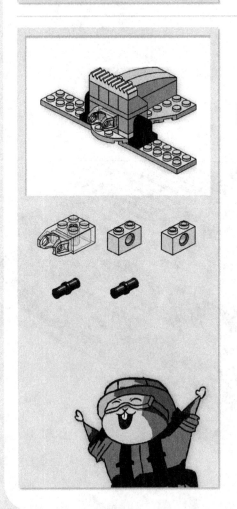

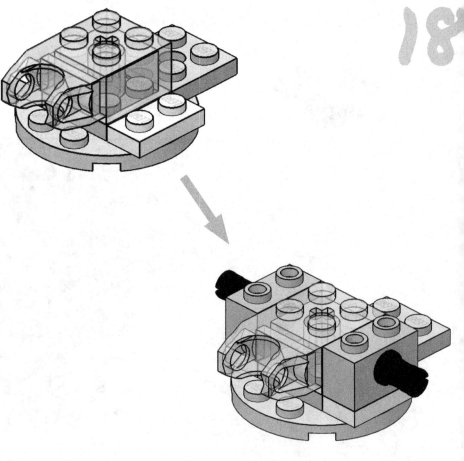

19

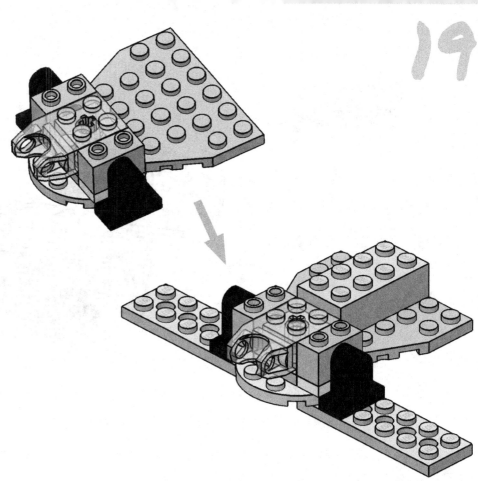

20

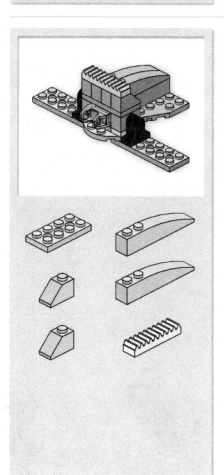

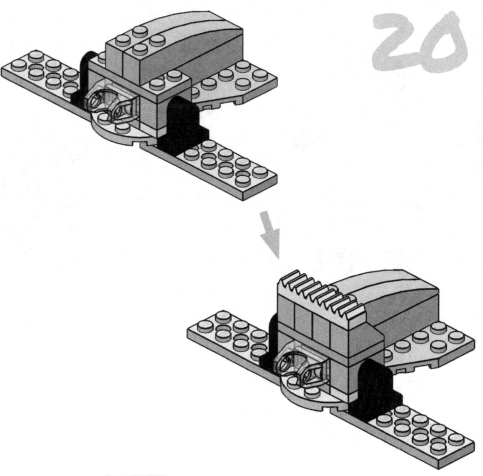

21

22

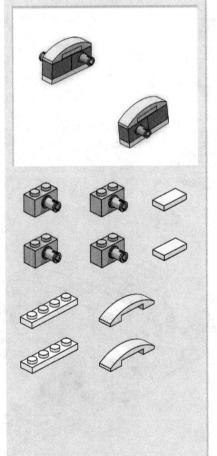

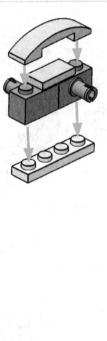

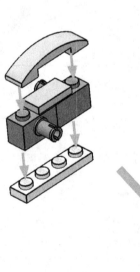

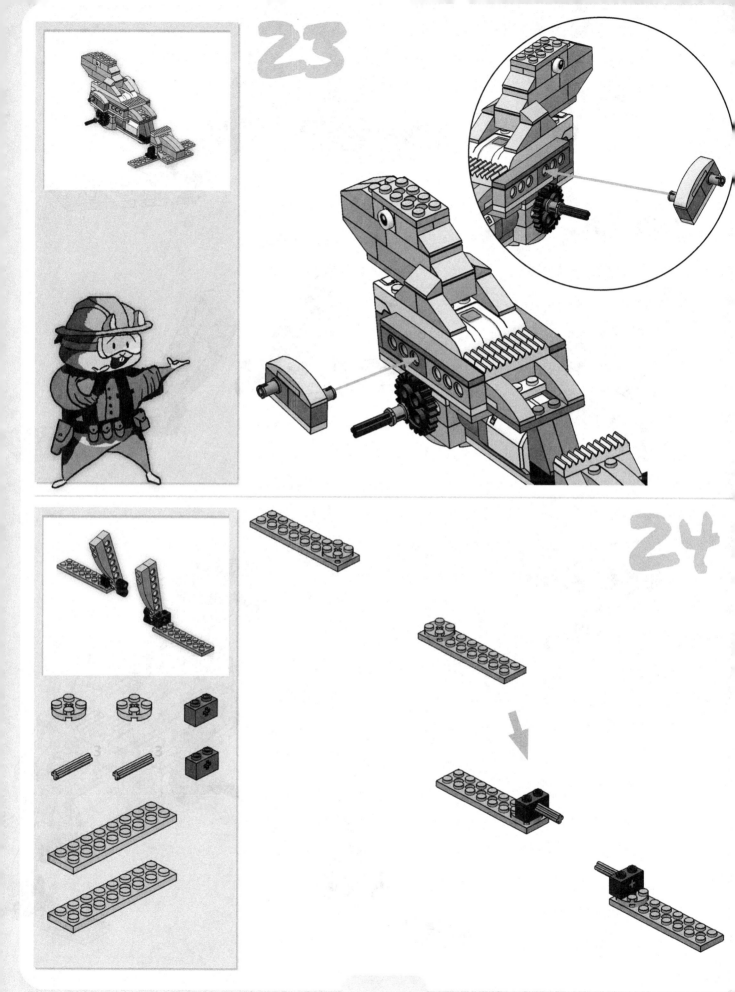

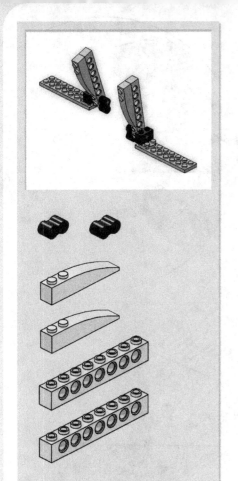

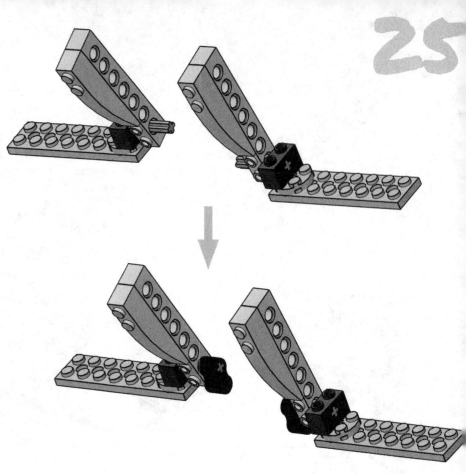

25

26

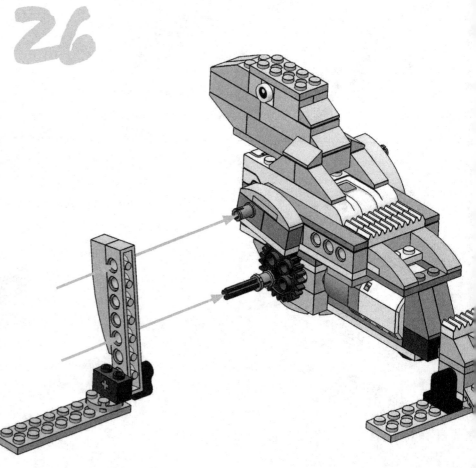

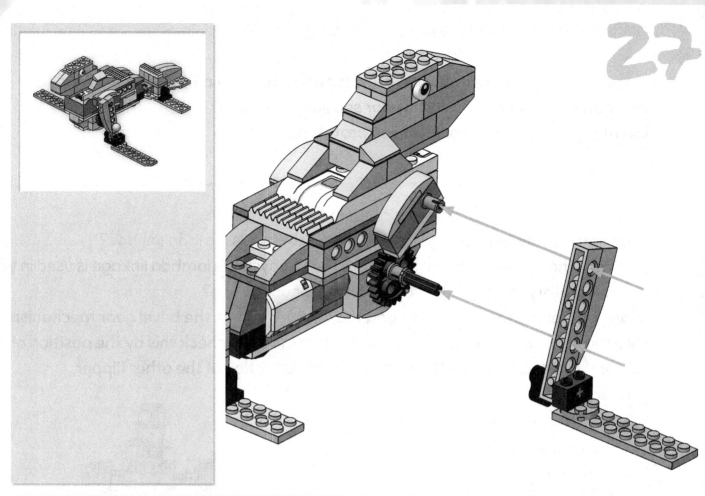

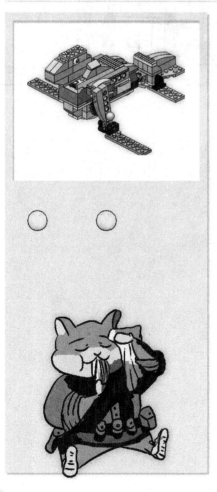

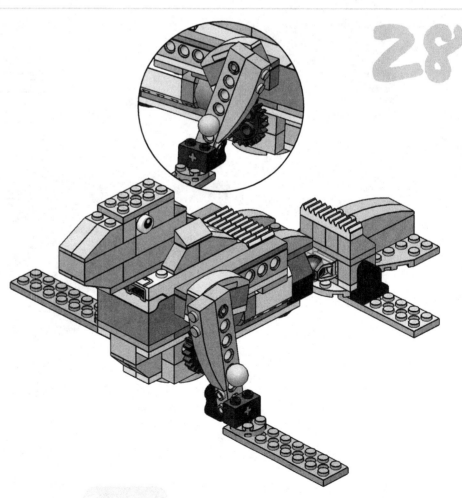

• Before going to the next phase, you can identify the mechanisms you are using in your se lion prototype.

• Can you predict how your sea lion prototype will move by only seeing the model?

• How many gears are you using in your sea lion prototype?

• How many flippers does your sea lion prototype have?

Design features

• Your sea lion uses the motor to drive its two front flippers.

• Can you identify the bevel gears and the Chebyshev's lambda linkage?

• Which of the three output motions from the Chebyshev's lambda linkage is used in your sea lion prototype: straight-curve, elliptical, or oscillating?

• Can you identify the driver gear and the follower gear in the bevel gear mechanism?

• Are the front flippers in an out-phase motion? You can check this by the position of the flippers. One flipper should be in the opposite direction of the other flipper.

Gearing down mechanism
     using bevel gears

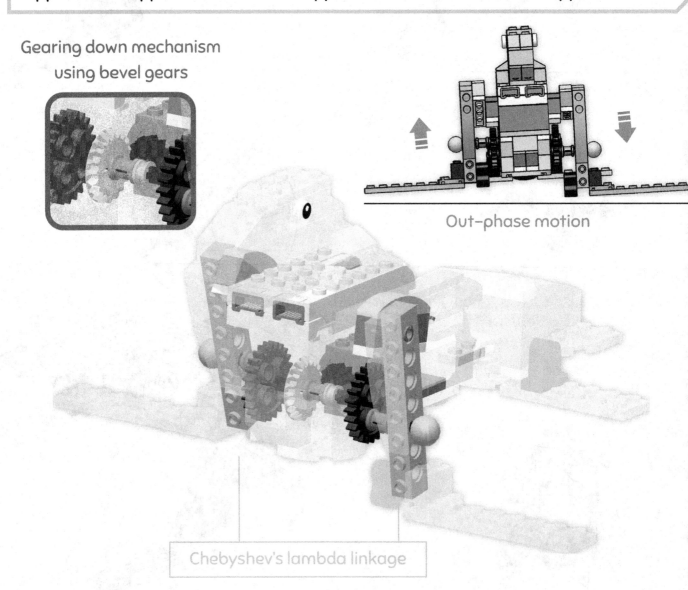

Out-phase motion

Chebyshev's lambda linkage

Program phase: Variables

· In this section, you will explore the use of variables in programming.

· The **program idea** consists of moving your sea lion forward, increasing or decreasing the motor power by pressing different keys from your keyboard as your sea lion moves.

· In a more detailed way, your sea lion will start moving forward with a motor power equal to 5. Simultaneously, if the key "U" is pressed, the motor power increases by 1 unit, and if the key "D" is pressed, the motor power decreases by 1 unit.

Flowchart

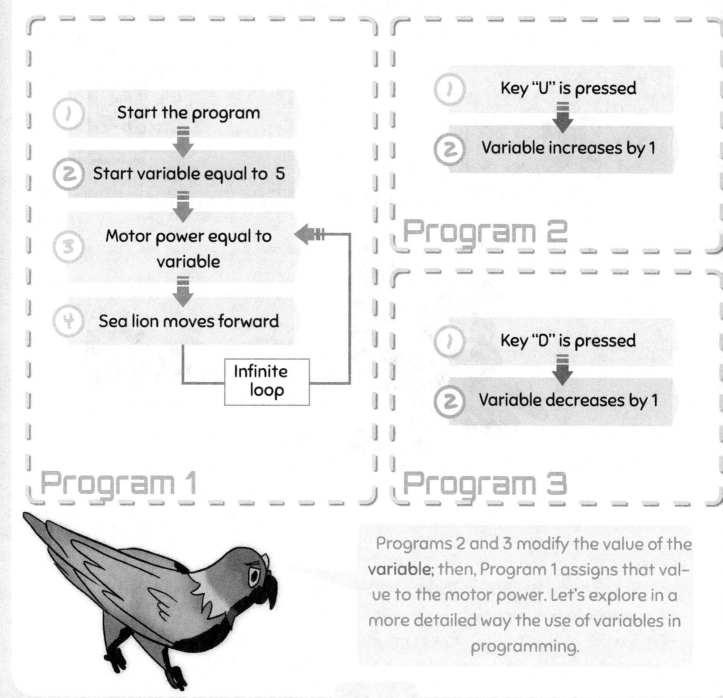

Program 1
1. Start the program
2. Start variable equal to 5
3. Motor power equal to variable
4. Sea lion moves forward
Infinite loop

Program 2
1. Key "U" is pressed
2. Variable increases by 1

Program 3
1. Key "D" is pressed
2. Variable decreases by 1

Programs 2 and 3 modify the value of the variable; then, Program 1 assigns that value to the motor power. Let's explore in a more detailed way the use of variables in programming.

Variable

- In programming, a variable is a **value** that **can change**, depending on conditions or on information during the **execution** of a program.
- Usually, a variable is a **number**, but it can be also a **nonnumerical** value.
- In your WeDo software, you can use the **display block**. In that case, your **variable** is the **number** shown on the **screen**.

- Using the programming blocks, the full program for your sea lion looks like this:

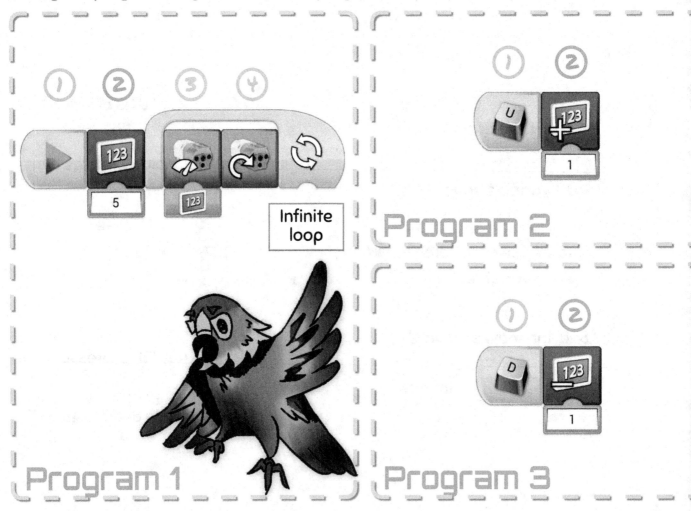

- **Program 1**: Tasks **1** and **2** are only executed **once**. Task **2** is called **variable initiation**, and i
purpose is to assign an **initial value** to your variable, in this case 5, meaning that if no othe
key from the keyboard is pressed, the motor power will be 5. **Task 3** assigns the value of th
variable to the motor power. **Tasks 3** and **4** are inside the infinite loop, so these two tasks a
being executed constantly.
- **Program 2**: Increases the number on your display (**variable**) by one.
- **Program 3**: Decreases the number on your display (**variable**) by one.

Test phase: Controlling motor power

· Remember to verify the **communication** between your WeDo software and the WeDo Hub before you start testing your prototype.

· Start testing your prototype by executing the program developed in the **program phase** by clicking the "Start" block.

TEST 1: Finding the right motor direction

· Identify in which direction your motor has to rotate to make your sea lion move forward and backward.

TEST 2: Beyond the limit

· From the previous chapter, you know that the motor power can have values from 0 to 10. However, the number on your display (variable) can have values lesser or greater than 0 and 10.
· What happens when your number on display (variable) is greater than 10? Does your motor go faster?
· What happens when your number on display (variable) is less than 0? Does your motor rotate?

TEST 3: Friction to walk

· Remove the rubber parts located at the bottom of your sea lion flippers.
· Execute your program and see how your sea lion moves without the rubber parts. Does it crawl better or worse than using the rubber parts?

Document & share phase

· Remember to collect all your **notes**, **videos**, and **photos** to report your **findings and results**.
· Write a report adding sketches, photos, or videos about the results obtained in the **three tests** from the **test phase**.
· Record a video comparing the motion of your sea lion using and not using the rubber parts.

Enhancing the experience

· **Build:** You can modify the flippers of your sea lion to try new motions.
· **Programming:** Instead of increasing and decreasing the motor power by 1 unit, try other numbers.

In the next chapter, you will
explore more about quadruped
motion!

QUADRUPED ROBOTS

Contents

PLESIOSAURUS

Design phase: Quadruped walking motion

· Remember to have a **white paper** and a **pencil** to start drawing your ideas!

Looking for inspiration

· **Plesiosaurus** was an aquatic reptile, **not a dinosaur**, though it coexisted with many dinosaurs during the Jurassic period.

· They had a **serpentine neck** with a **small head** at the end, and it used their four fins and short broad tail for mobility.

· They were usually about **11 feet in length**, full grown.

· The first Plesiosaurus fossil was discovered in **1821**. There have been fossils found off the coasts of Europe and throughout many areas of the **Pacific Ocean**. These include coasts of Asia, Australia, and North and South America.

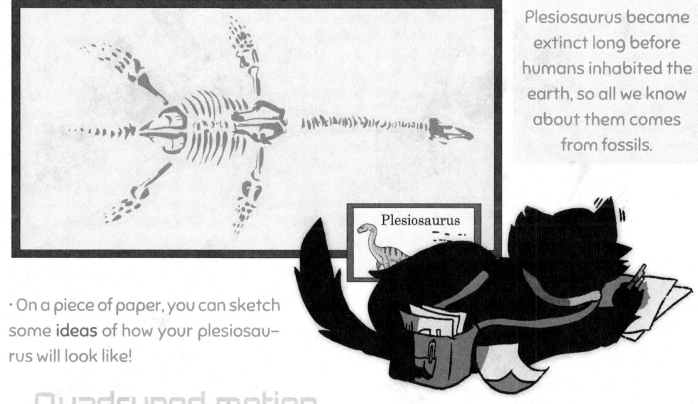

Plesiosaurus became extinct long before humans inhabited the earth, so all we know about them comes from fossils.

Plesiosaurus

· On a piece of paper, you can sketch some **ideas** of how your plesiosaurus will look like!

Quadruped motion

· Quadruped robots exhibit **high stability** because they rely on **four support points** to the surface to walk.

· Quadruped robots exhibit **better stability** than biped robots.

· Similar to a crawling robot, the **center of gravity** is not an issue in quadruped robots given its **high stability**.

· Given the following building instructions, you can build a **multiple Chebyshev's lambda** linkage.

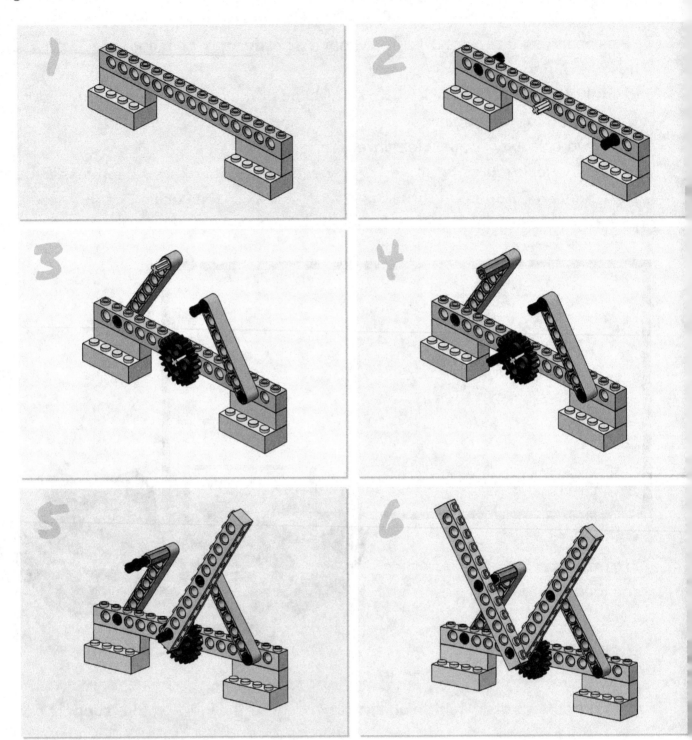

· Can you identify the two **Chebyshev's lambda** linkages?

· Which one out of the three motions that a **Chebyshev's lambda** linkage can produce is used in this particular mode: **straight–curve**, **elliptical**, or **oscillating**?

· Rotate the gear to see how the two beams move.

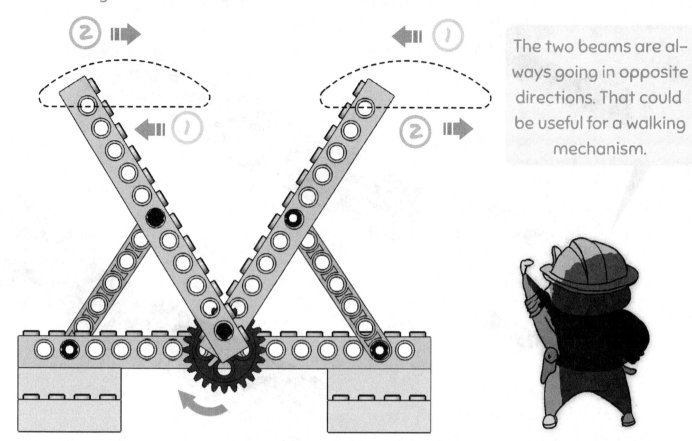

The two beams are always going in opposite directions. That could be useful for a walking mechanism.

· The two beams are going in **opposite directions**. We can divide the motion in two stages.
· **Stage 1:** The left beam is going over the straight motion, while the right beam is going over the curve motion.
· **Stage 2:** The left beam is going over the curve motion, while the right beam is going over the straight motion.

· Now you are ready to build your WeDo plesiosaurus prototype!
· Before you start building, prepare a **suitable workspace**.
· Keep in mind that the WeDo set has small pieces, so prepare a table with enough space to easily identify all the pieces and **prevent** them from getting lost.

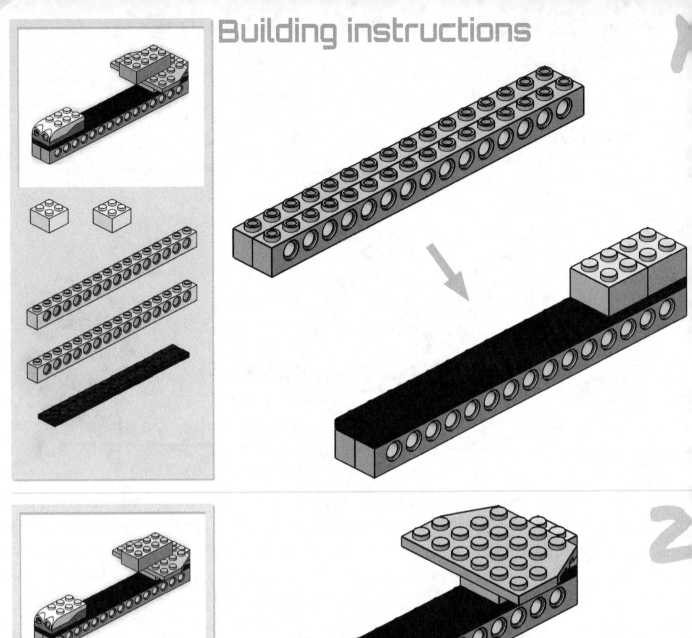

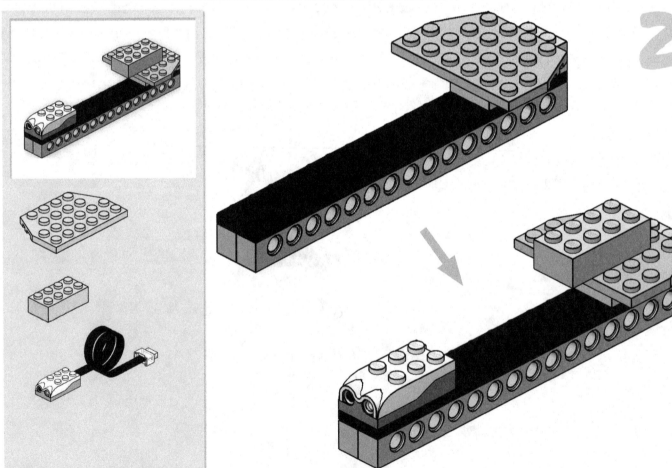

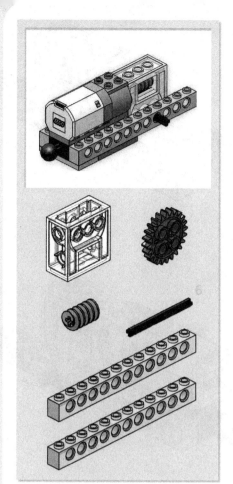

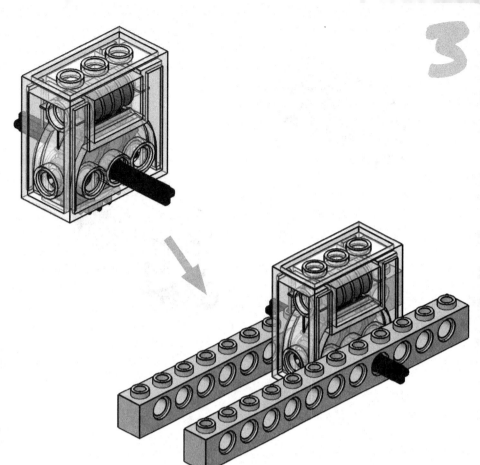

3

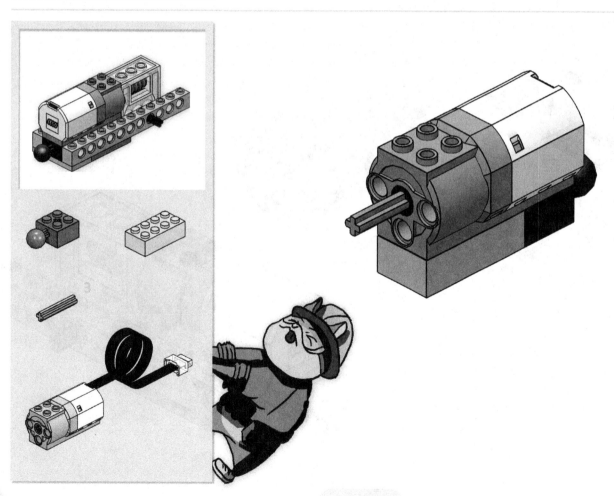

4

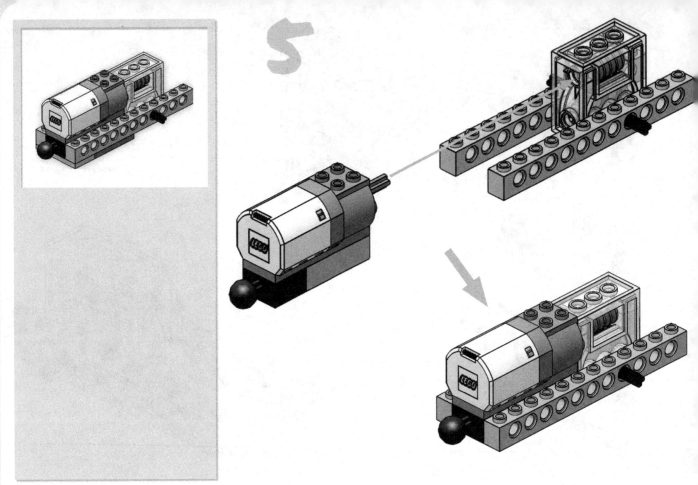

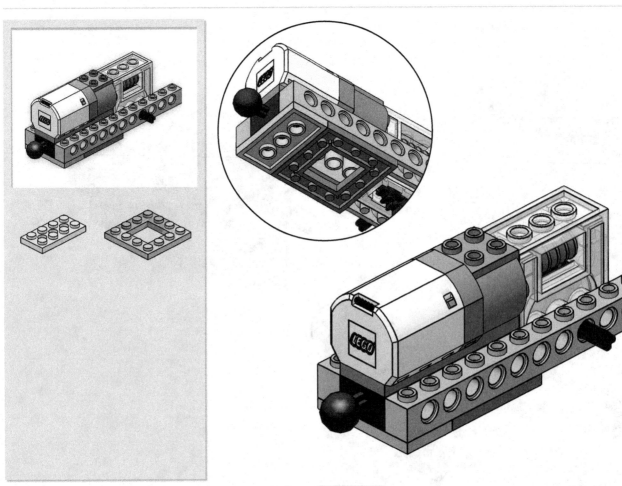

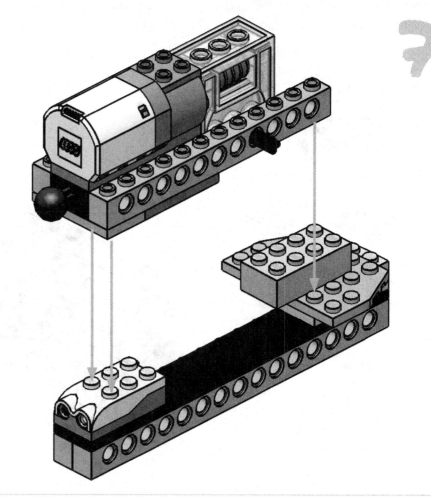

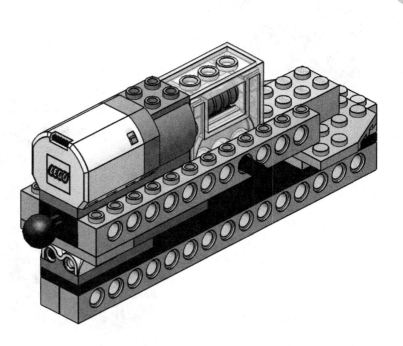

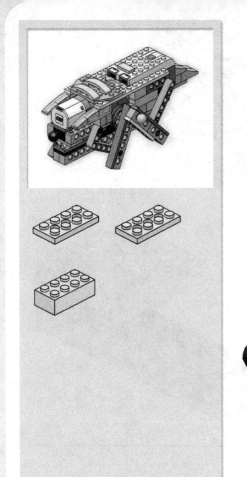

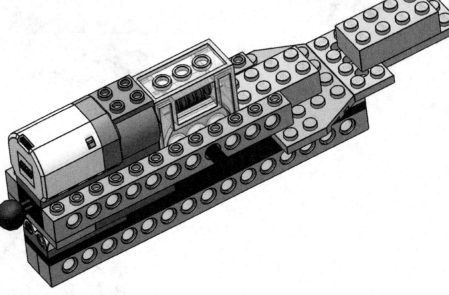

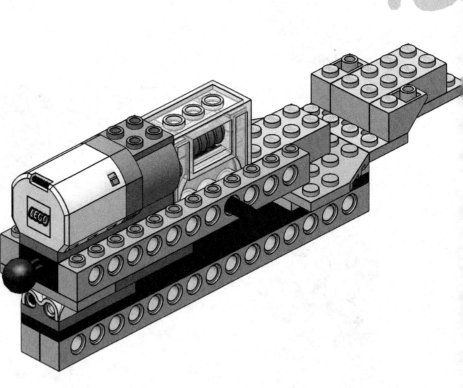

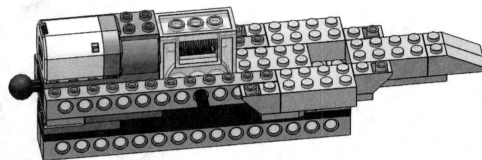

×2

Be careful! The plesiosaurus uses an "out–phase" motion, meaning that one of the axles is in the opposite position of the other one.

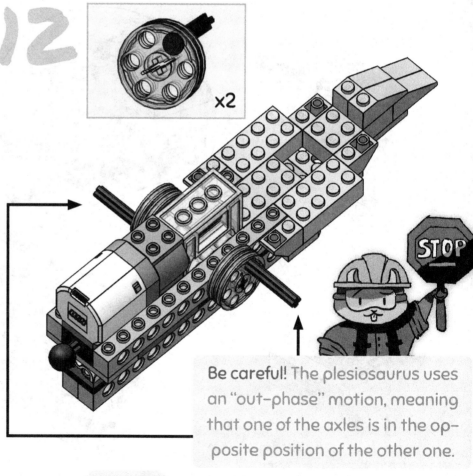

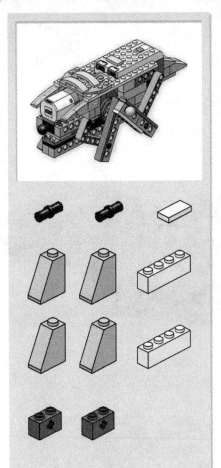

13

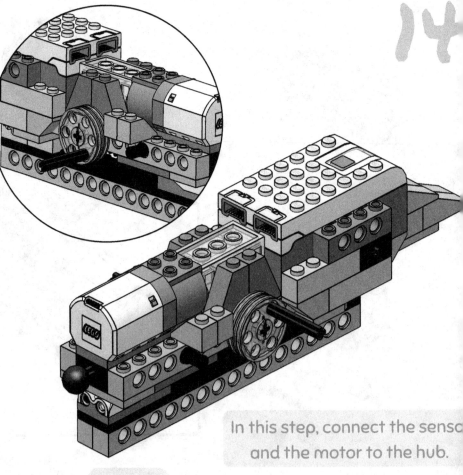

14

In this step, connect the sensor
and the motor to the hub.

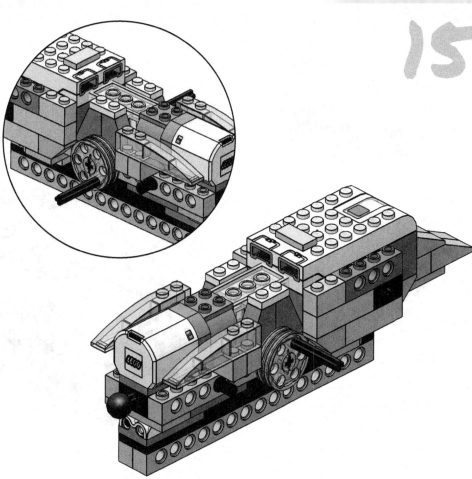

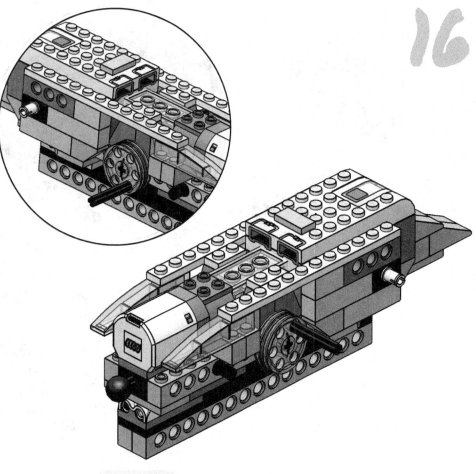

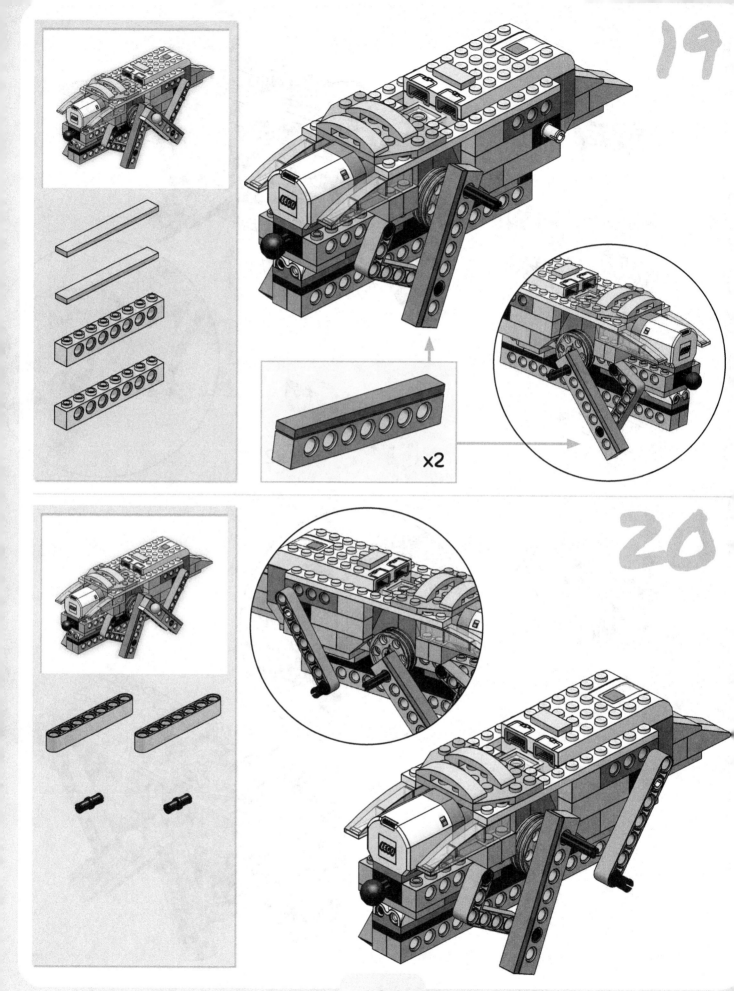

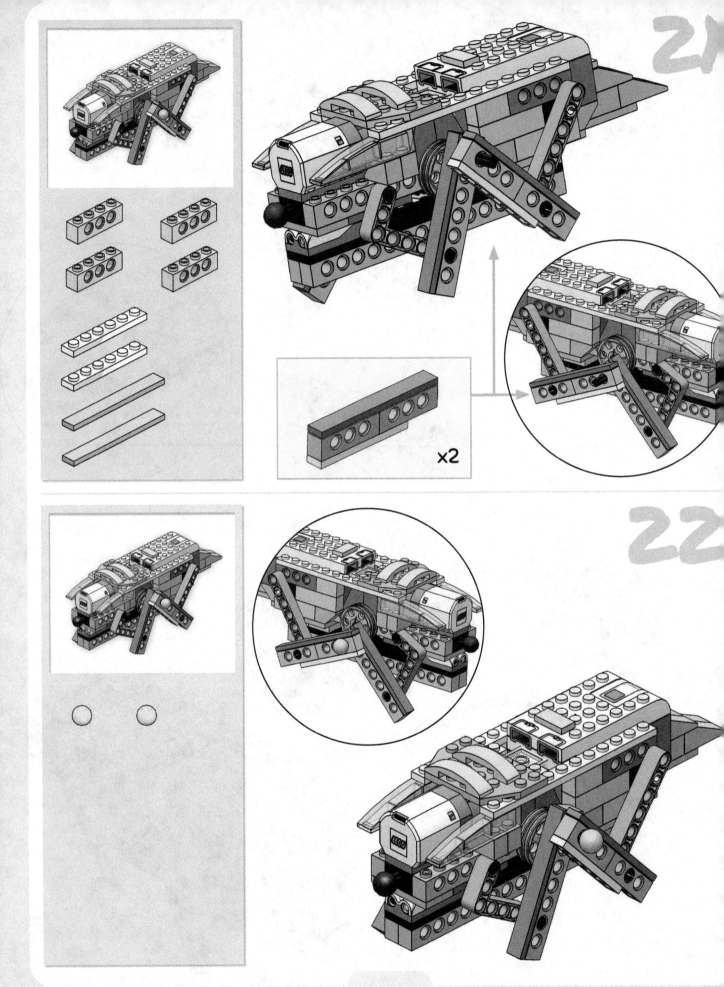

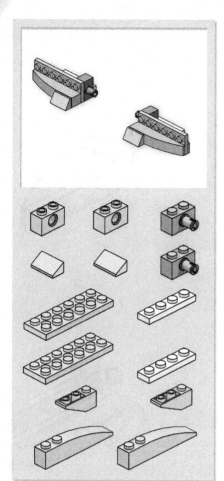

23

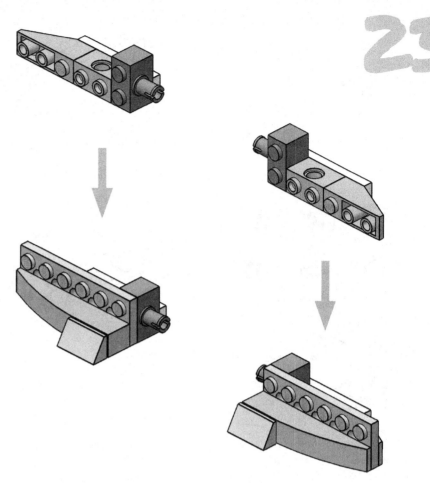

24

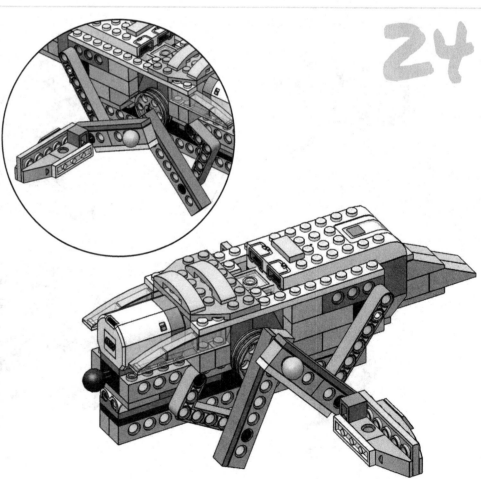

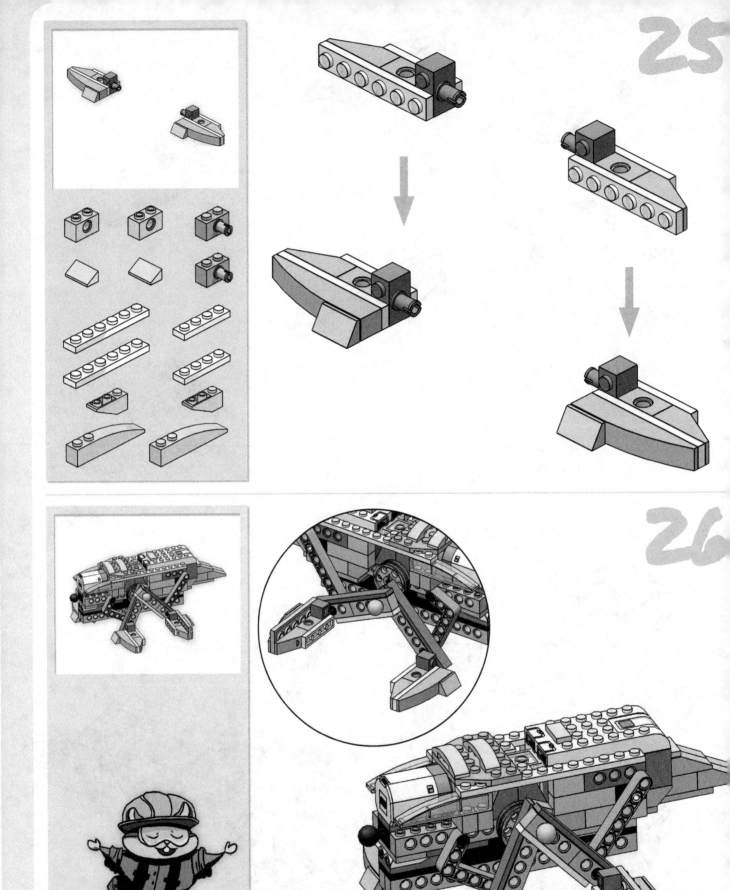

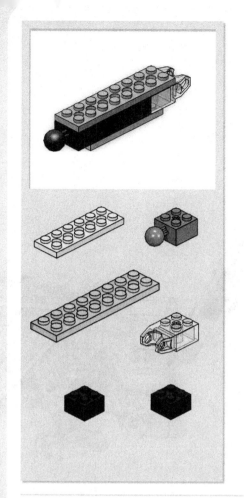

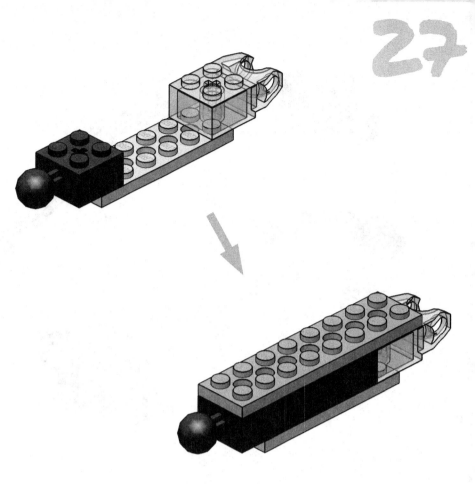

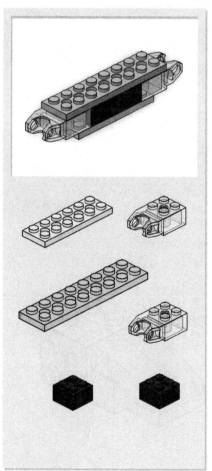

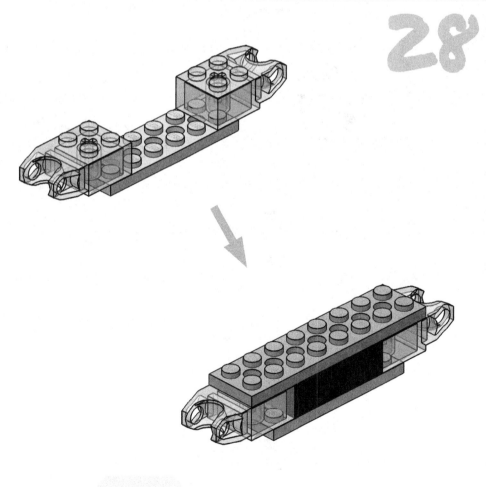

27

28

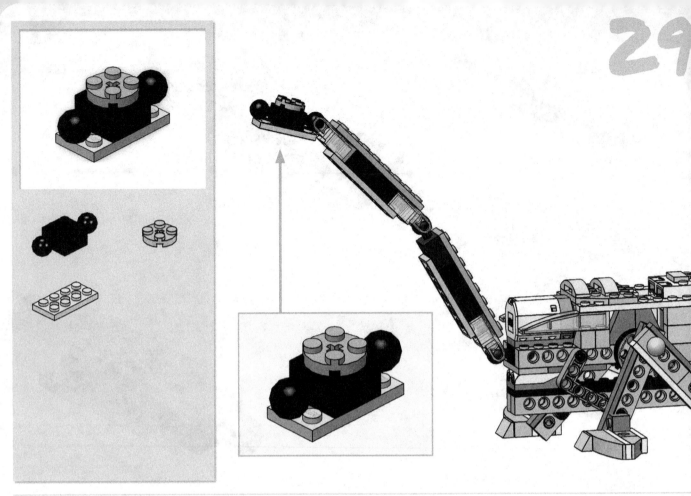

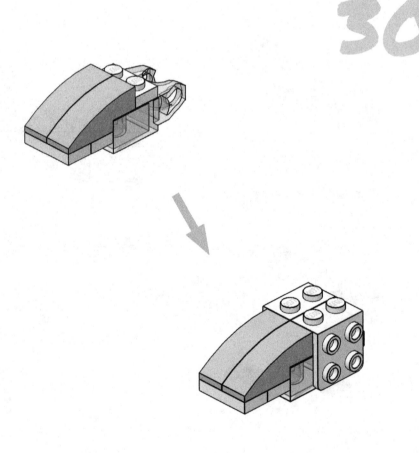

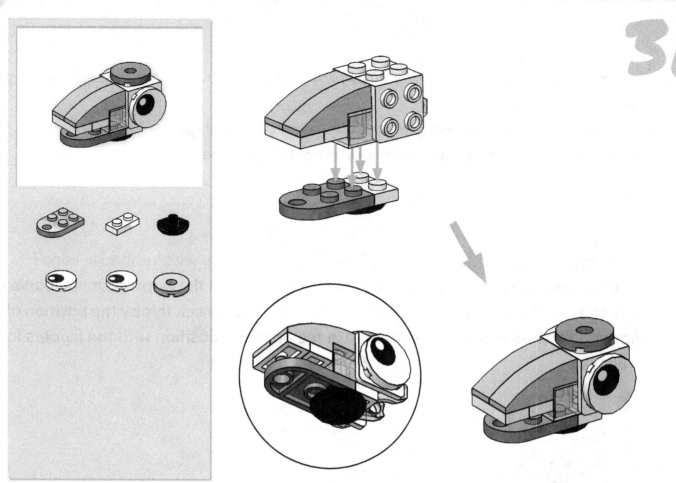

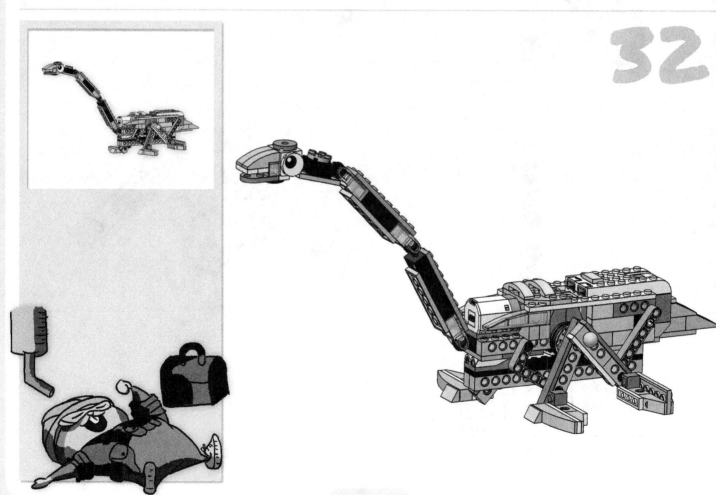

- Before going to the next phase, you can identify the mechanisms you are using in yo[ur] plesiosaurus prototype.
- Can you predict how your plesiosaurus prototype will move by only observing the prot[o]type?
- How many gears are you using in your plesiosaurus prototype?
- How many flippers does your plesiosaurus prototype have?

Design features

- Your plesiosaurus uses the motor to drive their four flippers.
- Can you identify the worm gear and the multiple Chebyshev's lambda linkage?
- Can you identify the driver gear and the follower gear in the worm gear mechanism?
- Are the four flippers in an out-phase motion? You can check this by the position of the flippers. Flippers in one side should be in the opposite position with the flippers in the other side.

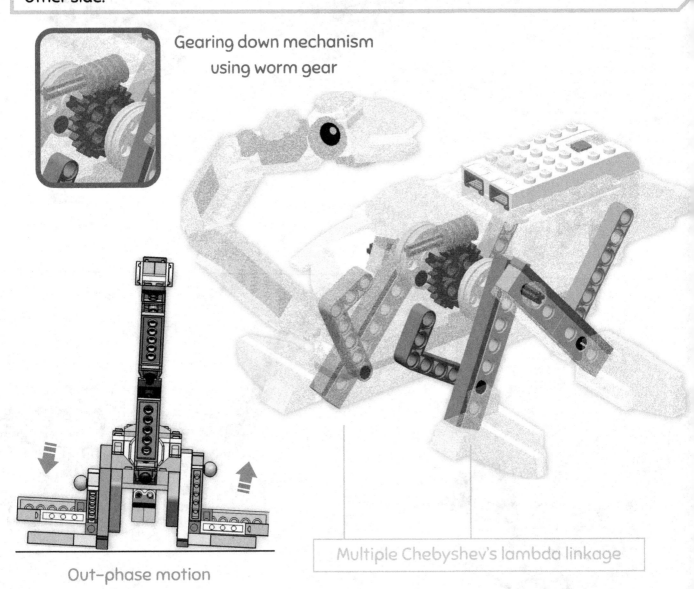

Gearing down mechanism
using worm gear

Out-phase motion

Multiple Chebyshev's lambda linkage

Program phase: Control on/off

· In this section, you will control the motor activation and deactivation (**on/off**) based on the readings from the distance sensor.

· The **program idea** consists of making your plesiosaurus stop every time its long neck is pointing downward and its head is touching the ground like it is drinking water. Once its neck is pointing upward, the plesiosaurus should start walking again. Thanks to the location of the distance sensor, your plesiosaurus prototype will know when its neck is pointing downward and upward.

The **algorithm** is as follows:

· The plesiosaurus with its neck pointing upward starts moving **forward**.

· The sensor **detects** if the neck is pointing downward.

·The Plesiosaurus **stops** moving.

· The sensor detects if the neck is pointing upward (**clear path**).

· The plesiosaurus starts moving **forward** again.

Flowchart

① Start the program

② Plesiosaurus moves forward

③ Set motor power

④ Sensor detects if neck is pointing downward

⑤ Plesiosaurus stops

⑥ Sensor detects if neck is pointing upward

Infinite loop

Distance sensor

· Similarly to the caiman program, you need to use the **distance change closer** and **distance change further** blocks to develop the plesiosaurus program.

· From the flowchart, you have **six tasks** plus an **infinite loop**. Therefore, your program have six blocks plus the infinite loop block.

· Now, you have everything ready to test your plesiosaurus prototype, so let's move to t next phase!

Test phase: Controlling motor on/off

· Remember to verify the **communication** between your WeDo software and your WeDo H Hub before you start testing your prototype.

TEST 1: Finding the right motor direction
· Identify in which direction your motor has to rotate to make your plesiosaurus move fc ward and backward.

· Before starting your program, move the neck of your plesiosaurus pointing upward:

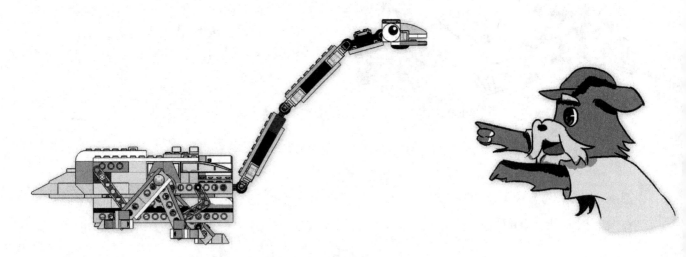

· Execute your program by clicking the "Start" block.

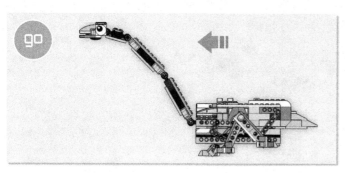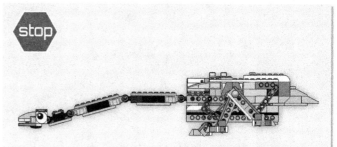

TEST 2: Initial conditions

· What happens if you start the program when your plesiosaurus is with its neck pointing downward? Do you observe any difference?

Could Plesiosaurus walk over land?

· The limbs of Plesiosaurus which were once legs in its ancestors evolved into **flippers** which make them better for **paddling** through the water than **walking** over ground.
· Similar to a sea lion, Plesiosaurus would be capable of pulling its body with the front flippers while pushing with the rear, being capable of **leaving the water** but not for any **great distance in land**.

Document & share phase

· Remember to collect all your **notes**, **videos**, and **photos** to report your **findings and results**.
· Write a report about your findings and observation from the **two tests** performed in the **test phase**.
· Record a video of your plesiosaurus performing given the **two different initial conditions**: starting with its neck pointing up-ward and starting with its neck pointing downward.

Enhancing the experience

· **Build:** Modify your plesiosaurus to an in-phase motion. How differently does it move?
· **Programming:** Instead of your plesiosaurus stopping when the neck is pointing down-ward, make it going backward, and when the neck is pointing upward, it should go forward.

DOG

Design phase: Multiphase synchronization

· Remember to have a **white paper** and a **pencil** to start drawing your ideas!

Looking for inspiration

· The dog is one of the most **popular pets** in the world. It is commonly referred to as "**man's best friend.**"

· Dogs are highly variable in **size** and **weight**.

· Dogs **defend** their **territories** and mark them by urinating on trees, rocks, fence posts, and other sites.

· Dogs **communicate** in several ways: body position, movement, and facial expression often convey a strong **message**.

Come on, Brolin; look how I walk using my four legs!
I am awesome!

I already know how to walk using my four legs! I better take a nap.

Multi phase synchronization

· In all previous prototypes, you did not have to use **synchronization** because only **one axle** was rotating to create the **walking motion**.

· Synchronization is really important to assure the **stabilization** of your quadruped when you have **multiple rotational axles**.

· An **out-phase motion** is based on how different or equal are the positions of opposite legs in one axle, but what happens if you have **two axles**? Let's explore in a more detailed way the **synchronization** concept.

Single-axle rotational motion

- Single-axle rotational motion means that you are only using **one single axle** to create the **walking motion**. You can see some examples using one axle (**red line**):

- As you can see in all previous prototypes, only one axle (**red line**) was rotating to create the **walking motion**.
- **Synchronization** is extremely important when you deal with more than one axle rotational motion.

Build phase: Multiple synchro and linkages

- In this section, you will explore two concepts: the **multiphase synchronization** motion and the **multiple lever linkage**.

Multiphase synchronization

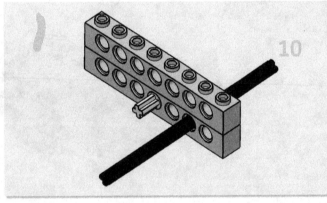

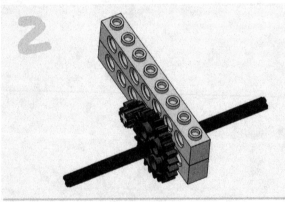

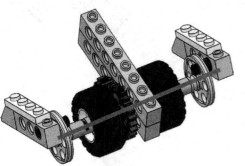

· Up to this point, you have a similar structure as the one developed in Chapter 4 to understand the **in-phase vs. out-phase** motion.

· **One single-axle** rotational motion (**red line**) is used, and the **in-phase** or **out-phase** motion is defined based on the **position of the legs** at opposite sides.

· Before continuing, **remove the legs** and leave them aside so you can add them at the end.

· Before adding the four legs, can you identify the **two-axle rotational motion**? For each axle, you can define an **in-phase** or an **out-phase** motion.

Different synchronization arrangements

①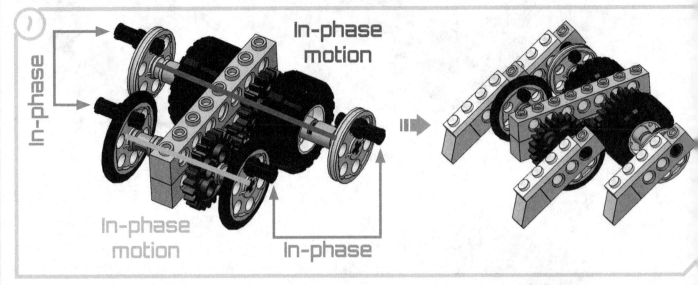

In-phase

In-phase motion

In-phase motion

In-phase

②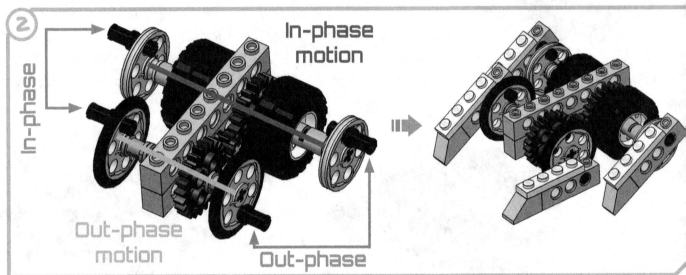

In-phase

In-phase motion

Out-phase motion

Out-phase

③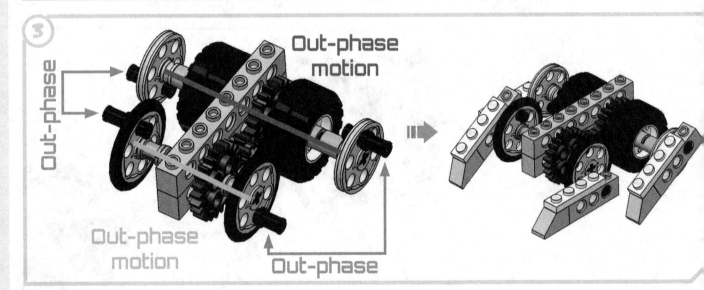

Out-phase

Out-phase motion

Out-phase motion

Out-phase

- How different are the movements of the legs for each of the **three cases**?
- Now you will explore a **new linkage** to use as a walking motion mechanism.

Multiple lever linkage

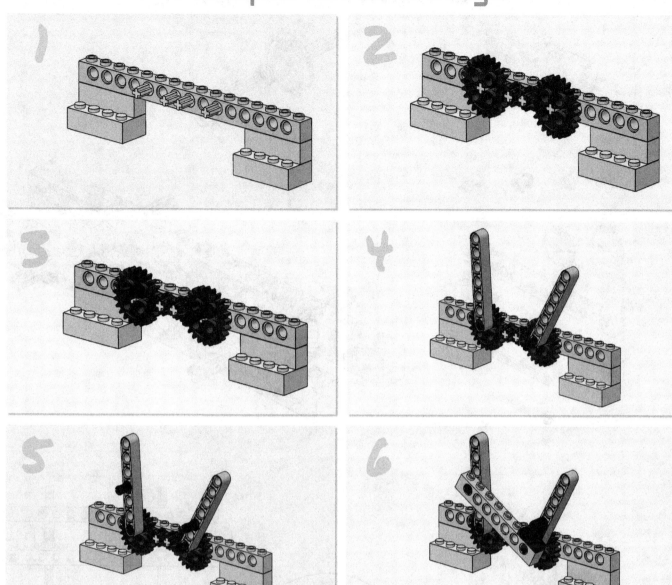

- Both gears must be **in-phase**, meaning that the connectors in both gears are located at the **same position**.

- The linkage is composed of **two beams**, one with an "I" shape and the other with an "L" shape.

- Before you start building your WeDo dog, prepare a **suitable workspace**.
- Keep in mind that the WeDo set has small pieces, so prepare a table with enough space to easily identify all the pieces and prevent them from getting lost.

Building instructions

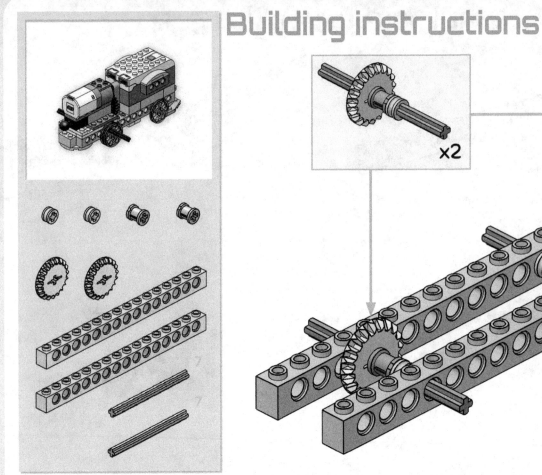

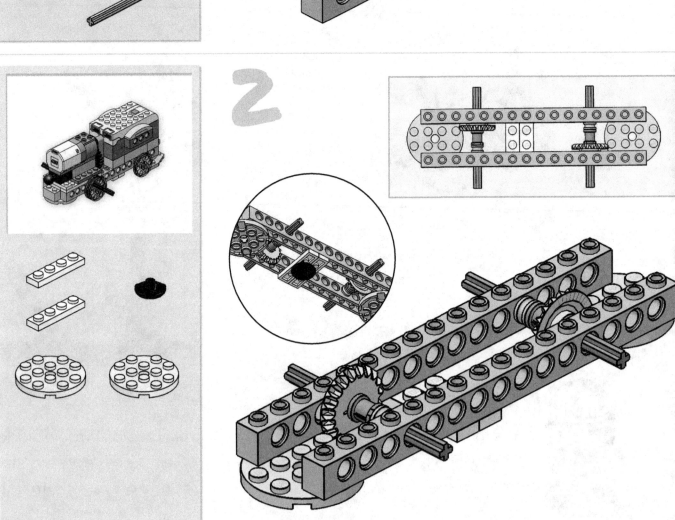

3

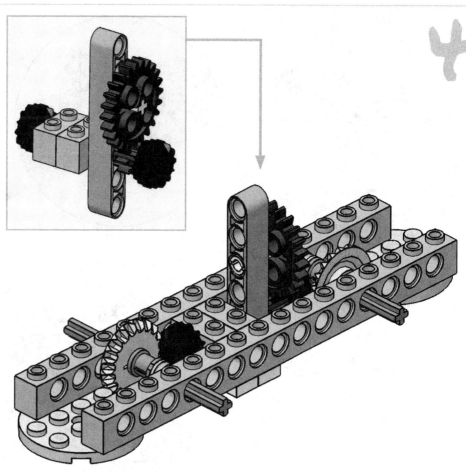

4

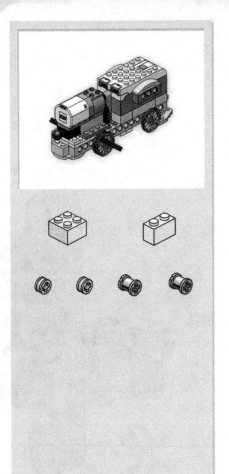

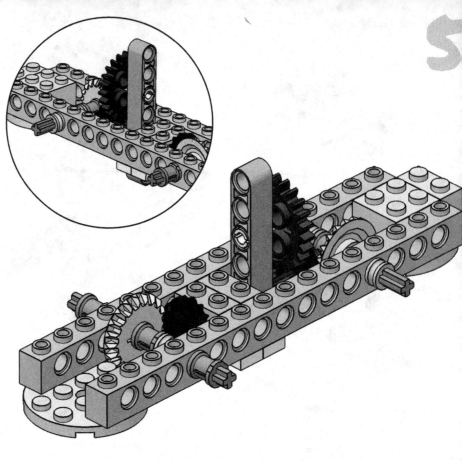

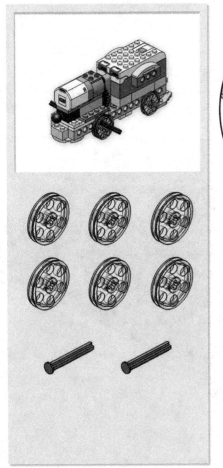

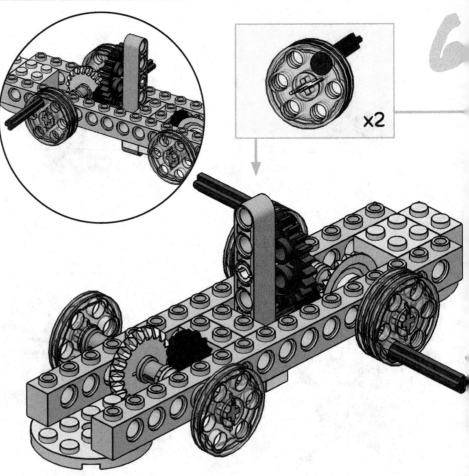

x2

Synchronizing the motion: The position of all the pulleys must be exactly as shown:

Left view:

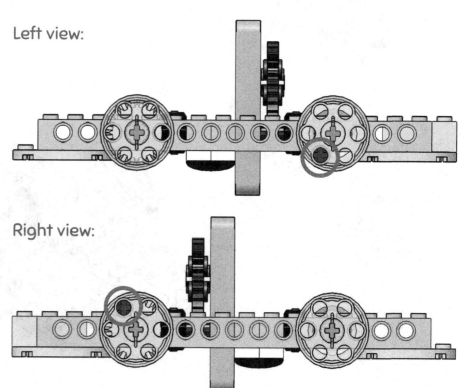

Right view:

Axles in an out–phase motion

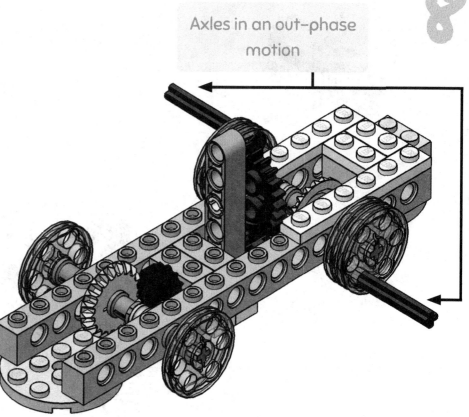

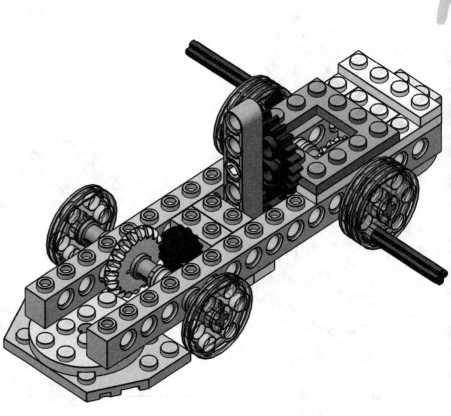

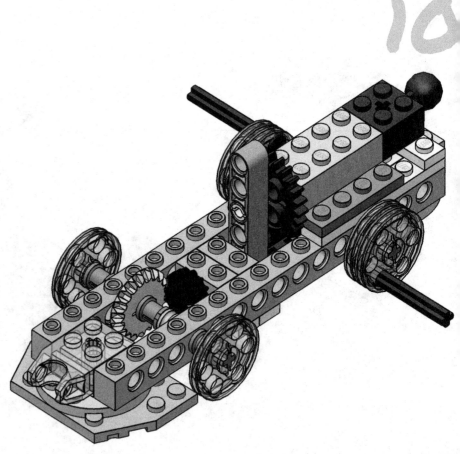

Push the axle into the motor.

11

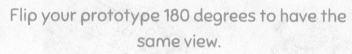

Flip your prototype 180 degrees to have the same view.

12

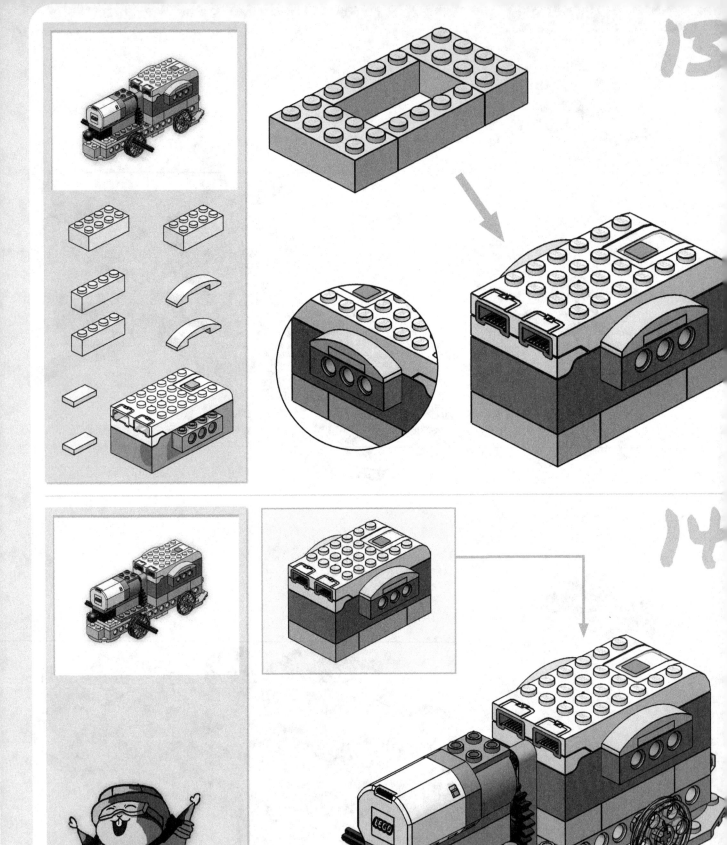

13

14

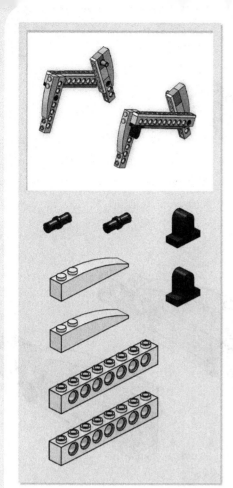

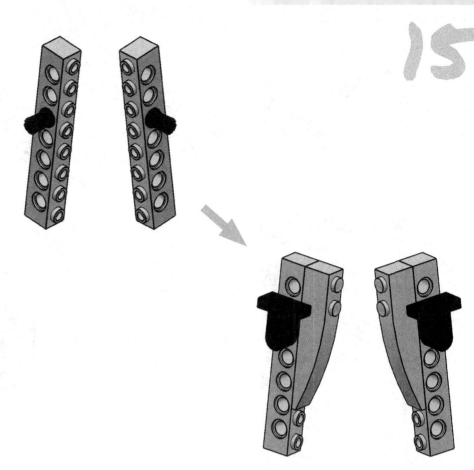

15

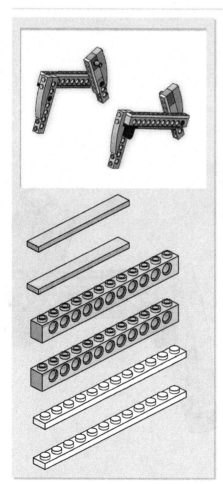

16

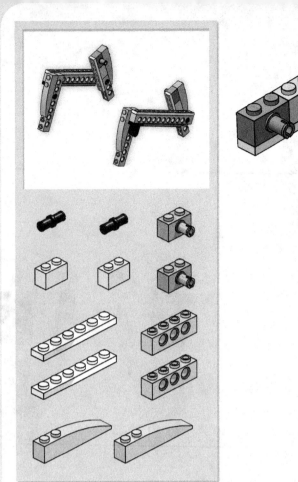

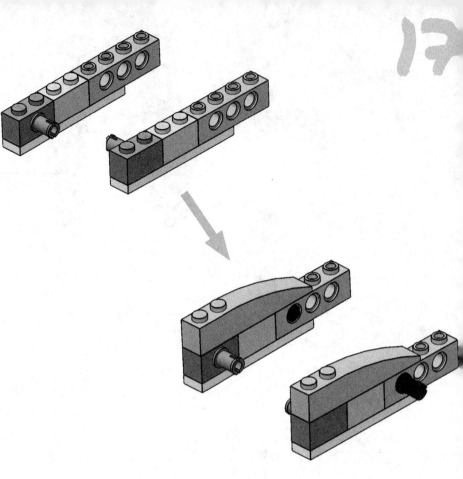

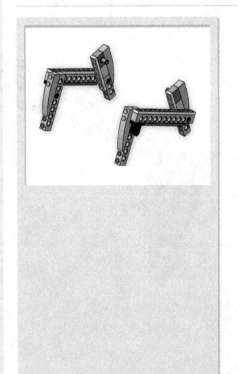

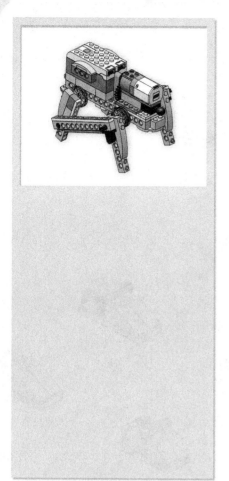

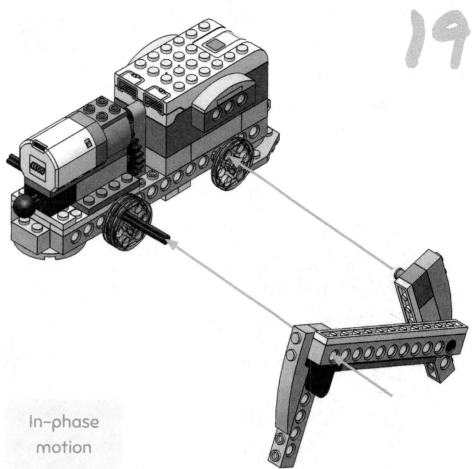

In-phase
motion

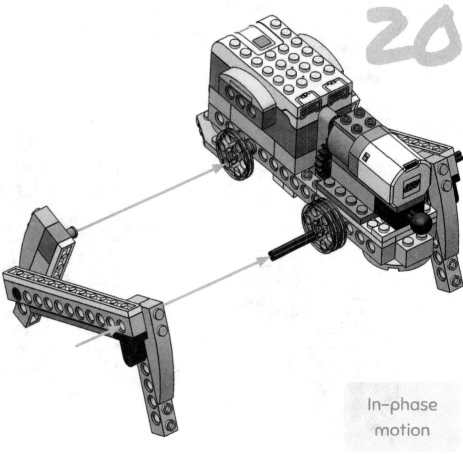

In-phase
motion

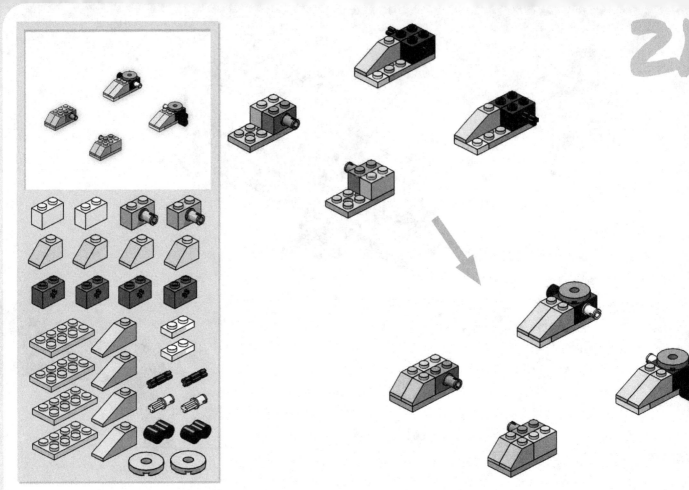

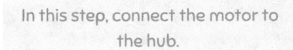
In this step, connect the motor to the hub.

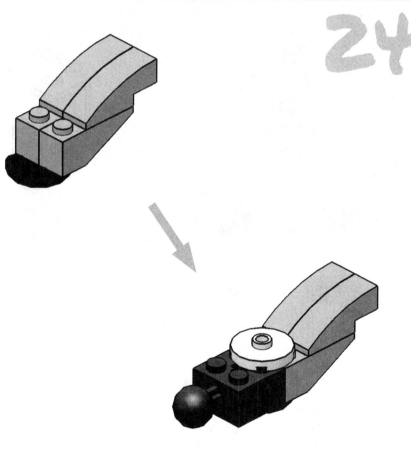

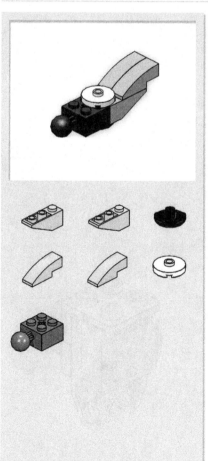

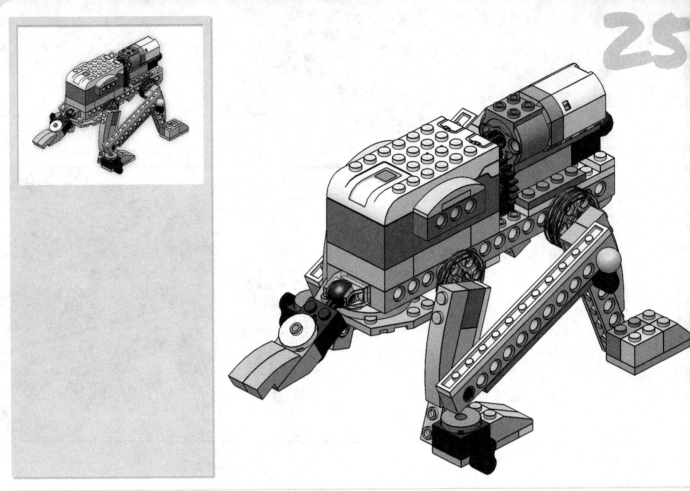

25

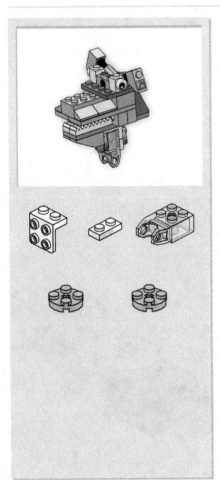

26

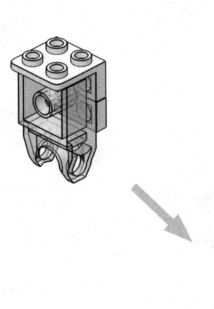

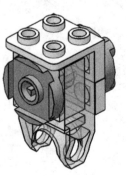

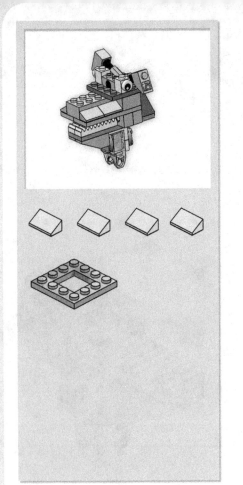

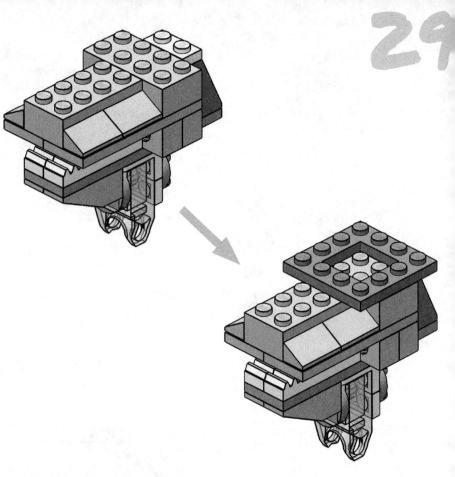

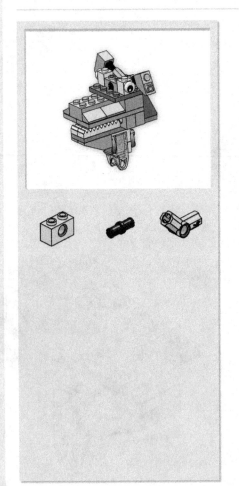

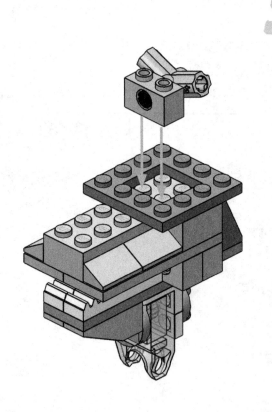

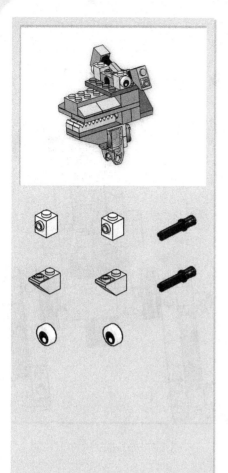

31

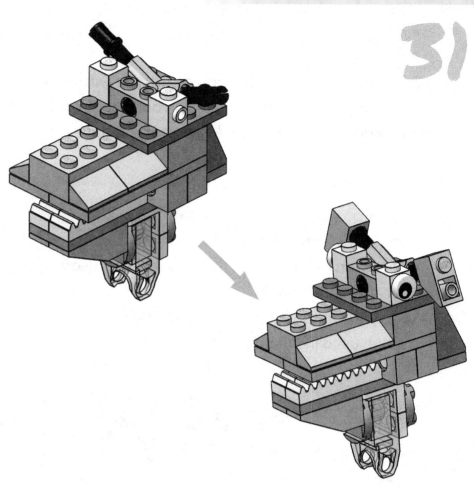

32

· Before going to the next phase, you can identify the mechanisms you are using in your d
prototype.

· Can you predict how your dog prototype will move by only seeing the model?

· How many gears are you using in your dog prototype?

· How many legs does your dog prototype have?

Design features

· Your dog uses the motor to drive its four legs.

· Can you identify the multiple lever linkage?

· How many bevel gear mechanisms are used in your dog prototype?

· Can you identify the multiphase synchronization motion used in your dog prototype?

Out-phase motion

Bevel gear mechanisms

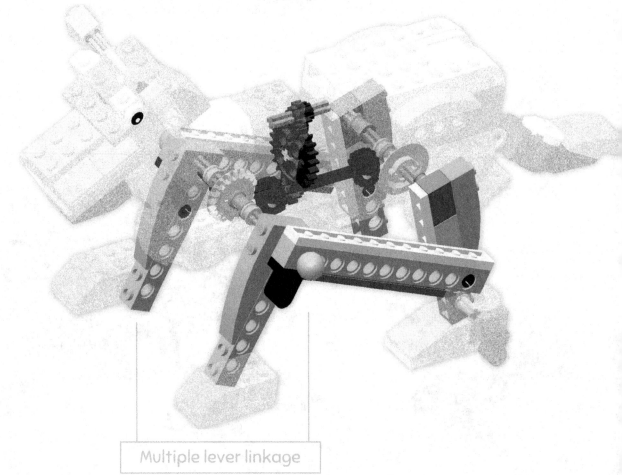

Multiple lever linkage

Let's analyze the synchronization arrangement used in your dog prototype!

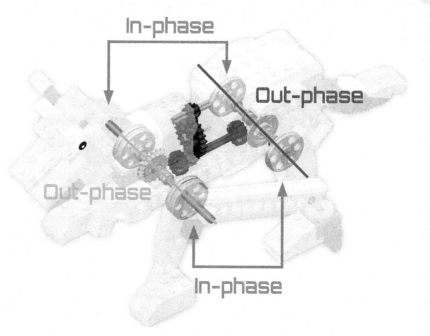

In-phase

Out-phase

Out-phase

In-phase

Program phase: Input sound block

· In this section, you will explore the use of an input **sound block**.

· The **program idea** consists of moving and stopping your dog by sound commands.

· In a more detailed way, your dog will move forward until "**hearing**" a strong noise such as a clap; after that, the dog will stop and will remain like that until "**hearing**" another strong noise. Then, it will start walking forward again.

Flowchart

You can program your dog to follow some sound commands!

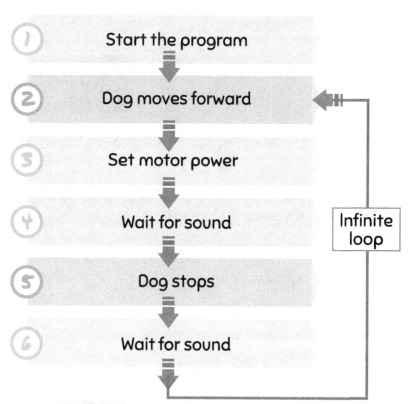

① Start the program

② Dog moves forward

③ Set motor power

④ Wait for sound

⑤ Dog stops

⑥ Wait for sound

Infinite loop

Microphone

- **Microphones** are **sound sensors** used in phones, computers, baby monitors, and music systems like karaoke machines.
- **Sound sensors** work by mimicking the human body process that involves the **ears** and signal transmission to the brain.
- In your WeDo software, you can use the **microphone block** to program tasks using your microphone signal as an input (**sensor**).

- The flowchart indicates **six tasks** and an infinite block. Therefore, you assign a **programming block** for **each task**:

- **Task 2** indicates that your dog goes forward. Which of **these blocks** will make your dog forward?

- You will find out the answer to this question on the **test phase**!

Test phase: Motor control by sound

- Remember to verify the **communication** between your WeDo software and your WeDo hardware before you start testing your prototype.

- Start testing your prototype by executing the program developed in the **program phase** by clicking the "Start" block.

TEST 1: Finding the right motor direction

· Identify in which direction your motor has to rotate to make your dog move forward and backward.

TEST 2: Sound commands

· Test your program. Check if your dog moves or stops by making sounds such as clapping.

TEST 3: Friction to walk

· Remove the rubber parts located at the bottom of your dog's legs:

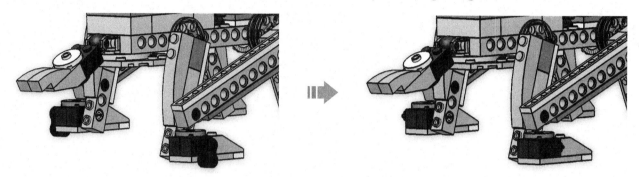

· Execute your program and see how your dog moves without the rubber parts. Does it walk better or worse than using the rubber parts?

TEST 4: Modifying the synchronization arrangement

· Modify the position of yous dog's legs to test different synchronizations between each of the four legs. How does the walking movement change by trying new synchronization arrangements?

Document & share phase

· Remember to collect all your **notes, videos**, and **photos** to report your **findings and results**.
· Record a video of your dog using and not using the rubber parts and make a comparison.
· Record a video of your dog walking using different synchronization arrangements. How different is the motion for each synchronization arrangement?

Enhancing the experience

· **Build:** Try to modify the legs of your dog. Can you make your dog sit?
· **Programming:** Add another option to make your dog walk backward.

In the next chapter, you will build
and program robots that look
like humans; they are called
humanoids!

6

HUMANOIDS

Contents

SKIER

Design phase: Humanoids

· Remember to have a **white paper** and a **pencil** to start drawing your ideas!

Looking for inspiration

· Skiing is a **recreation**, **sport**, and **mode of transportation** that involves moving over snow by the use of a pair of long, flat runners called **skis**, attached or bound to shoes or boots.

· Different techniques (**motions**) are used depending on if the skier is going **downhill** or **uphill**. In a **downhill**, the skier slides down on skis with fixed-heel bindings. In an **uphill**, the skier uses a classical diagonal stride that emulates a walking motion.

Skiers move differently depending on if they are in an uphill or a downhill.

· On a piece of paper, you can sketch some **ideas** of how your skier will look like and how it will move!

· For your skier prototype, you will be resembling an **uphill walking motion**.

Humanoids

· A humanoid robot is a robot with its appearance built to resemble the **human body** and replicate **human motion**.

Build phase: Multiphase synchro motion

· Similarly to your dog prototype built in the previous chapter, your skier uses a multiphase synchronization motion with a **Chebyshev's lambda linkage**.

· Before you start building your WeDo skier, prepare a **suitable workspace**.

· Keep in mind that the WeDo set has small pieces, so prepare a table with enough space to easily identify all the pieces and prevent them from getting lost.

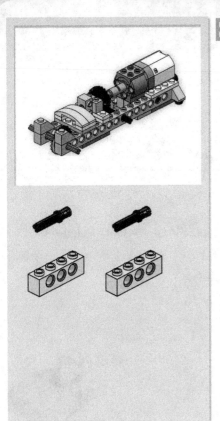

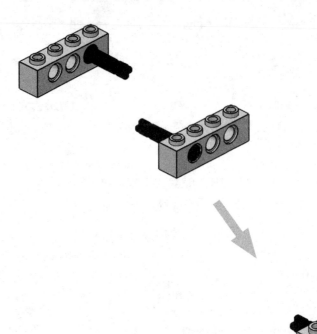

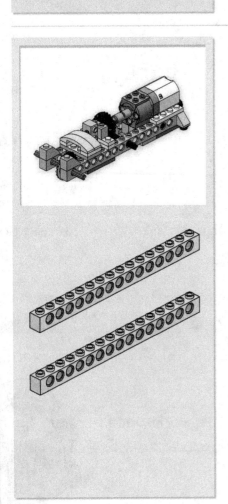

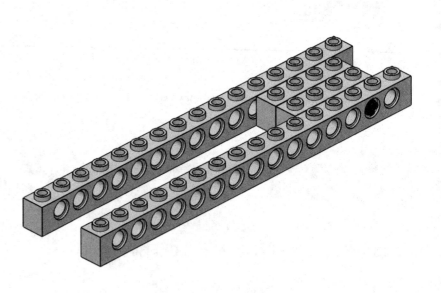

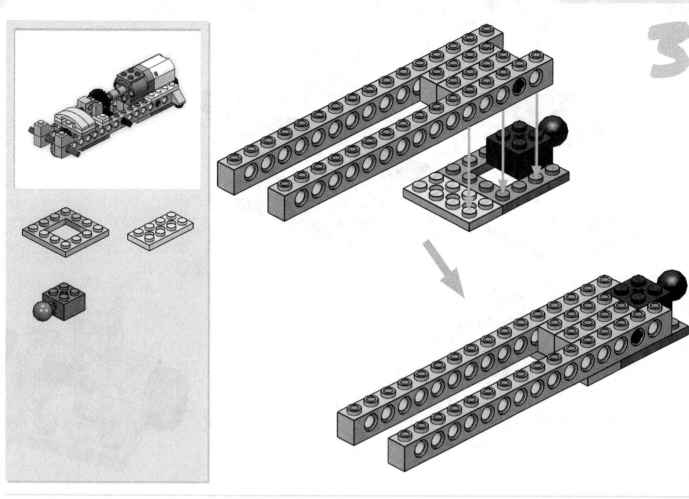

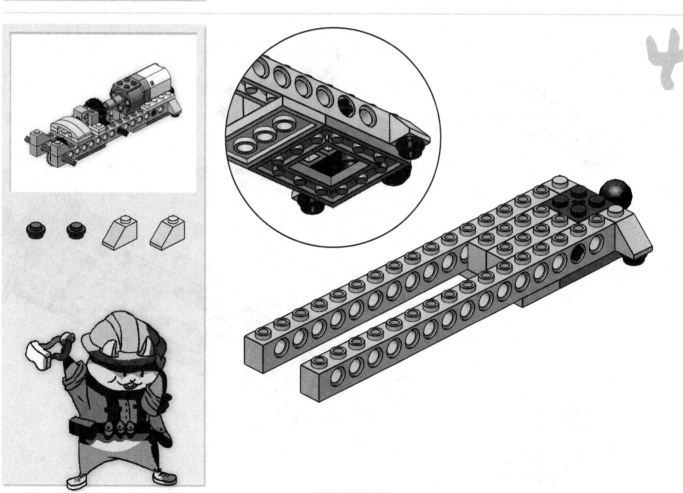

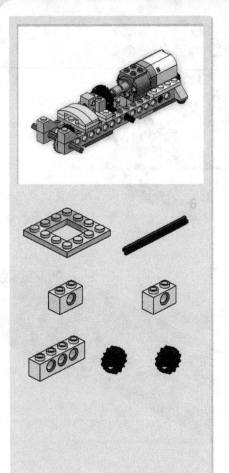

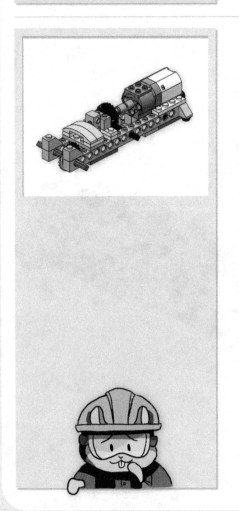

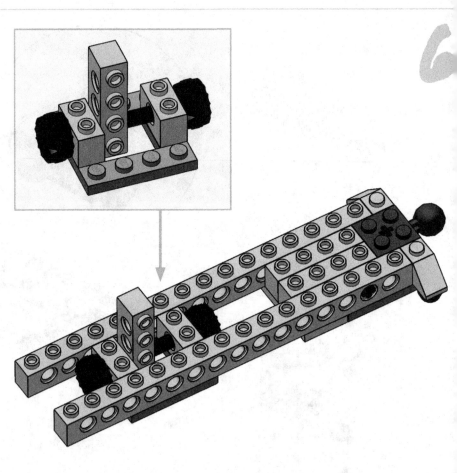

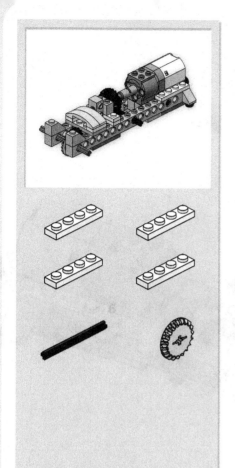

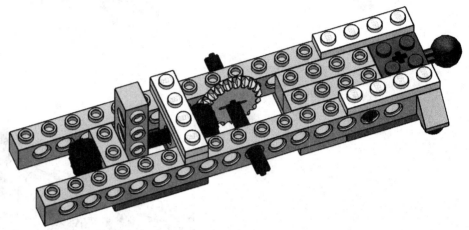

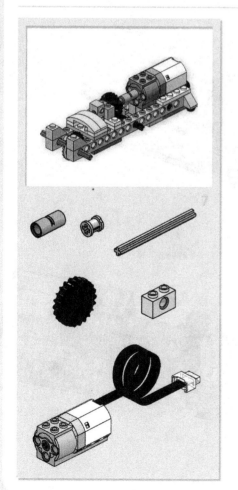

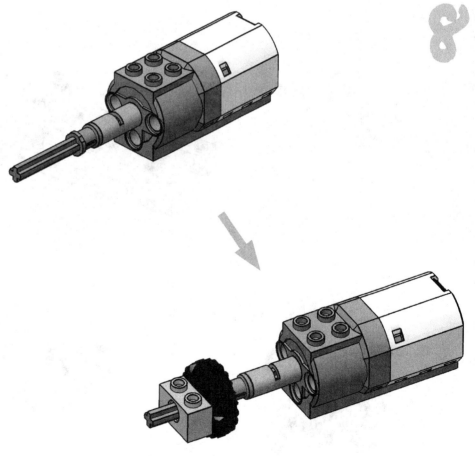

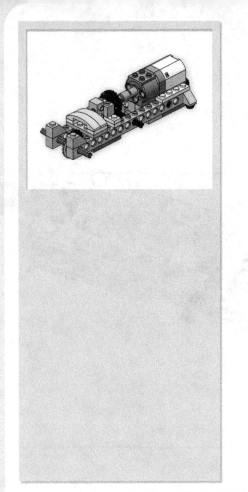

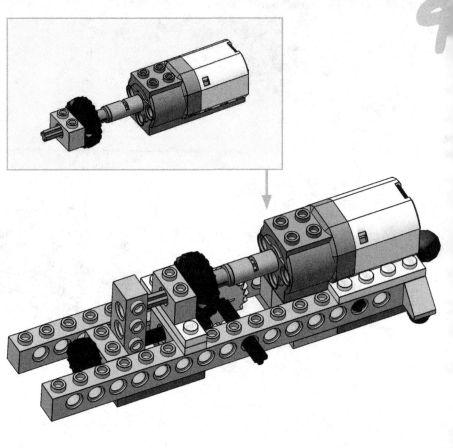

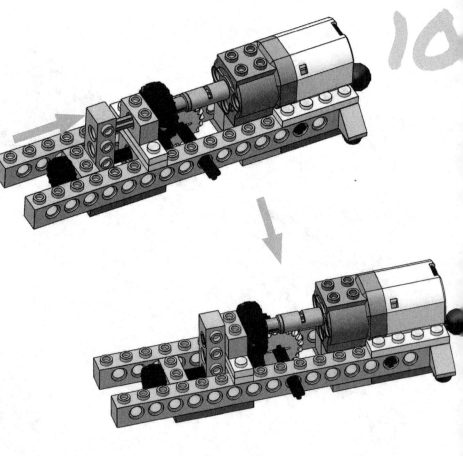

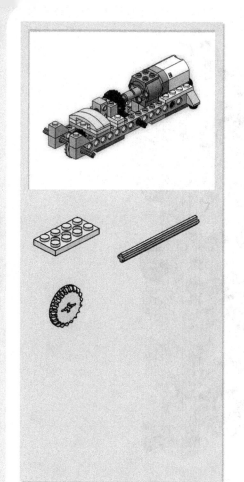

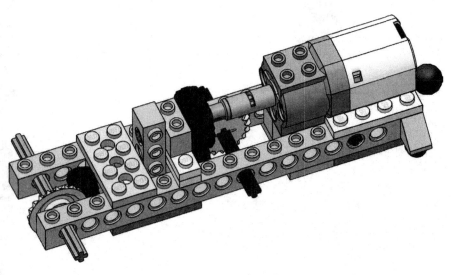

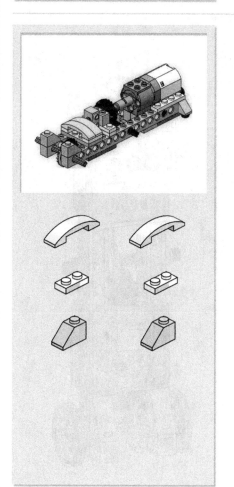

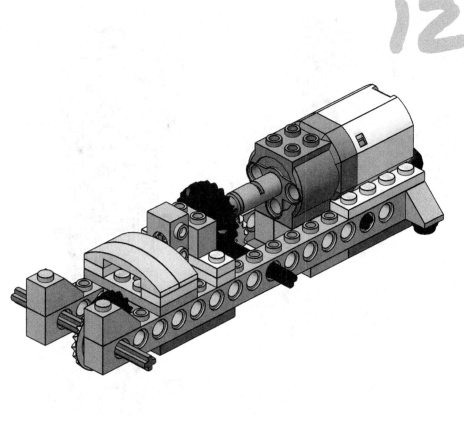

Flip over your prototype to have the same view.

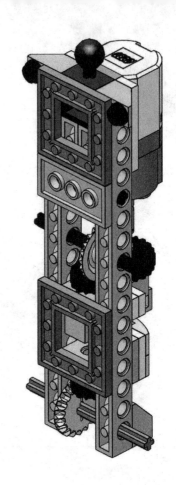

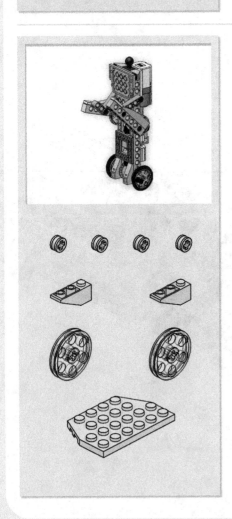

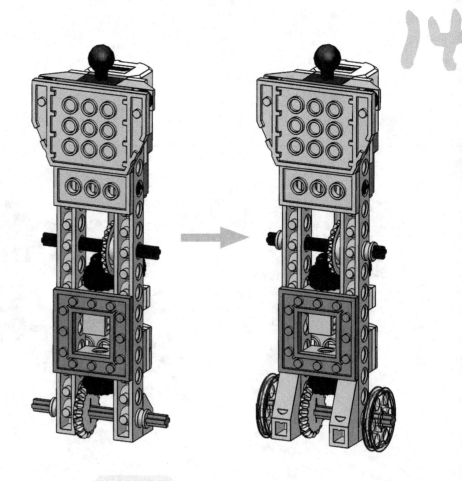

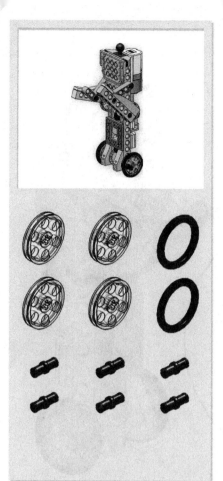

15

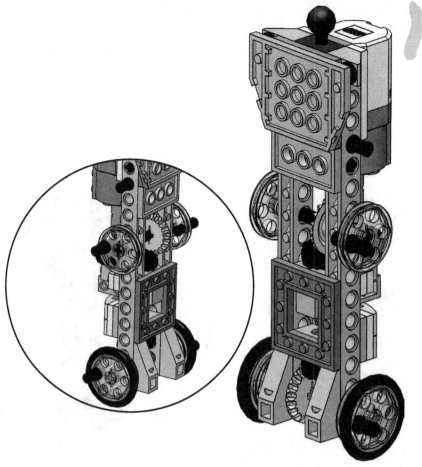

16

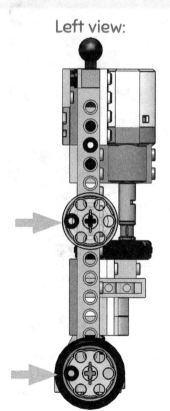

Synchronizing the motion: The position of all the pulleys must be exactly as shown:

Left view:

Right view:

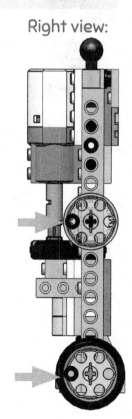

17

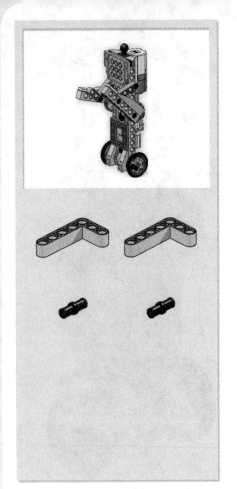

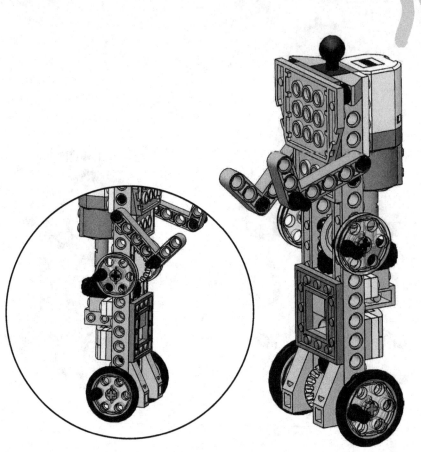

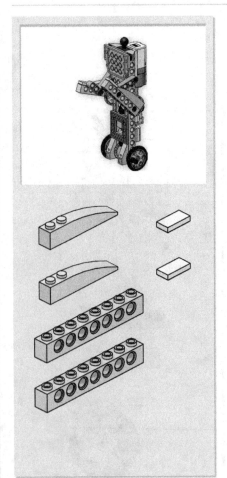

18

x2

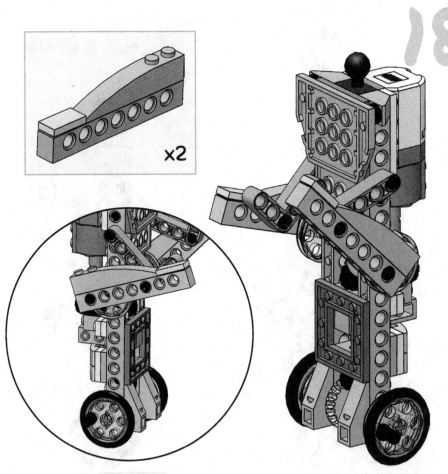

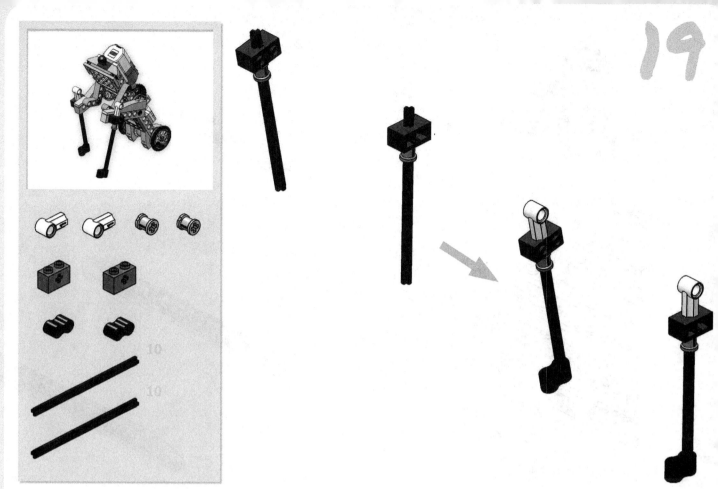

19

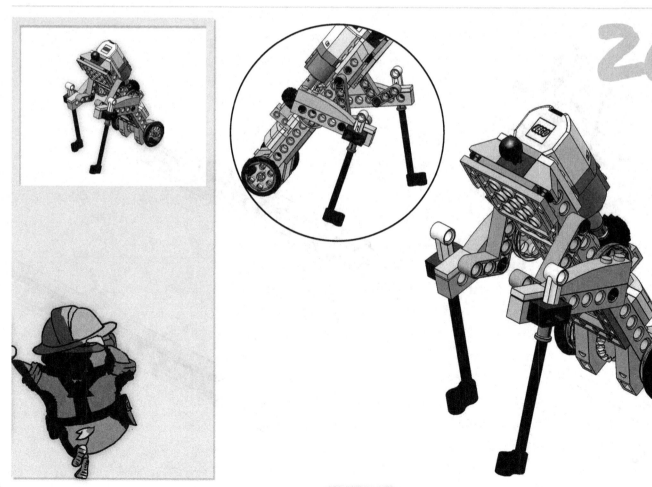

20

241

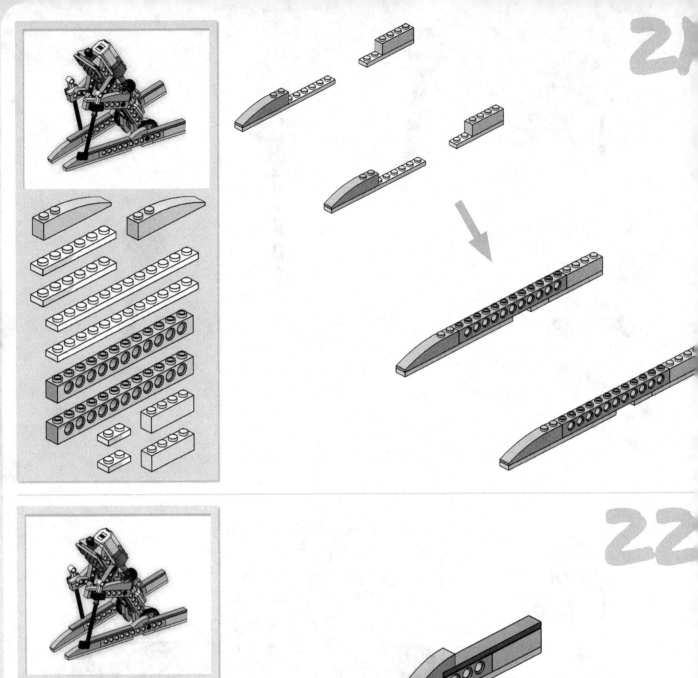

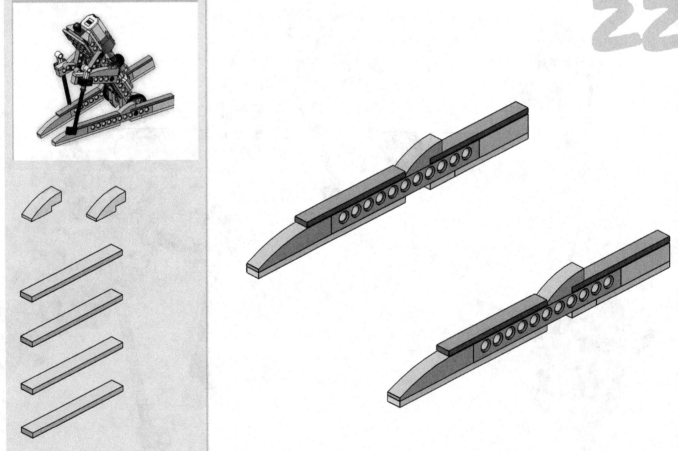

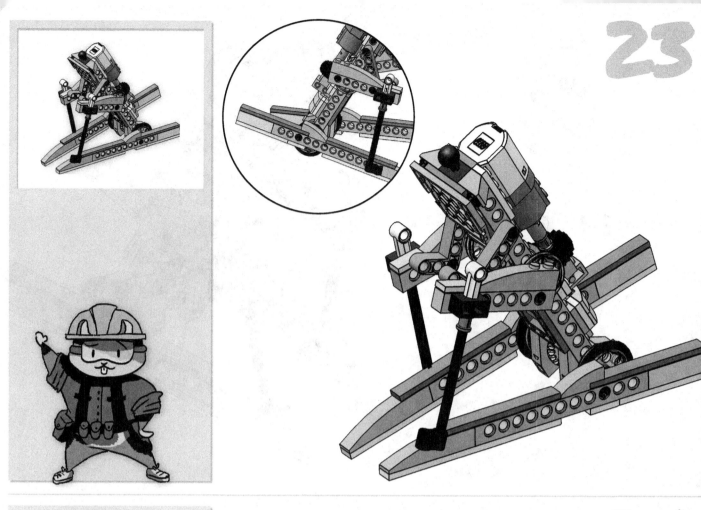

23

24

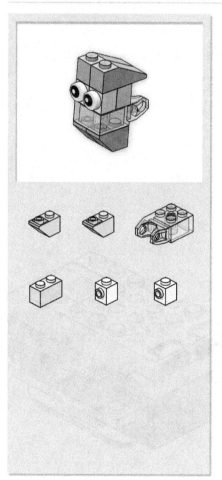

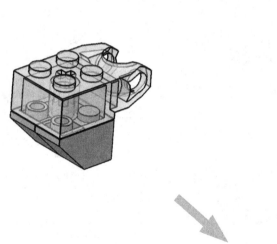

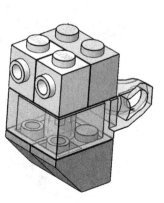

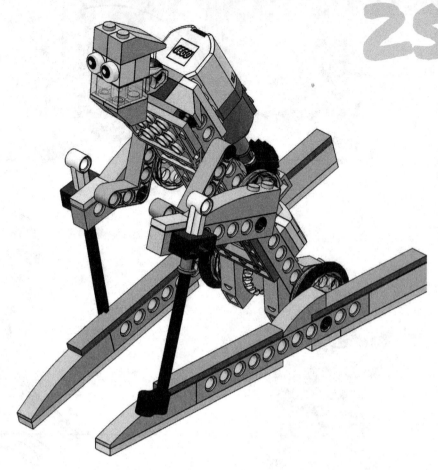

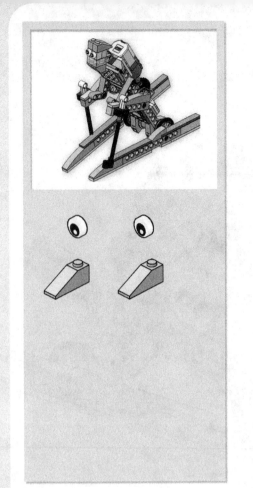

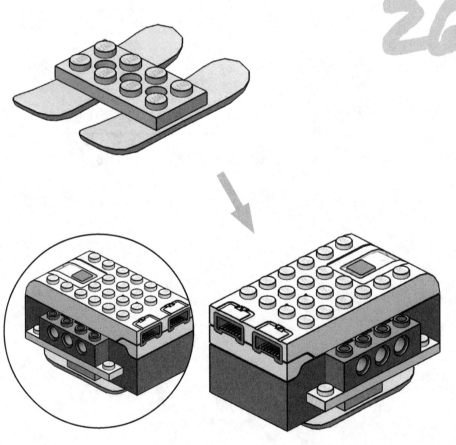

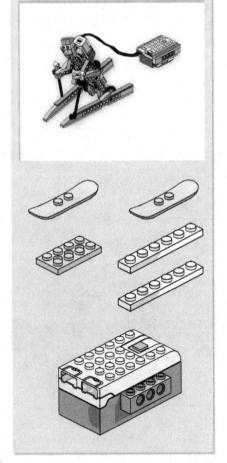

25

26

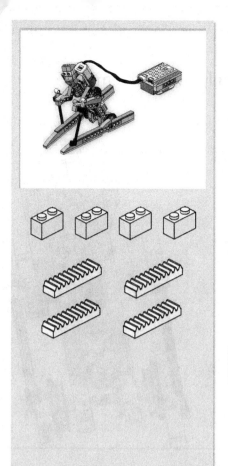

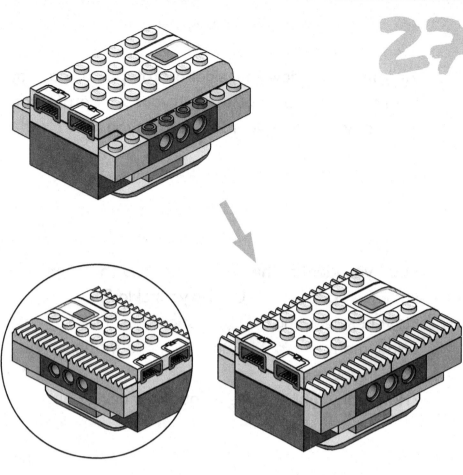

In this step, connect the motor to the hub.

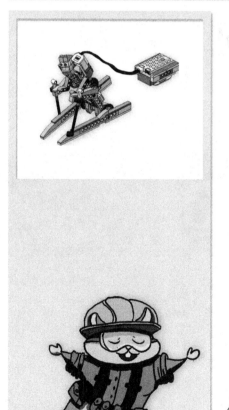

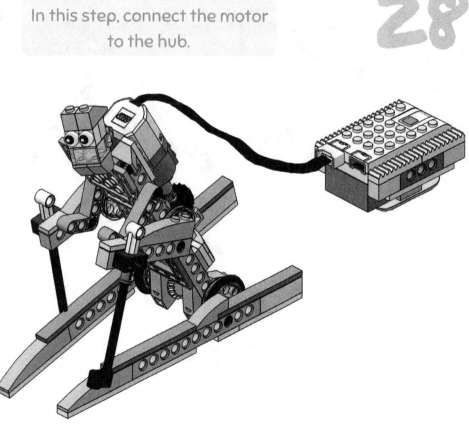

• Before going to the next phase, you can identify the mechanisms you are using in yc skier prototype.

• Can you predict how your skier prototype will move by only seeing the model?

• How many gears are you using in your skier prototype?

• How many legs does your skier prototype have?

Design features

• Your skier uses the motor to drive its two legs and two arms.

• Can you identify the bevel gears and the Chebyshev's lambda linkage used in your skier?

• Is your skier using multiple synchronization?

• How many out-phase and in-phase motions are used in your skier?

• How many rubber parts is your skier using?

Out-phase motion

Bevel gears mechanism

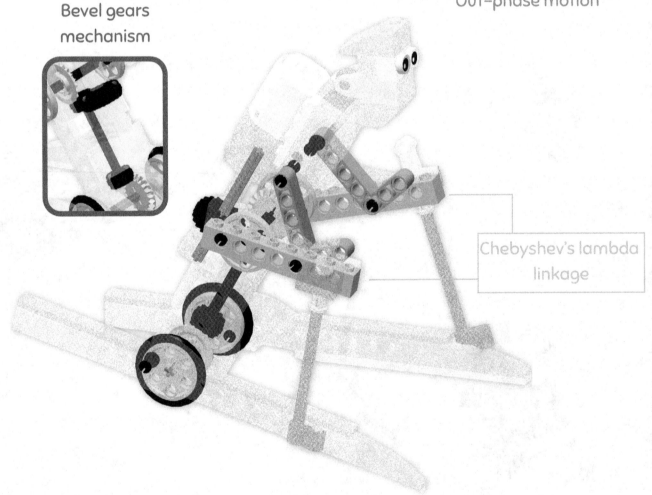

Chebyshev's lambda linkage

Let's analyze the synchronization arrangement used in your skier prototype!

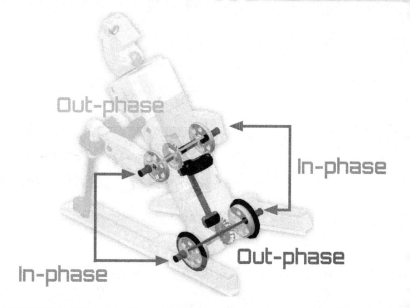

Out-phase

In-phase

In-phase

Out-phase

Program phase: Motor ramp starting

· In this section, you will explore the use of ramp starting for your motor.

· The **program idea** consists of moving forward your skier increasing its speed. Your skier will start moving very slow, and it will accelerate until reaching the maximum power. We will be using a **variable** to develop the program.

Flowchart

· Tasks 1, 2, 3, and 4 are called **initial conditions** since they are only **executed once** at the beginning of your program.

· Tasks 5, 6, and 7 are executed 10 times, taking the **motor power** from a value of **0** up to a value of **10**.

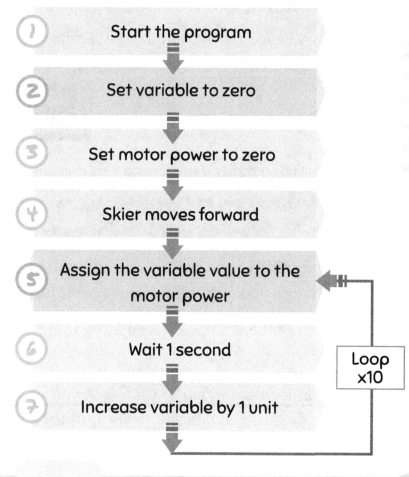

1. Start the program
2. Set variable to zero
3. Set motor power to zero
4. Skier moves forward
5. Assign the variable value to the motor power
6. Wait 1 second
7. Increase variable by 1 unit

Loop x10

- The flowchart indicates **7 tasks**. Therefore, you assign a **programming block** for **each ta**

Are variables useful?

- Variables can be used to **reduce the size of our code**.
- If you want to develop the same program for your skier without the use of variables your program would look like this:

- With variables, you have **7 tasks** in your program; without variables, you have **23 tasks**
- When you decrease the number of tasks, you are performing a **code optimization**.

- **Task 4** indicates that your skier is moving forward. Which of **these blocks** will move yo skier **forward?**

- You will find out the answer to this question on the **test phase!**

Test phase: Accelerate motion

- Remember to verify the **communication** between your WeDo software and your We hub before you start testing your prototype.

- Start testing your prototype by executing the program developed in the **program pha** by clicking the "Start" block.

TEST 1: Finding the right motor direction
- Identify in which direction your motor should rotate for your skier to move forward a backward.

TEST 2: 23-block program vs. 7-block program

· Do you find any difference between the program using 23 programming blocks and the program using 7 programming blocks?

TEST 3: Increasing or decreasing the acceleration rate

· You can accelerate or decelerate your **motor ramp starting** by increasing or decreasing the wait time in task 6:

Accelerating:

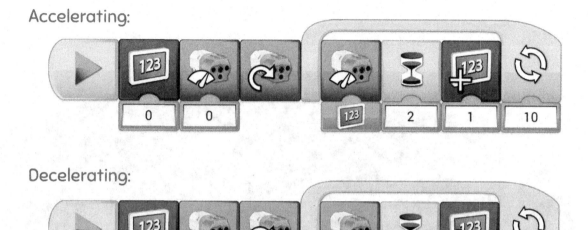

Decelerating:

TEST 4: Removing the friction

· Remove all the rubber parts from your skier, including the two located on its sticks and the tires located on its legs. Start your program and see how the motion has changed.

Document & share phase

· Remember to collect all your **notes**, **videos**, and **photos** to report your **findings and results**.
· Record a video with and without your skier moving using the rubber parts and make a comparison.
· Write your findings and results of all the **four tests** performed in the **test phase**.

Enhancing the experience

· **Build:** Try to modify the arm and leg positions of your skier into an in-phase motion. Now your skier should perform a downhill motion instead of an uphill motion.
· **Programming:** Can you think about another program using a variable?

ASTRONAUT

Looking for inspiration

- Humans are driven to **explore the unknown**, and the **space** is a territory that has a **lot of mysteries** that have called humans' attention since **ancient times**.
- **Human space exploration** helps to unravel the mysteries about our place in the Universe.
- On **July 20, 1969**, the US Apollo 11 mission made the first **moon landing**.
- The term "**astronaut**" derives from Greek and means "space sailor."
- An **astronaut** is someone who has been launched as a crew member aboard a **spaceship** into **outer space** to investigate it.

Nazca lines

- The Nazca was a culture located in a **southern desert of Peru**, and it is famous due to its inexplicable and impressive **lines drawn in the ground**.
- The lines are known as **geoglyphs** – drawings on the ground made by removing rocks and earth to create an **image**.
- The lines are drawn in **geometric patterns** and distinct animal and humanoid shapes.

- The size of the straight lines runs up to **30 miles**, while the animals and humanoids range from **50 to 1200 feet** in length. Given their sizes, the lines are best seen from the air.
- Scientists believe that the majority of lines were made by the **Nazca people**, around A.D. 1 to 700.
- One of the most popular lines is a humanoid figure nicknamed "The Astronaut."

- On a piece of paper, you can sketch some **ideas** of how your astronaut prototype will look like!

> I will design an astronaut prototype inspired by the ones drawn by the Nazca people!

Humanoid bipedal motion

- The humanoid robot overall design is a very complex task since they are designed and manufactured to **resemble the human body**.
- When a humanoid performs biped walking, the **stability** must be guaranteed at any moment.
- The **center of gravity** is very important in the development of walking humanoids.

- In the **1970s**, **Honda** started wide research on humanoid bipedal robots, and nowadays there are numerous **research projects** performed by companies and universities to develop better humanoid robots.

Build phase: Parallel Chebyshev's lambda

- Follow the building instructions to build your own **parallel Chebyshev's lambda linkage**.

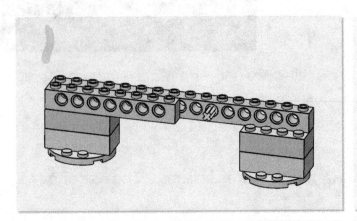

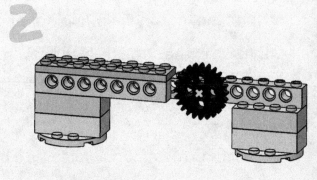

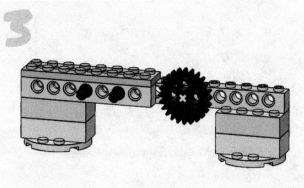

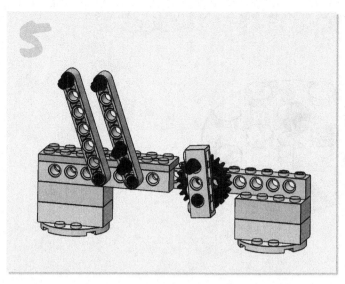

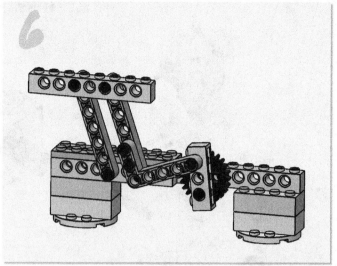

· Turn the gear to see the motion generated by your **parallel Chebyshev's lambda linkage**.

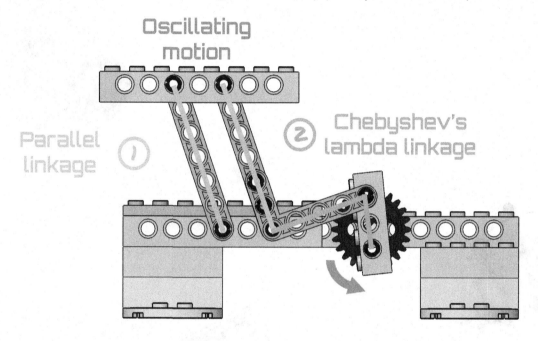

Oscillating motion

Parallel linkage ① ② Chebyshev's lambda linkage

· The **parallel Chebyshev's lambda linkage** changes the **rotational motion** of the gear into an **oscillating motion** of the green beam.

· The particularity of the **oscillating motion** generated is that the beam always keeps its **horizontal position** at any moment.

· The parallel Chebyshev's lambda linkage is a **multiple linkage** since it is composed of two: a **parallel linkage** and a **Chebyshev's lambda linkage**.

· Now you are ready to build your WeDo astronaut prototype!

· Before you start building, prepare a **suitable workspace**.

· Keep in mind that the WeDo set has small pieces, so prepare a table with enough space to easily identify all the pieces and prevent them from getting lost.

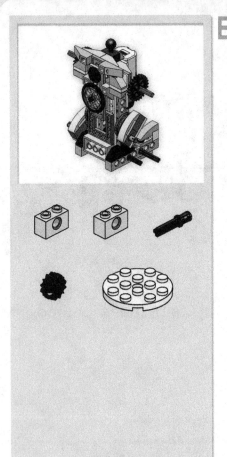

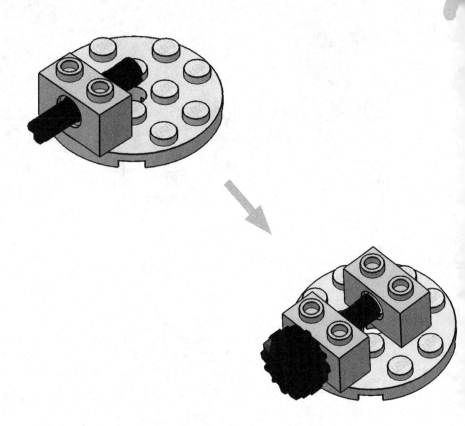

2

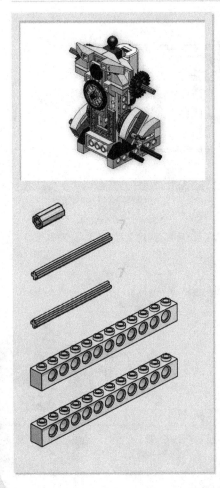

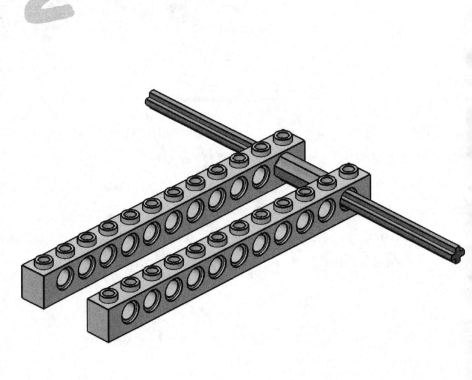

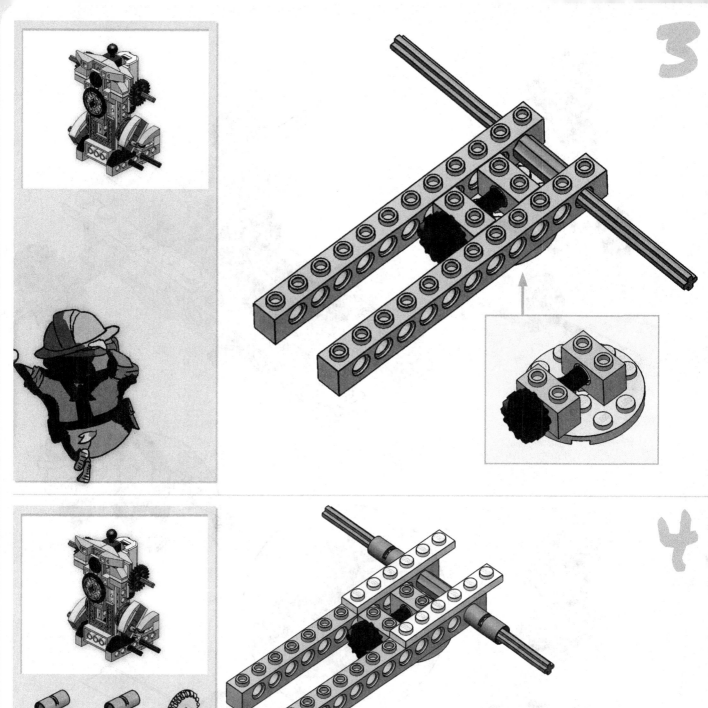

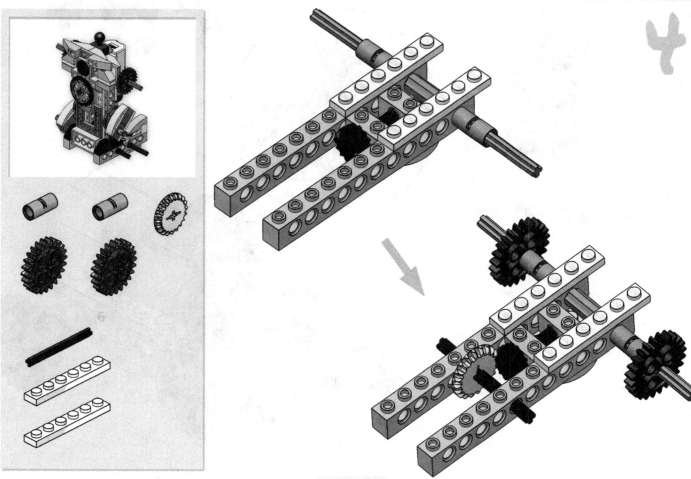

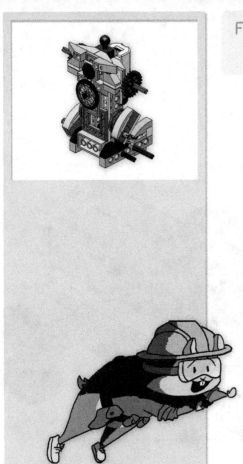

Flip over your prototype to have the same view.

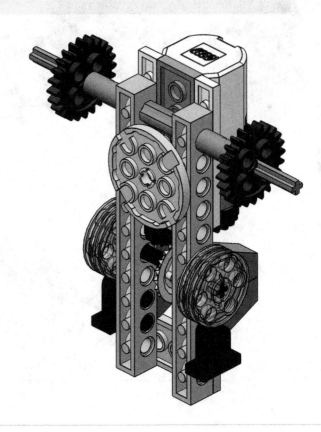

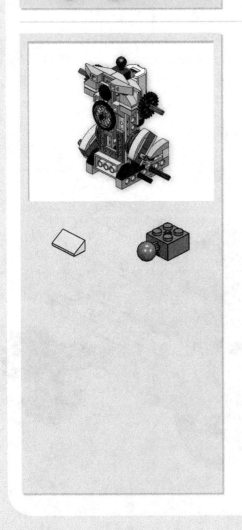

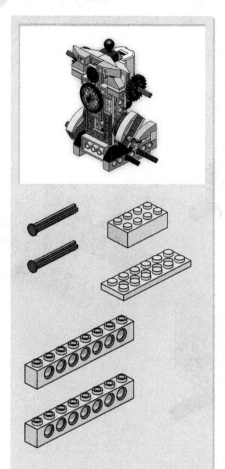

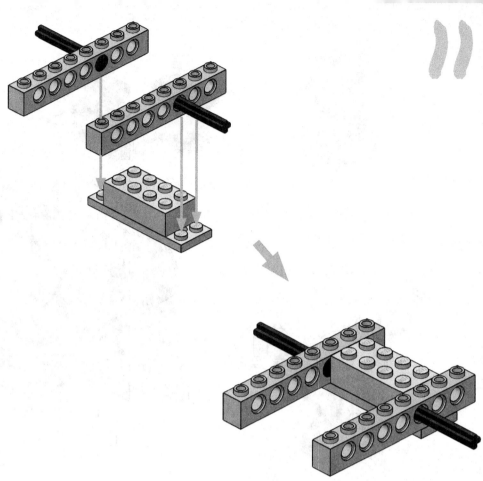

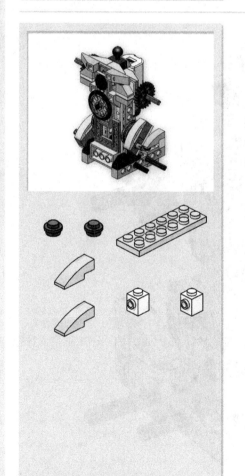

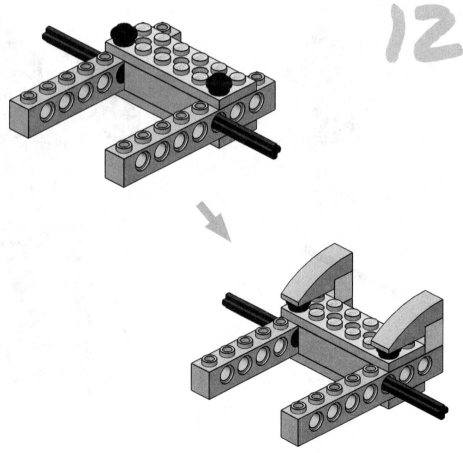

10

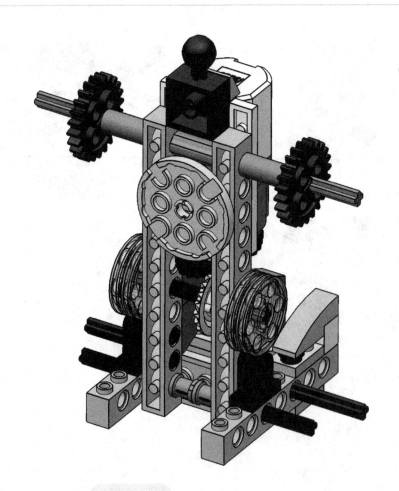

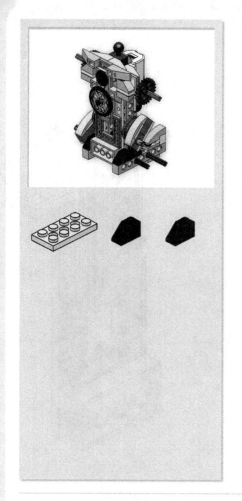

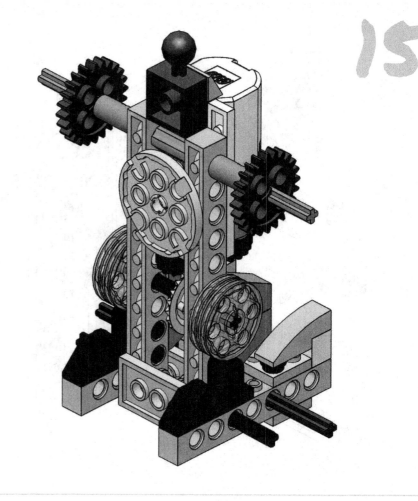

15

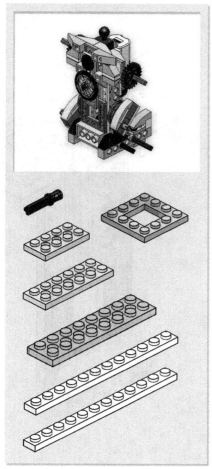

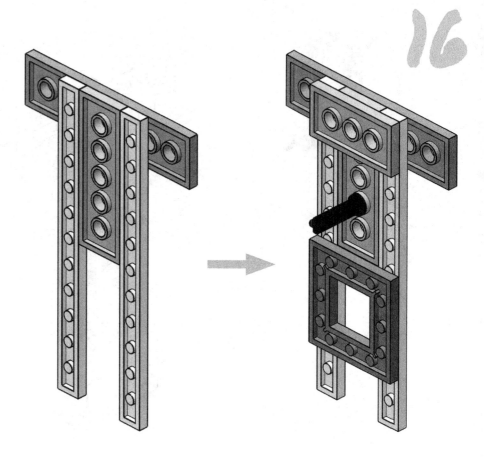

16

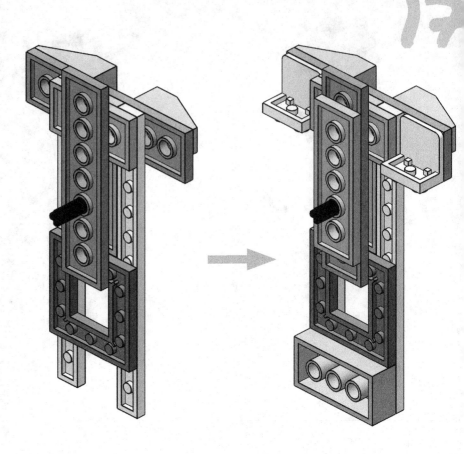

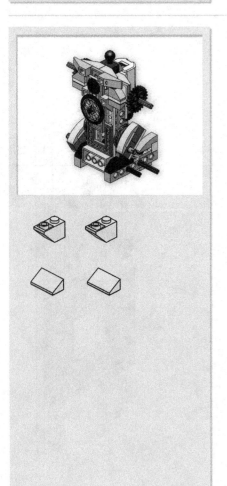

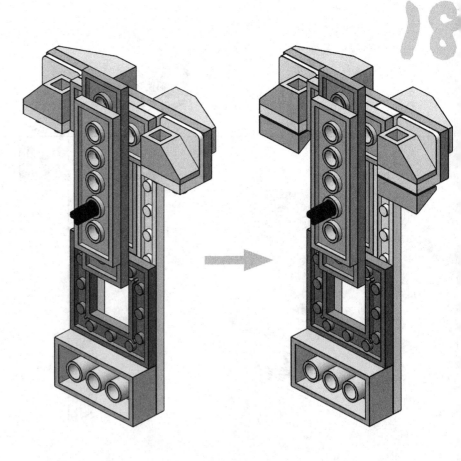

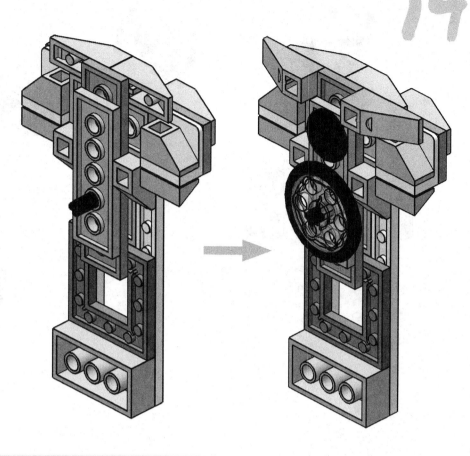

19

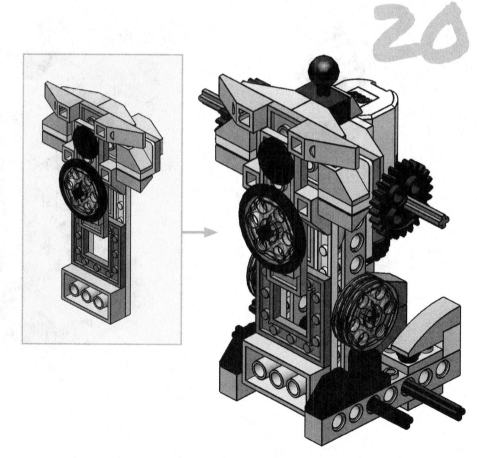

20

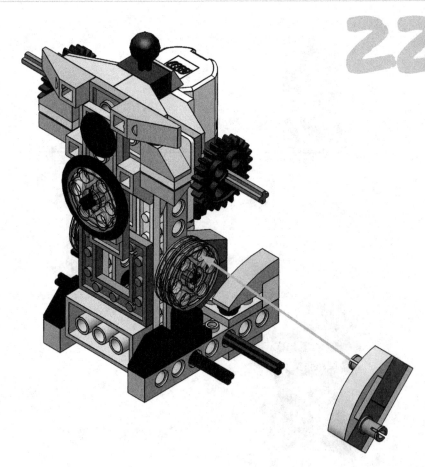

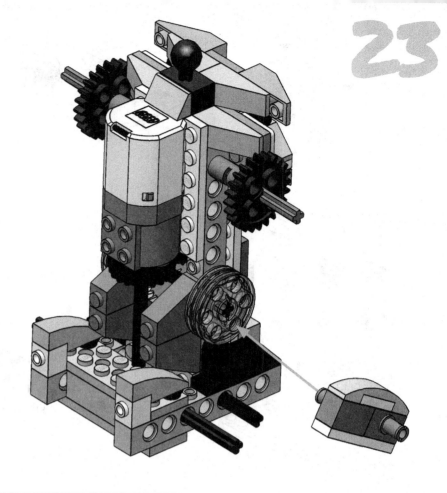

Be careful! The astronaut uses an "out-phase" motion, meaning that one of the connectors is in the opposite position of the other one.

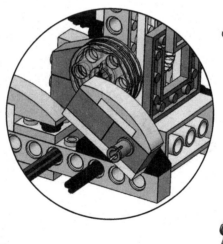

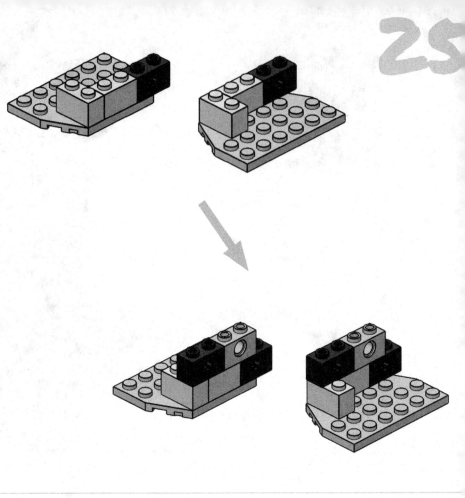

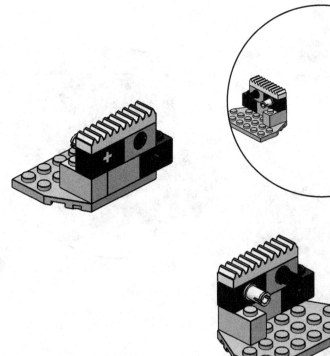

27

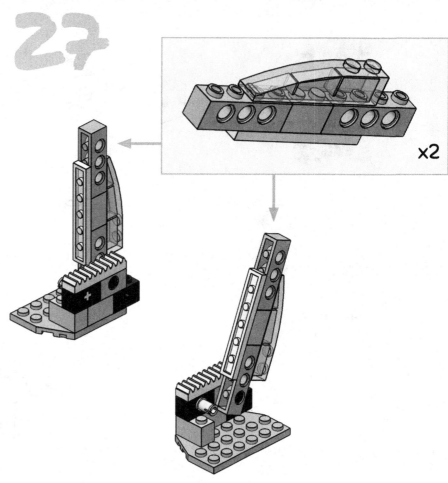

x2

28

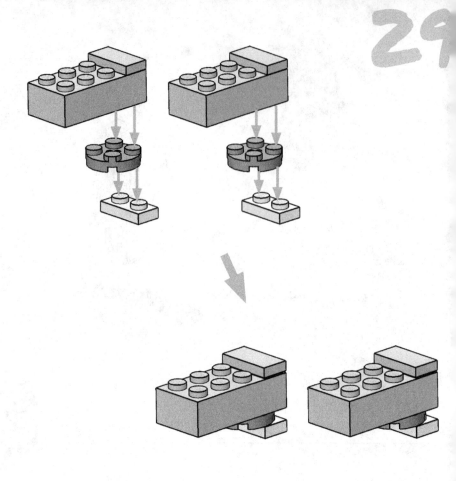

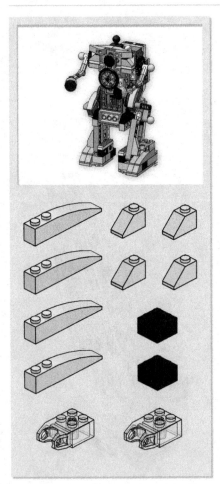

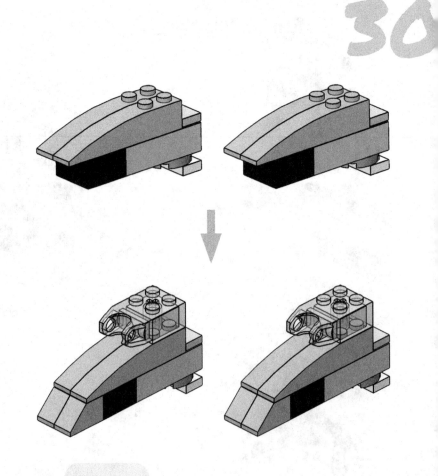

31

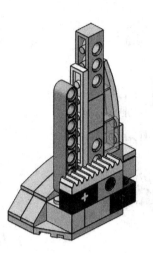

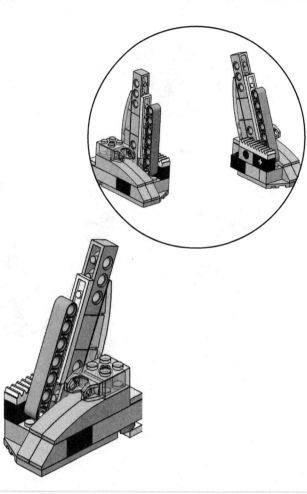

32

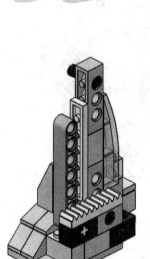

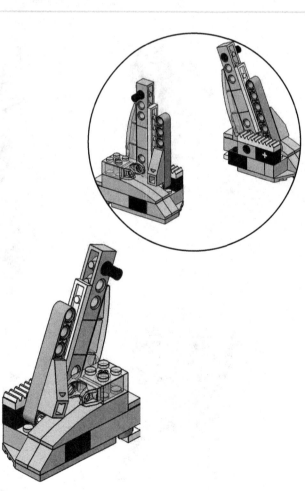

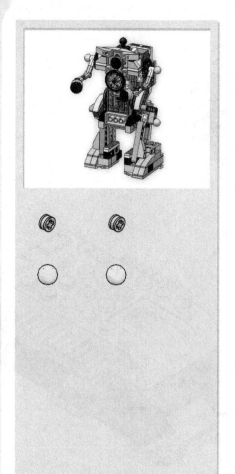

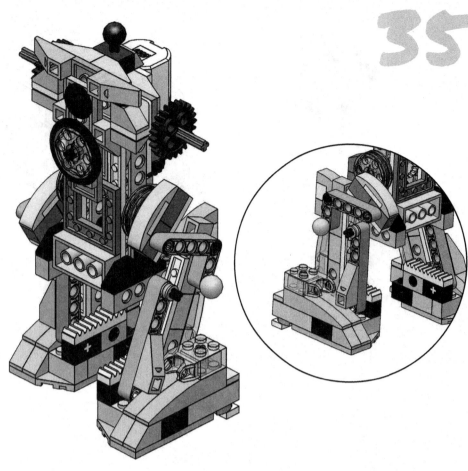

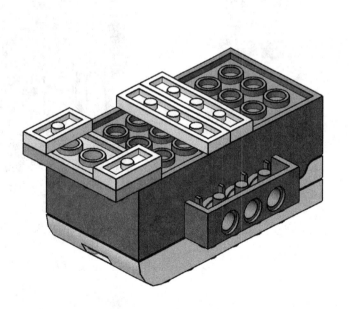

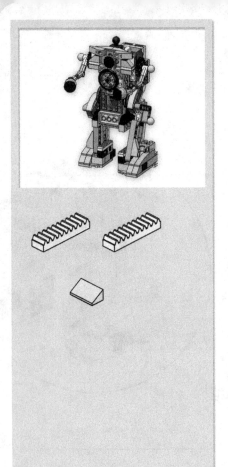

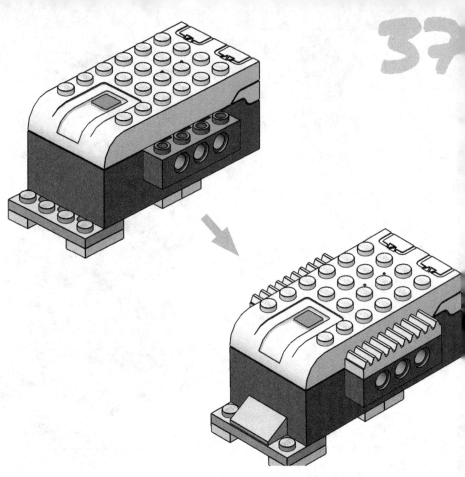

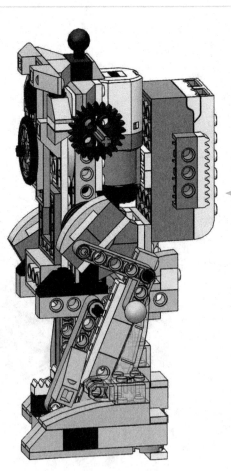

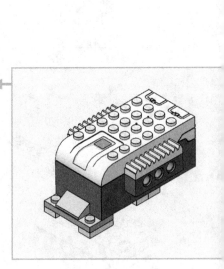

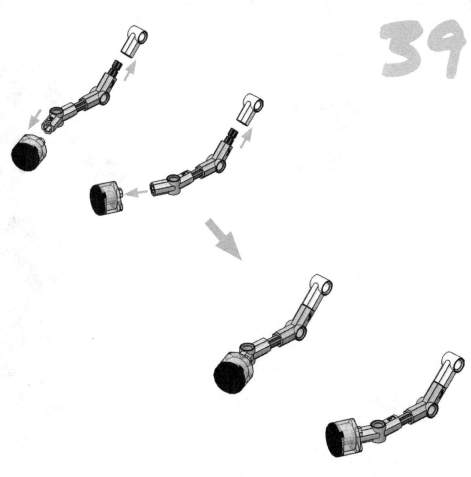

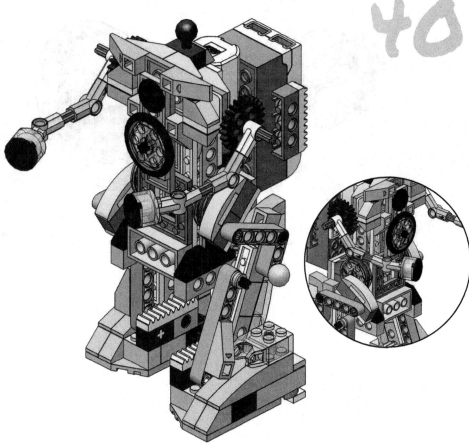

○   ○

41

42

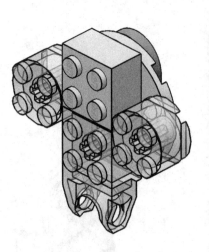

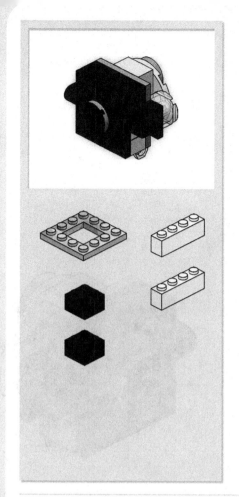

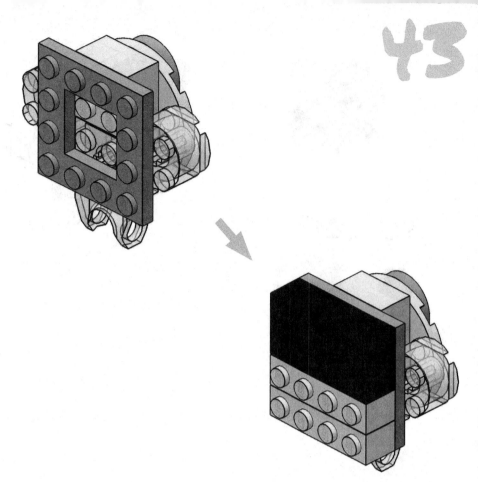

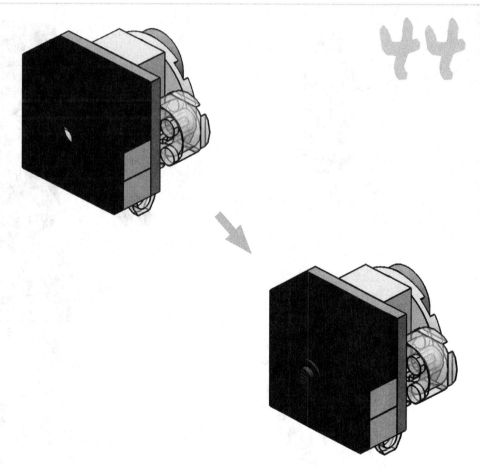

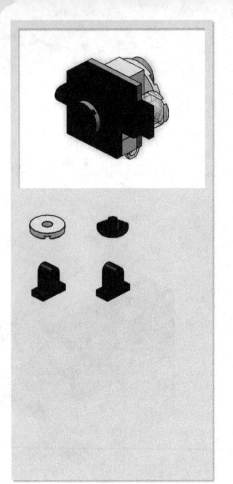

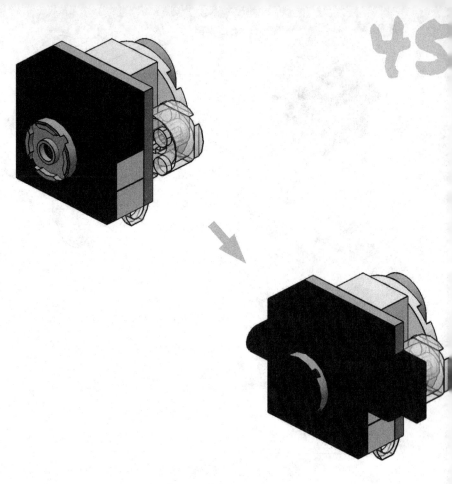

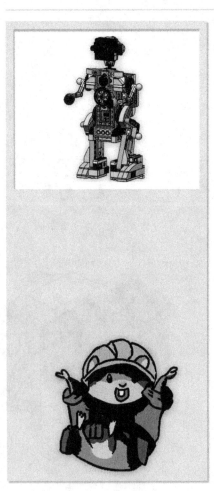

· Before going to the next phase, you can identify the mechanisms you are using in your astronaut prototype.

· Can you predict how your astronaut prototype will move by only seeing the model?

· How many gears are you using in your astronaut prototype?

· How many legs does your astronaut prototype have?

Design features

· Your astronaut uses the motor to drive its two legs.

· Can you identify the bevel gears and the parallel Chebyshev's lambda linkage?

· Can you identify the driver gear and the follower gear in the bevel gear mechanism?

· Are the two legs in an out-phase motion? You can check this by the position of the legs. In an out-phase motion, one leg should be in the opposite direction of the other one.

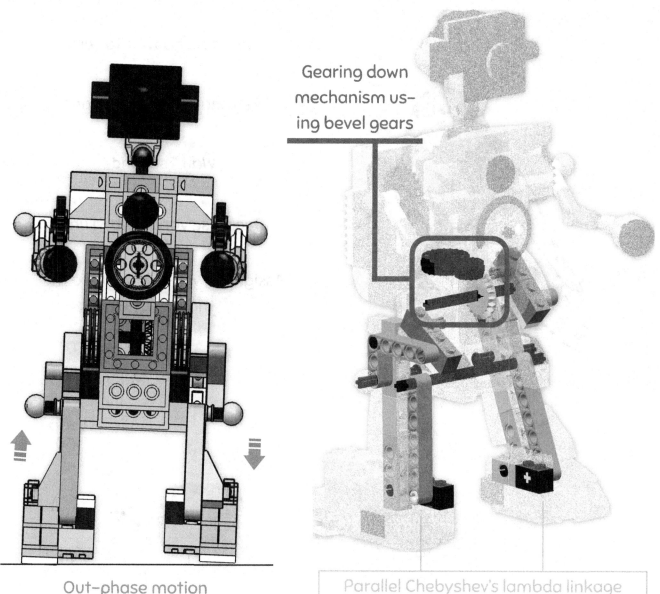

Gearing down mechanism using bevel gears

Out-phase motion

Parallel Chebyshev's lambda linkage

· In this section, you will explore the use of ramp stopping for your motor.
· The **program idea** consists of moving your astronaut forward decreasing its speed. Your atronaut will start moving first very fast, and it will continue decelerating until reaching zepower. Similarly to the skier program, you will be using a **variable** to develop the progra

Flowchart

· Tasks 1, 2, 3, and 4 are called **initial conditions** since they are only **executed once** at the beginning of your program.
· Tasks 5, 6, and 7 are executed 10 times, taking the **motor power** from a value of **10** to a value of **0**.

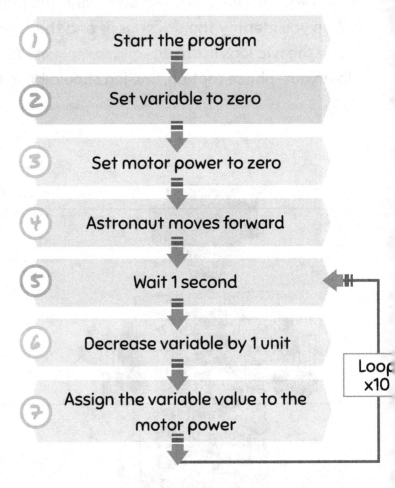

①	Start the program
②	Set variable to zero
③	Set motor power to zero
④	Astronaut moves forward
⑤	Wait 1 second
⑥	Decrease variable by 1 unit
⑦	Assign the variable value to the motor power

Loop x10

· The flowchart indicates **7 tasks**. Therefore, you assign a **programming block** for each ta

① ② ③ ④ ⑤ ⑥ ⑦   Loop x10

Test phase: Decelerate motion

· Remember to verify the **communication** between your WeDo software and your WeDo hub before you start testing your prototype.

· Start testing your prototype by executing the program developed in the **program phase** by clicking the "Start" block.

TEST 1: Finding the right motor direction

· Identify in which direction your motor has to rotate to make your astronaut move forward ward and backward.

TEST 2: Increasing or decreasing the deceleration rate

· You can accelerate or decelerate your **motor ramp stopping** by increasing or decreasing the wait time (task 5).

TEST 3: From out-phase motion to in-phase motion

· Modify the position of your astronaut legs to perform an **in-phase motion** and execute your program. How differently does your astronaut move?

Document & share phase

· Remember to collect all your **notes, videos,** and **photos** to report your **findings and results.**
· Report your findings and results from the **three tests** performed in the **test phase.**
· Record a video of your astronaut moving using an **out-phase** and an **in-phase** motion to compare how different the motions are.

Enhancing the experience

· **Build:** You can add a sensor to your astronaut prototype so it can interact with the environment.
· **Programming:** Program the sensor added to your astronaut prototype.

279

So far, you have explored a lot of walking mechanisms; however, there are other types of motions, such as the wing motion while flying.

BIOMIMETIC ROBOTS

Contents

DOLPHIN

Design phase: Diving motion

· Remember to have a **white paper** and a **pencil** to start drawing your ideas!

Looking for inspiration

· Dolphins are **small-toothed aquatic mammals** easily recognizable by their curved mouths, which give them a **permanent "smile."**

· Most dolphins live in the **ocean** or brackish waters along **coastlines**; however, there are some species that can be found in the Amazon River.

· They feed chiefly on **fish** and **squid**.

· They communicate with **clicks**, **squeaks**, and **whistles**.

Dolphins can jump really high from the water!

· On a piece of paper, you can sketch some **ideas** of how your dolphin will look like!

· So far, you have built several prototypes inspired by animals, focusing only on their **walking** and **crawling** motions. However, animals can perform other kinds of motions, such as **swim**, **fly**, **climb**, and so on.

Biomimetic robots

· Biomimetic robot **designs** attempt to develop robots inspired by **biological systems** such as animals, plants, insects, and so on.

· One of the most common applications in the development of biomimetic robots is to **replicate animal motions** such as swimming, flying, walking, climbing, and crawling.

· In this chapter, you will explore two new bio-inspired motions: **swimming and flying.**

283

Build phase: Parallel free-joint linkage

- Given the following building instructions, you can build your own **parallel free-joint linkage**

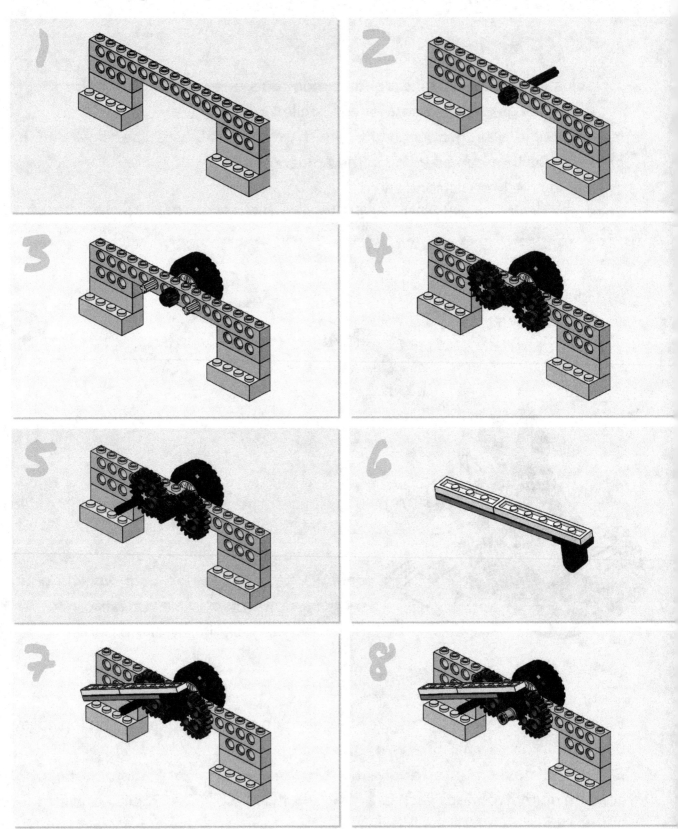

- Spin the wheel to see the generated motion.

Different diving motions

· You can change the position of the connectors of one of the gears to generate four different motions:

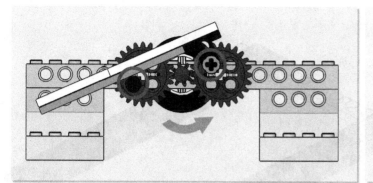
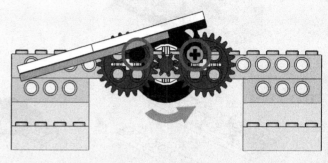

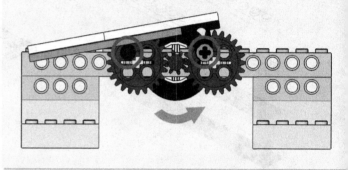

Parallel free-joint linkage

· By observing the mechanism, you can see that it is only connected to one connector (**fixed-joint**); the other connector only works as a support, and it is not attached to the structure (**free-joint**).

Fixed-joint

Free-joint

· Now you are ready to build your WeDo dolphin prototype!
· Before you start building, prepare a **suitable workspace**.
· Keep in mind that the WeDo set has small pieces, so prepare a table with enough space to easily identify all the pieces and prevent them from getting lost.

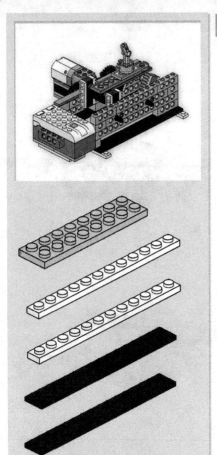

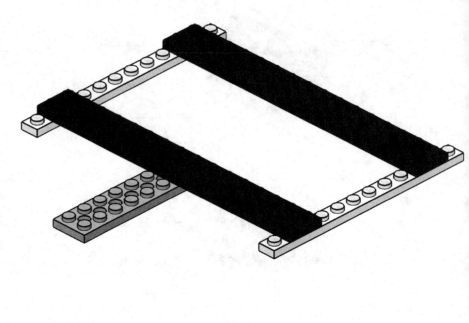

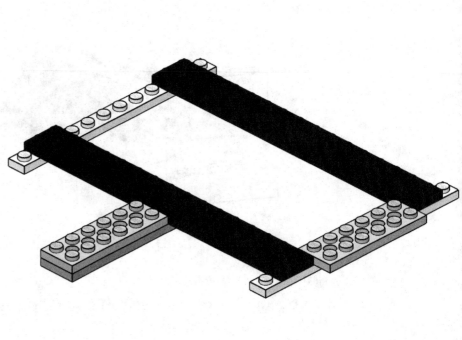

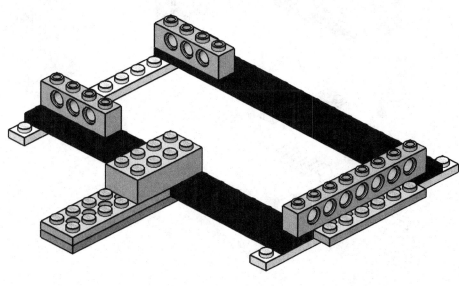

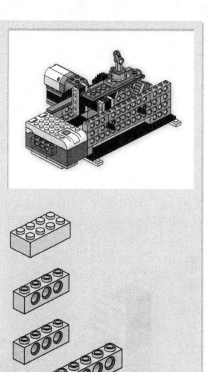

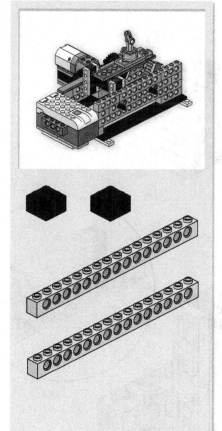

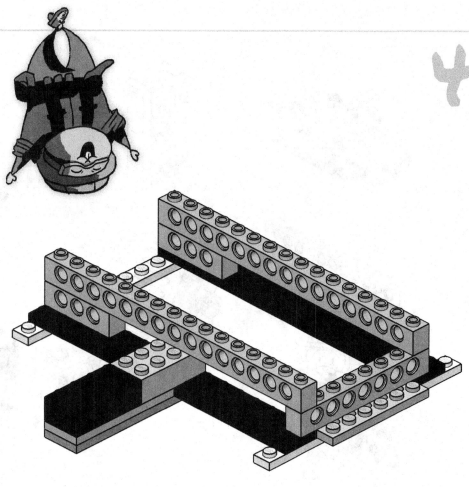

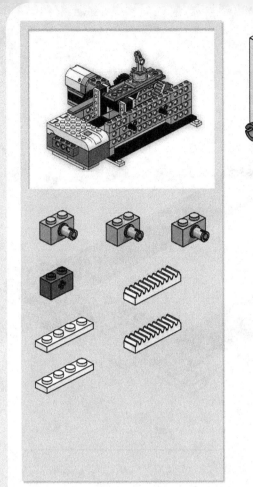

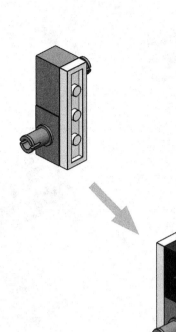

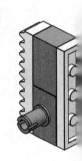

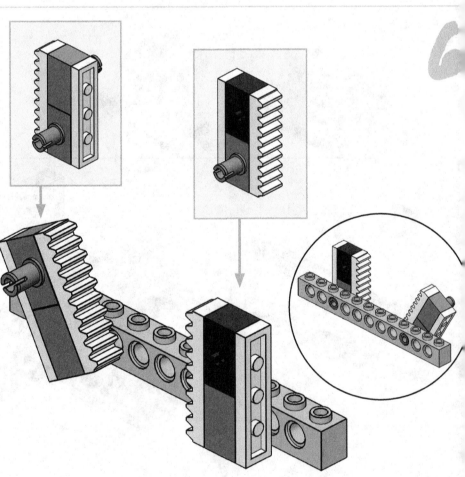

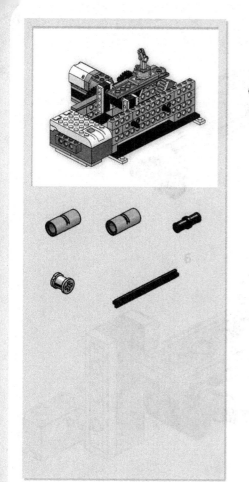

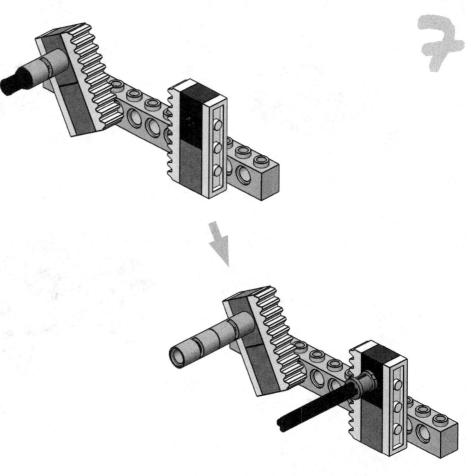

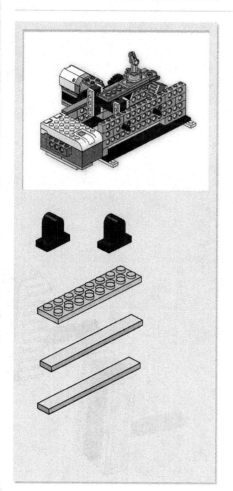

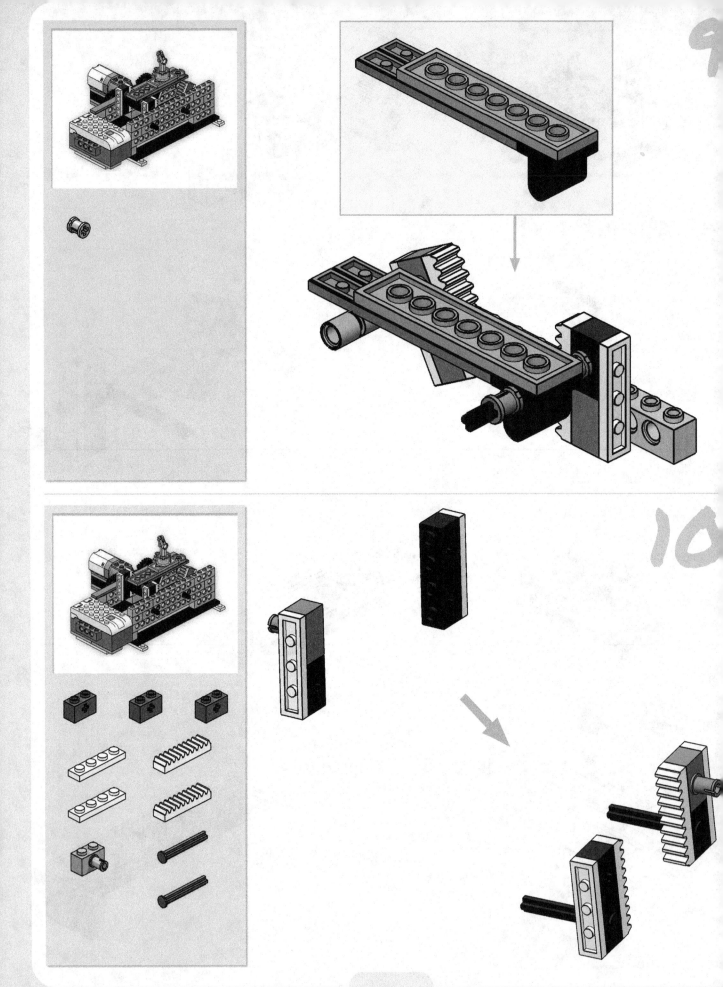

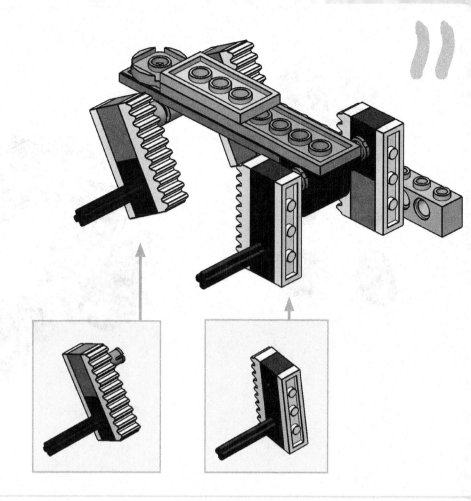

11

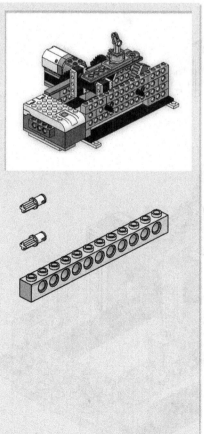

12

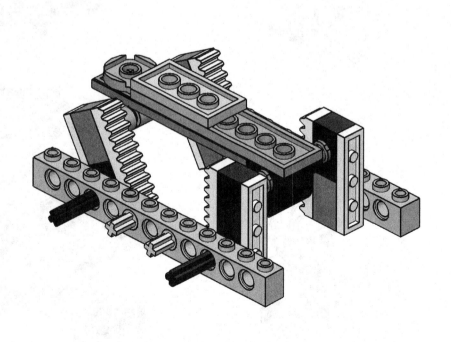

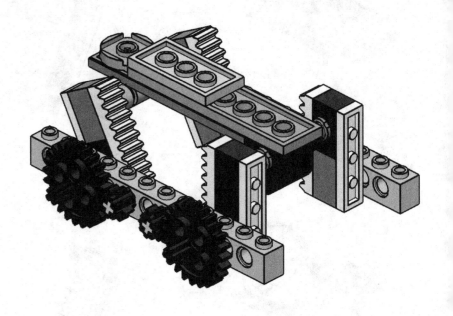

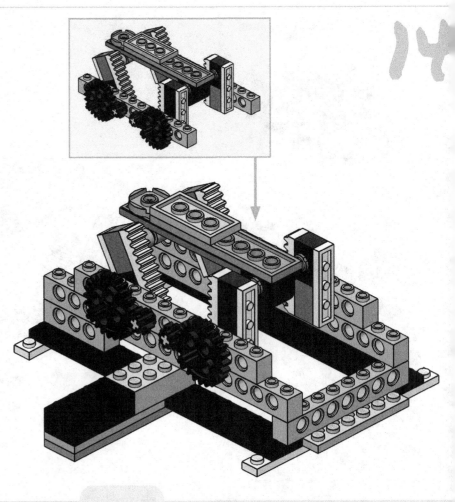

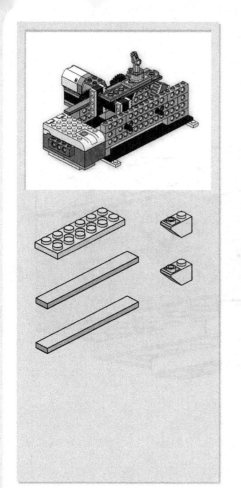

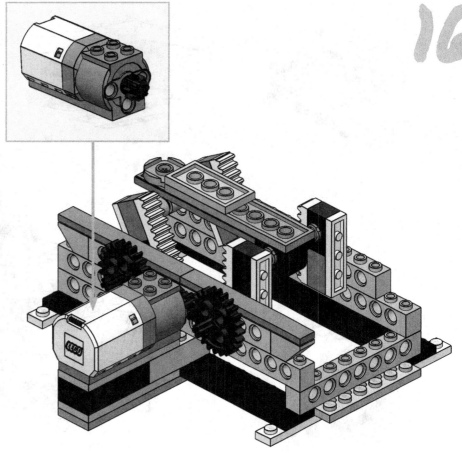

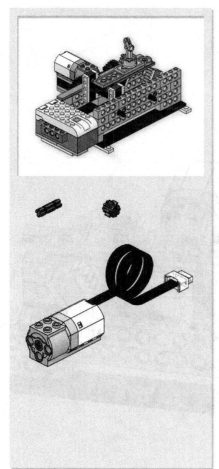

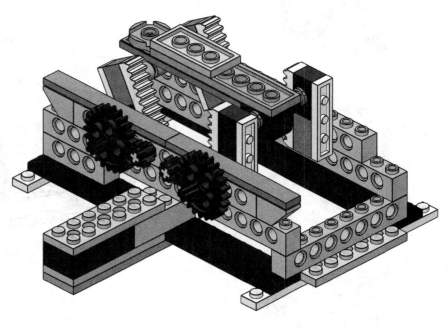

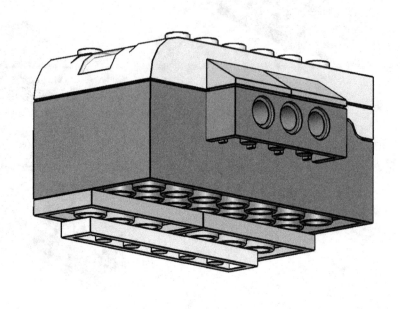

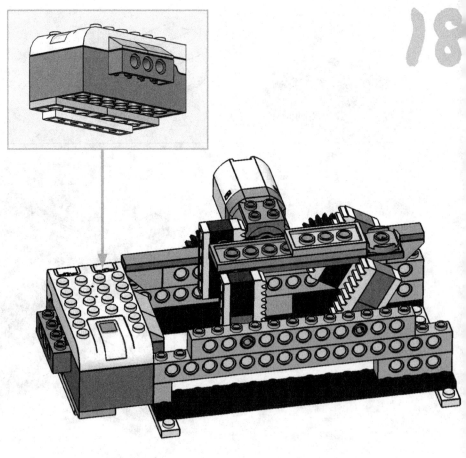

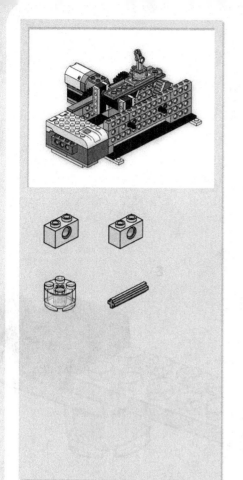

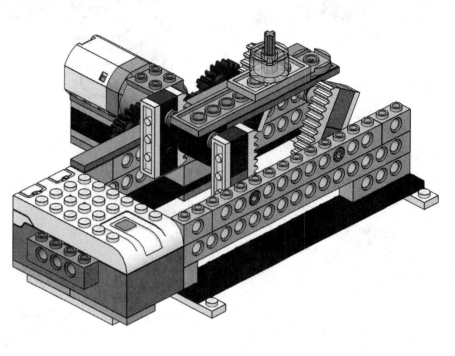

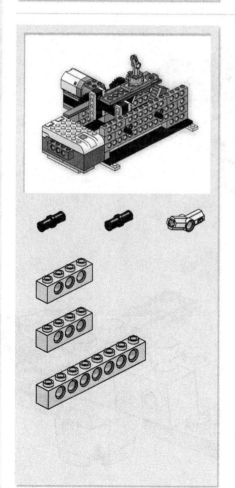

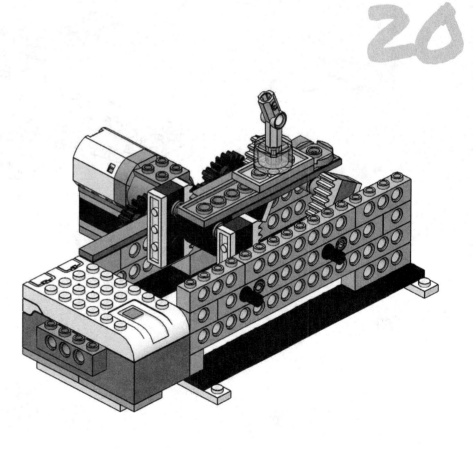

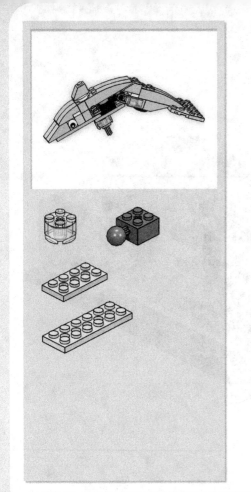

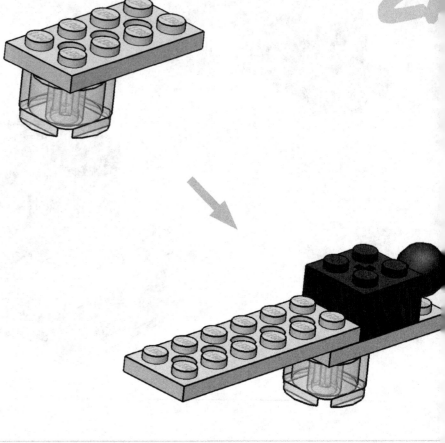

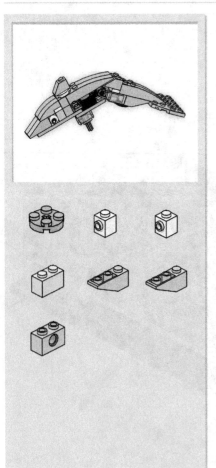

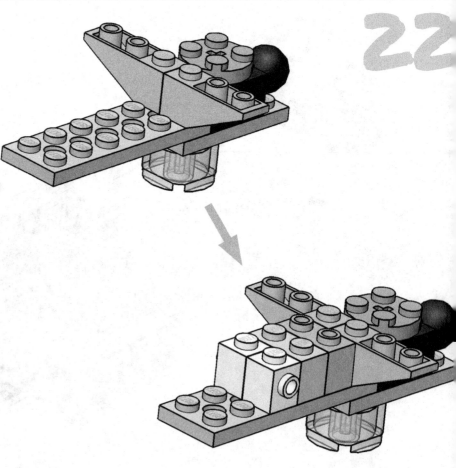

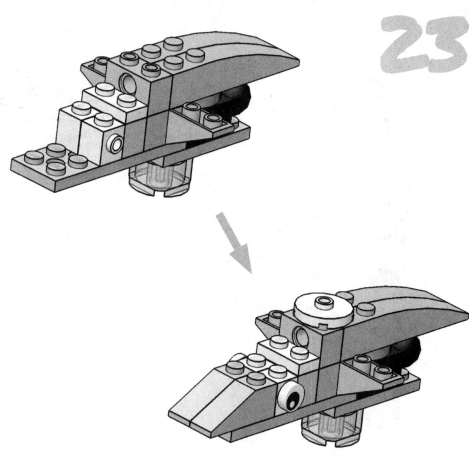

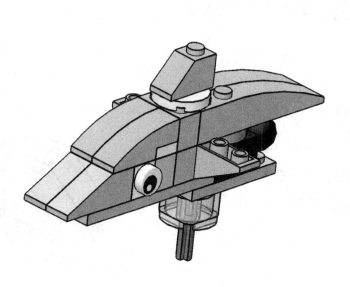

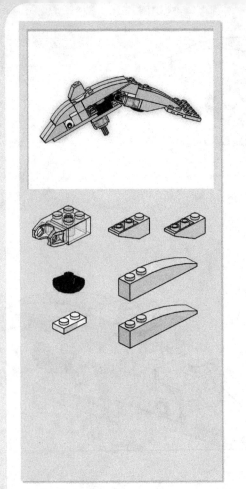

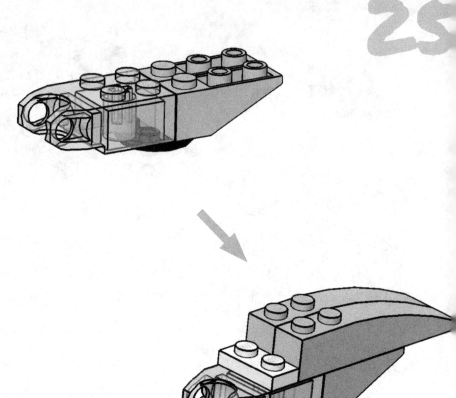

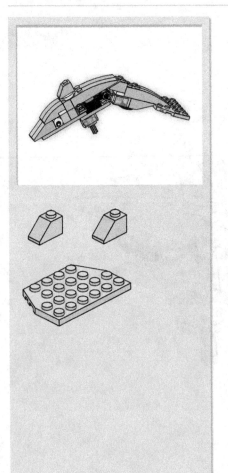

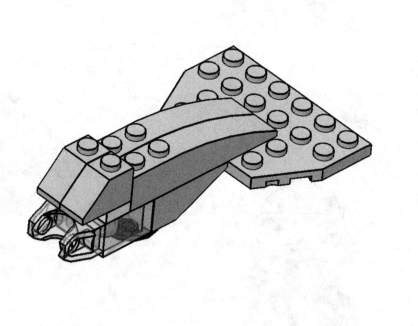

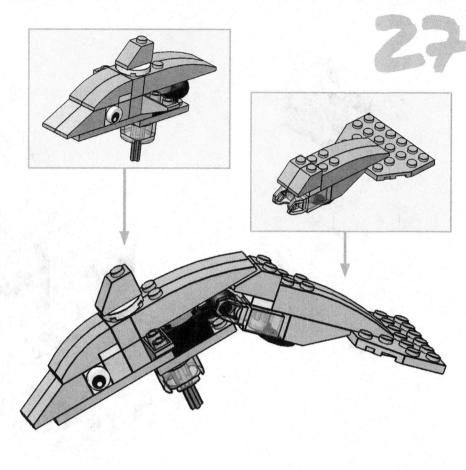

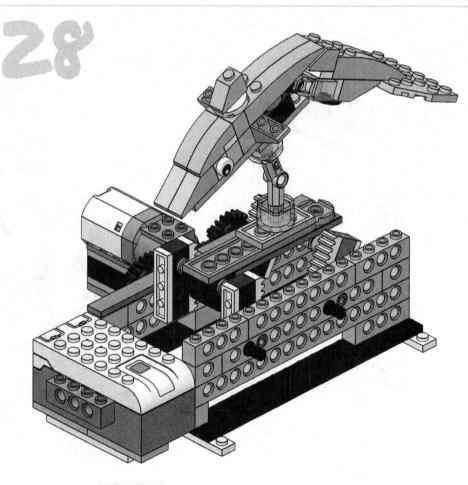

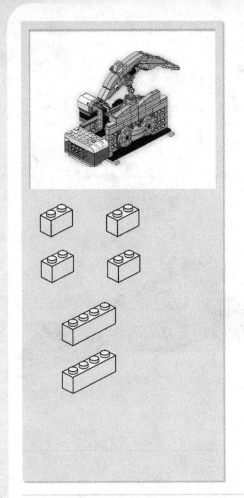

29

30

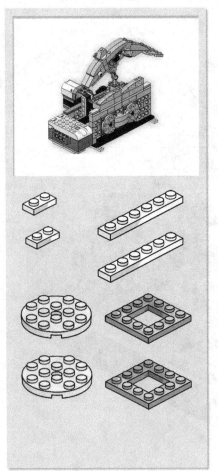

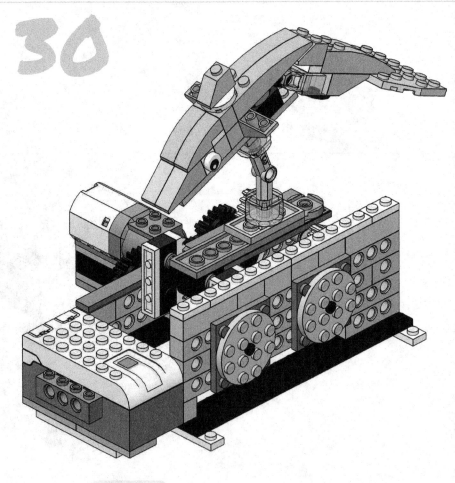

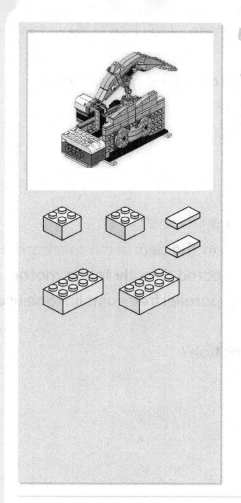

31

32

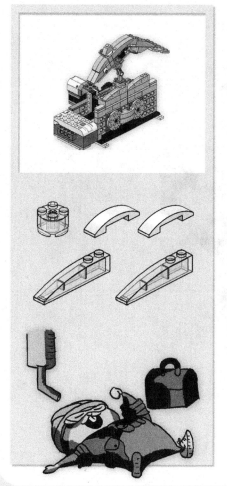

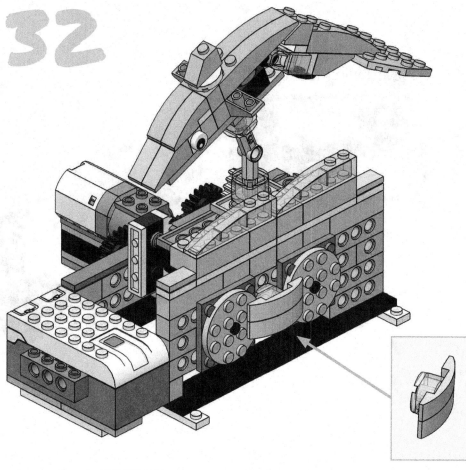

• Before going to the next phase, you can identify the mechanisms you are using in y[...]
dolphin prototype.

• Can you predict how your dolphin prototype will move by only seeing the model?

• How many gears are you using in your dolphin prototype?

Design features

• Your dolphin uses the motor to emulate a diving motion.

• Can you identify the gear train and the parallel free-joint linkage?

• Can you identify the driver gear and the follower gears in the gear train mechanism[...]
Keep in mind that the driver gear is usually the one connected directly to the motor.

• Can you identify the fixed-joint and the free-joint in the parallel free-joint linkage use[...]
in your dolphin?

• Does your dolphin use an out-phase or an in-phase motion?

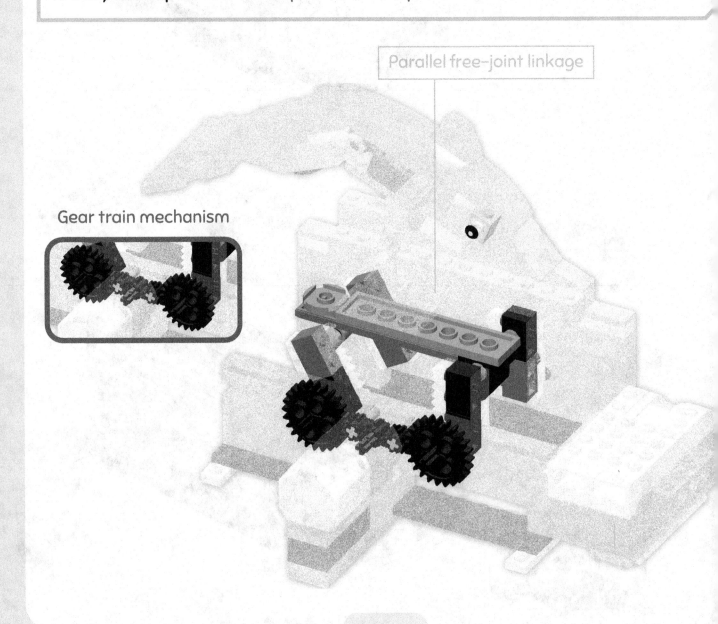

Parallel free-joint linkage

Gear train mechanism

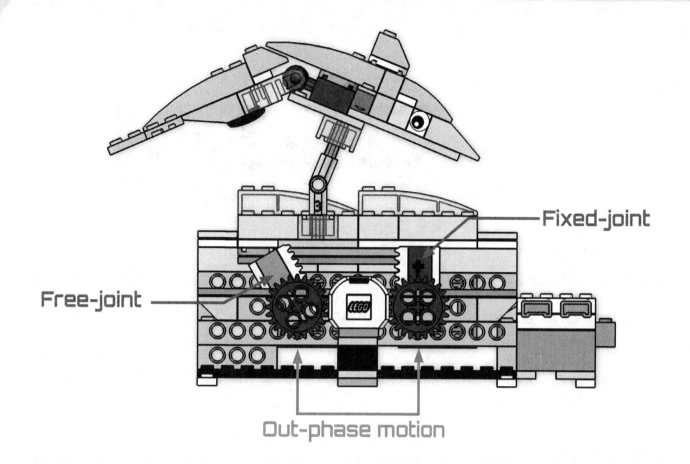

Fixed-joint

Free-joint

Out-phase motion

Program phase: Random and LED blocks

· In this section, you will explore the use of the random and LED blocks.

· The **program idea** consists of moving your dolphin, but you will not know for how long or how fast until you execute your program. Additionally, you will use the LED block just to explore the different colors that it can display.

· In a more detailed way, first, you have to create a random variable and define the rotation of the motor, then assign the value of the random variable to the three blocks: LED block, motor power block, and wait for block.

Flowchart

① Start the program

② Create a random variable

③ Dolphin starts moving

④ Assign variable to LED

⑤ Assign variable to motor power

⑥ Assign variable to motor time on

• The flowchart indicates **six tasks**. Therefore, you assign a **programming block** for **each ta**

Test phase: Dealing with randomness

• Remember to verify the **communication** between your WeDo software and your We
hub before you start testing your prototype.

• Start testing your prototype by executing the program developed in the **program pha**
by clicking the "**Start**" block.

TEST 1: Changing the motor direction

• Do you find any difference in changing the direction of your motor in task 3?

TEST 2: Finding the LED colors

• The LED located in your Hub can display several different colors. When you execute yo
program, you will see a number on the screen; this number is generated randomly. Based
the value of the number on the screen, the LED will display a particular color:

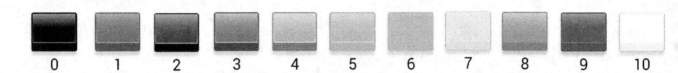

0	1	2	3	4	5	6	7	8	9	10

TEST 3: A different randomness

• In your program, at the beginning, you assign the generated random number to the disp
block (variable). Then you use that value for the other three blocks: tasks 4, 5, and 6. That w
the number shown on the screen will always correspond to the color shown by your L
as experienced in **TEST 2**.

· Modify your program, so now you use three random blocks instead of the **display input blocks**

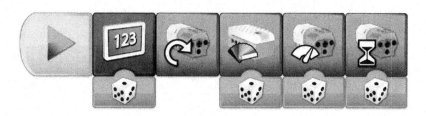

· Execute your program several times. After each execution, check if the number shown on your screen corresponds with the color of your LED.

TEST 4: Out-phase vs. in-phase
· Modify your dolphin from an out-phase motion to an in-phase motion and execute your program.

Why do dolphins jump out of the water?

· Dolphins are mammals, so they need to **breathe oxygen** from the air as they remain in the water. **Jumping out of the water** allows dolphins to remain wet while also taking in oxygen.
· Dolphins must **swim** really fast below the surface to get the **required speed** to push themselves up through the surface of the water.
· Dolphins jump out of the water for several reasons: have **fun**, increase **visibility**, remove parasites, and **improve navigation**.

Document & share phase

· Remember to collect all your **notes**, **videos**, and **photos** to report your **findings and results**.
· Record a video of your dolphin moving the motor clockwise and counterclockwise. Do you observe any difference in your **dolphin motion**?
· Record a video of your dolphin moving using an out-phase and an in-phase motion to compare the results.

Enhancing the experience

· **Build:** You can replace the dolphin with other marine animals.
· **Programming:** In your WeDo software, you have sound blocks that you can add to your dolphin prototype so it can be more realistic. Also, you can add a good background while you execute your program.

PELICAN

Design phase: Flapping wings motion

· Remember to have a **white paper** and a **pencil** to start drawing your ideas!

Looking for inspiration

· Pelicans are **large birds** characterized by a **long beak** and a **large throat** pouch.
· They are found on **coastlines** and also along lakes and rivers.
· Pelicans like **fishing in groups**; they can use their **elastic pouches** to **catch fish**.
· Most of the different pelican species have **pale plumage**; however, there are some exceptions as the **brown pelican** and the Peruvian pelican.
· They can **fly for hours** or even days looking for feeding areas.

Wow! Pelicans can fly low over stretches of water; this kind of flying is called skim.

· On a piece of paper, you can sketch some **ideas** to replicate the wings motion observed in pelicans.

Flapping wings

· **Flapping wings** are used by a wide variety of animals such as birds and bats and a variety of insects to fly both **quickly** and **slowly**.
· Birds flap their wings to **land** and **take off** from anywhere. For example, birds flap their wings at a large angle of attack to push themselves away from the ground during take-off.
· The principle behind the flapping wings motion is: the two wings are flapped to produce both **lift and thrust**, to **overcome gravity**, and to provide a **sustained flight**.

Build phase: Crank-rocker four-bar linkage

· Given the following building instructions, you can build a **crank–rocker four-bar linkage**.

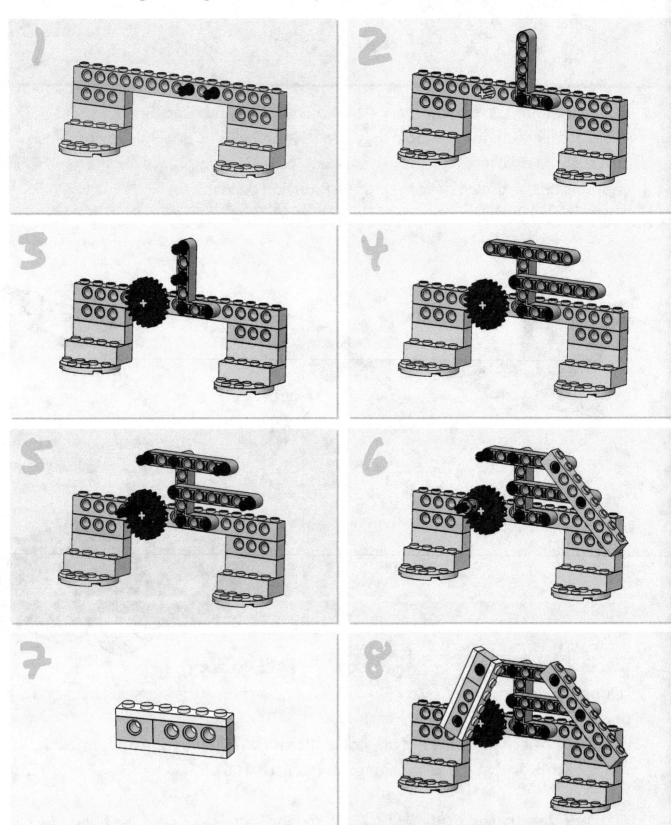

· Spin the gear to see the generated **flapping wings motion**.

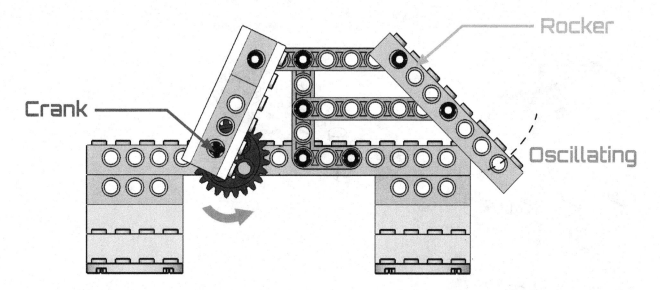

Crank

Rocker

Oscillating

Crank-rocker four-bar linkage

- **Crank**: A side link which revolves relative to the frame is called a crank.
- **Rocker**: Any link which oscillates is called a rocker.
- **Crank–rocker mechanism**: It is a four–bar linkage; if the shorter side link revolves and the other one rocks (oscillates), it is called a crank–rocker mechanism.

Four-bar linkage variations

- A variety of useful linkages can be formed from a **four–bar linkage**. Through slight variations, such as changing the characteristics of the pairs or proportions of the bars, you can generate **different kinds of motions**.
- In previous chapters, you have used several variations of a **four–bar linkage** to create different prototypes. All of the following are four–bar linkages:

  - The **Chebyshev's lambda linkage** used in your American rhea, plesiosaurus, sea lion, skier, and astronaut prototypes.
  - The **parallel linkage** used in your frog and turtle prototypes.
  - The **parallel free–joint linkage** used in your dolphin prototype.

- Now you are ready to build your WeDo pelican prototype!
- Before you start building, prepare a **suitable workspace**.
- Keep in mind that the WeDo set has small pieces, so prepare a table with enough space to easily identify all the pieces and prevent them from getting lost.

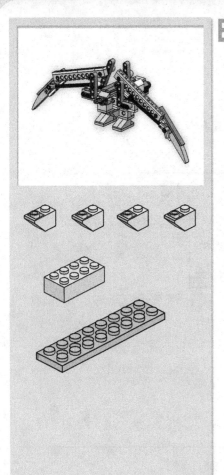

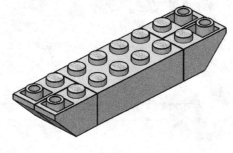

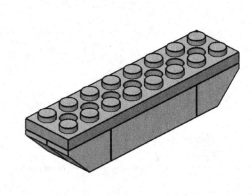

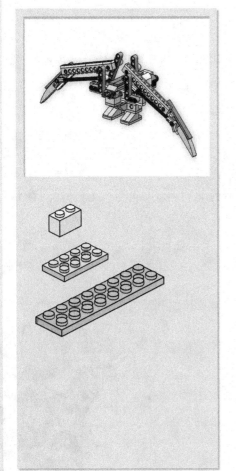

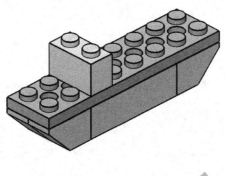

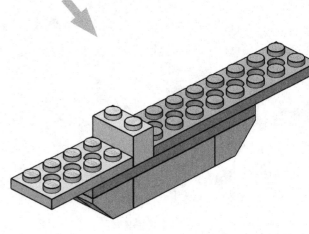

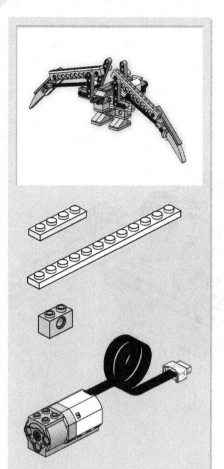

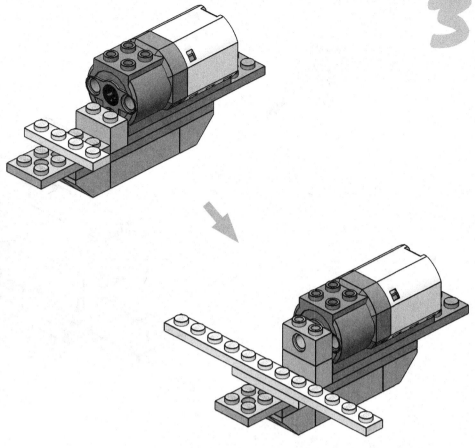

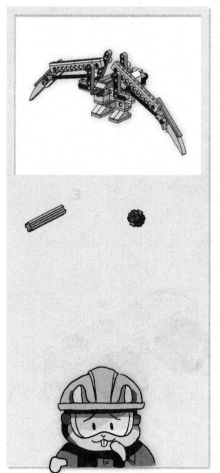

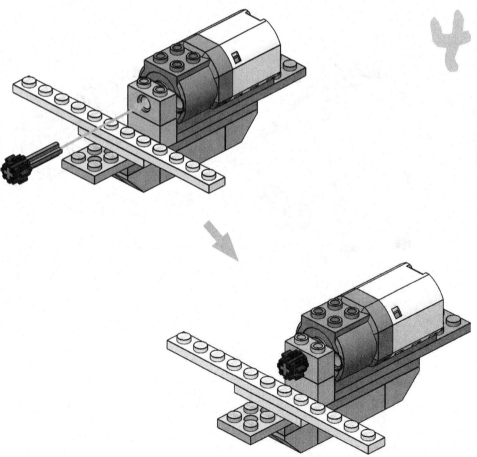

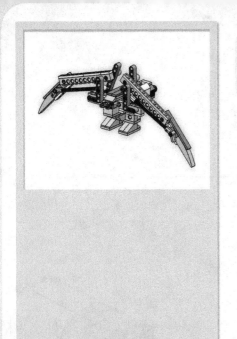

Flip your prototype 180 degrees to have the same view.

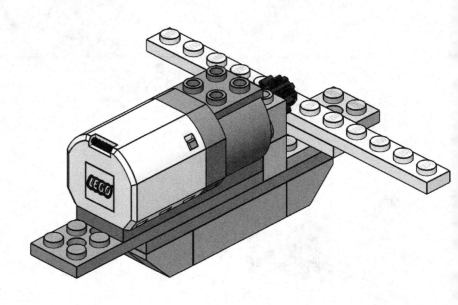

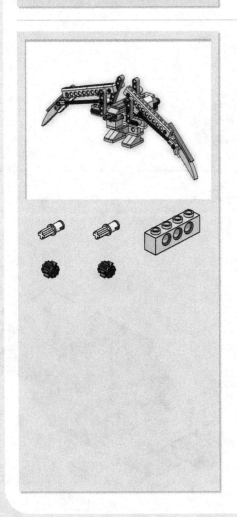

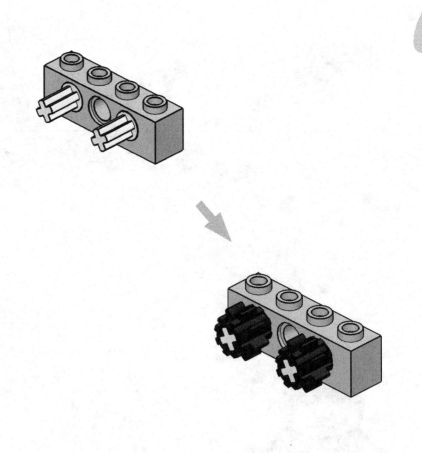

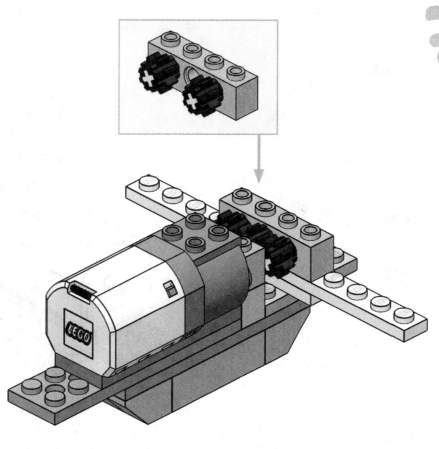

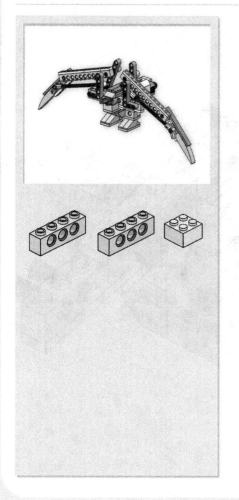

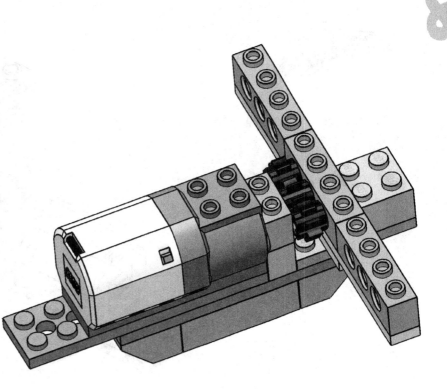

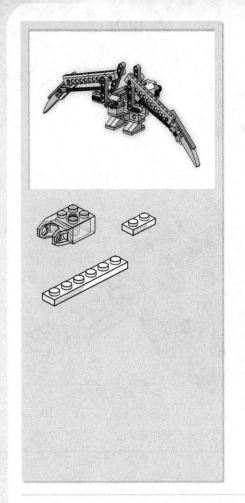

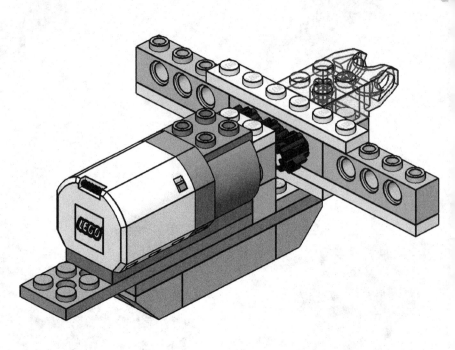

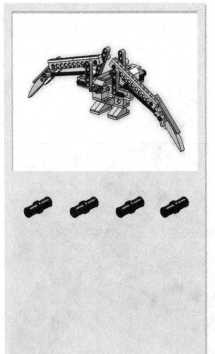

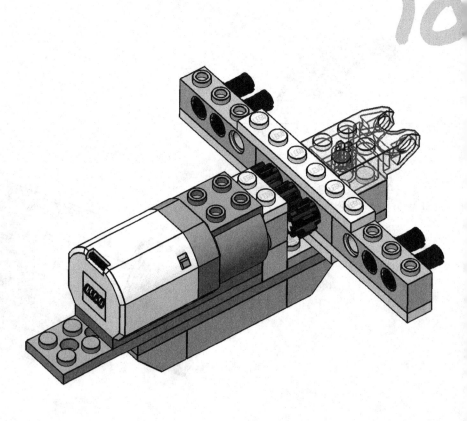

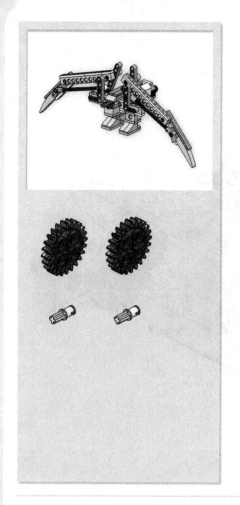

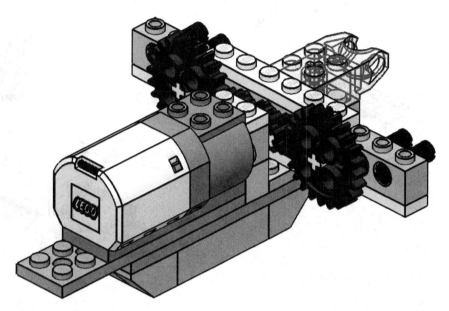

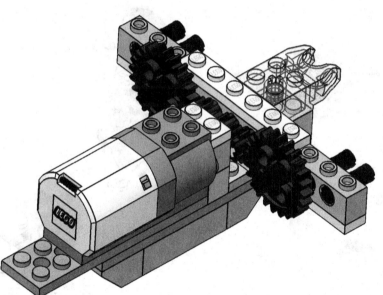

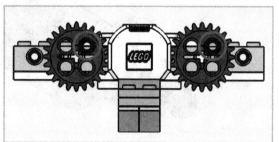

Be careful! The pelican uses an "in-phase" motion, meaning that one of the axles is in the exact same position of the other one.

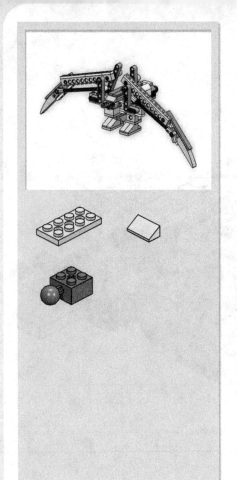

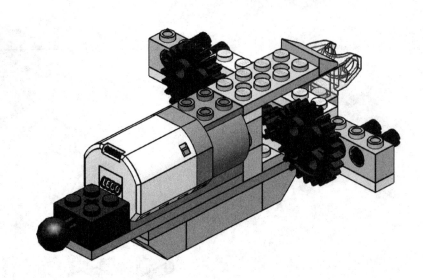

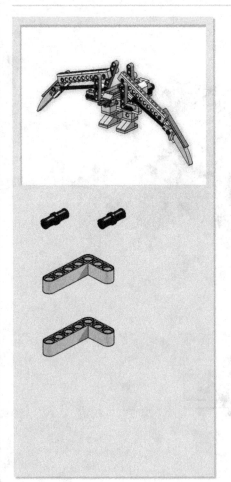

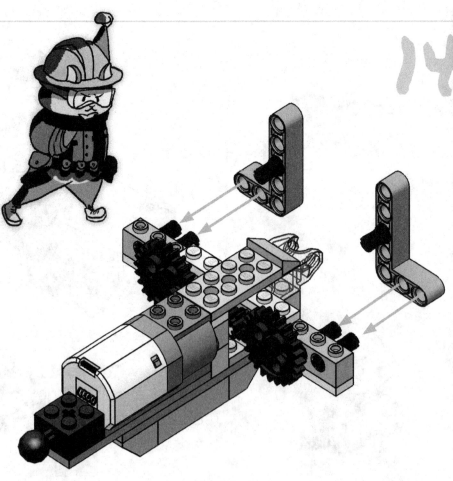

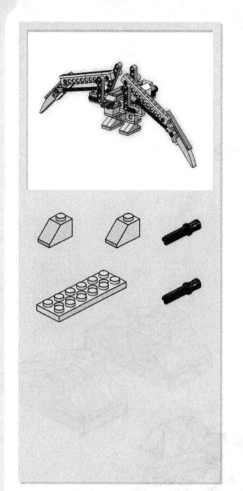

15

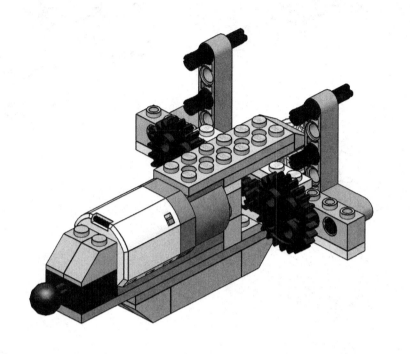

16

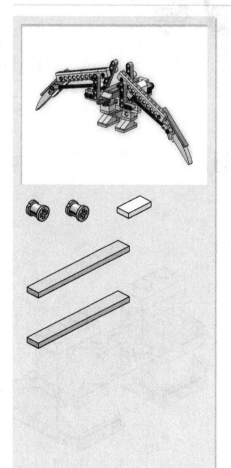

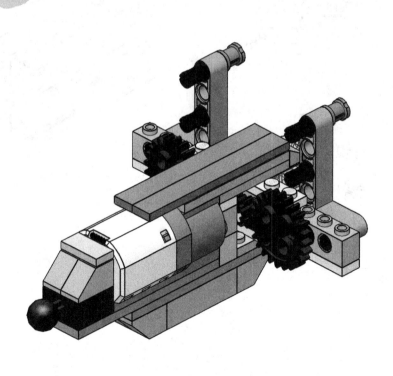

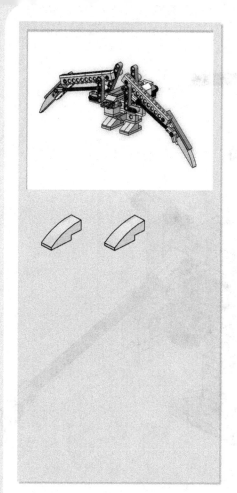

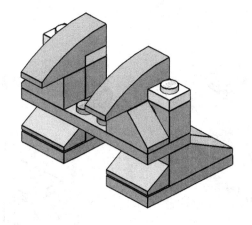

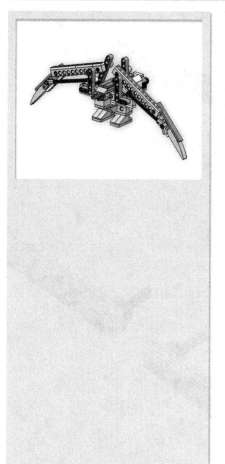

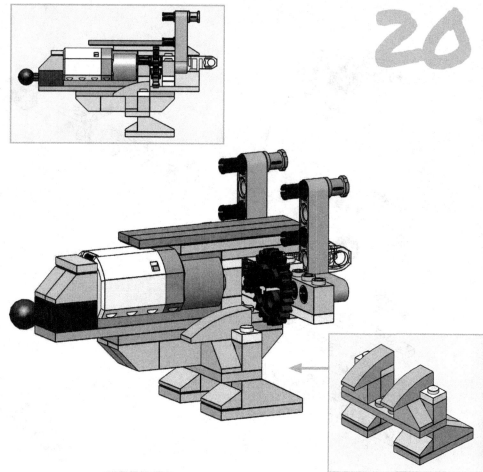

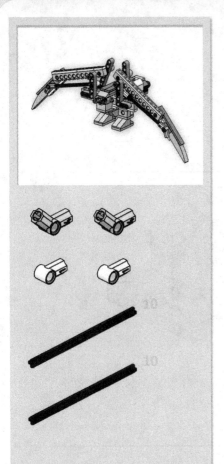

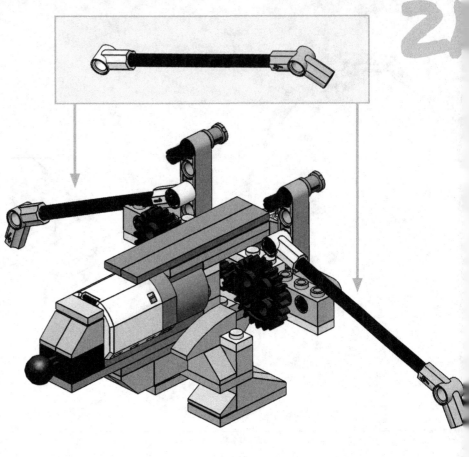

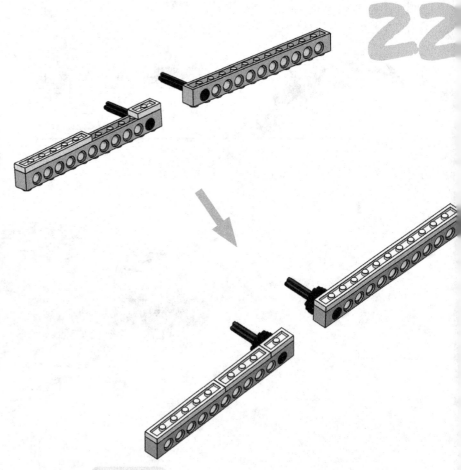

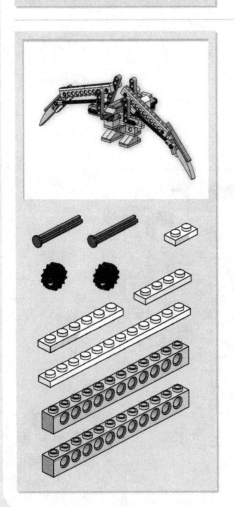

10

10

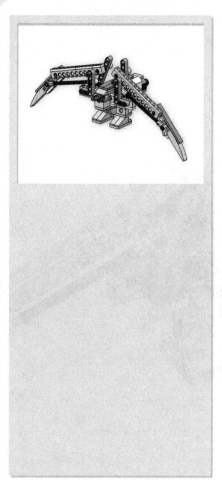

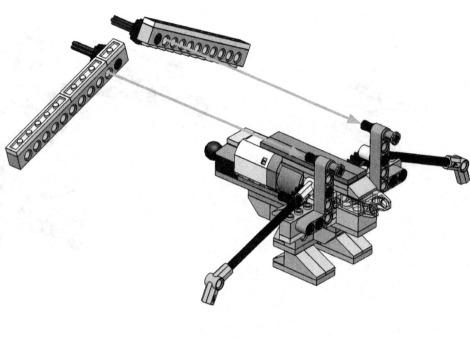

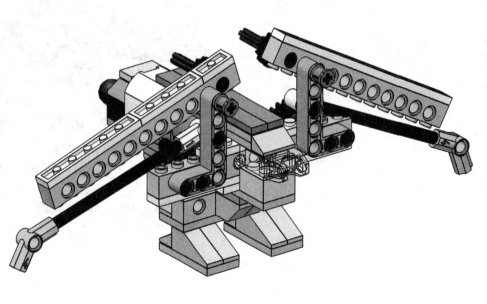

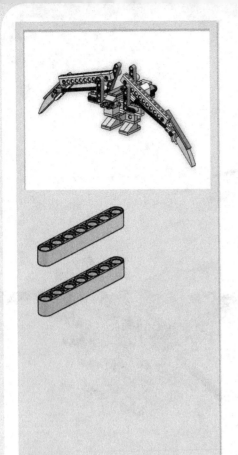

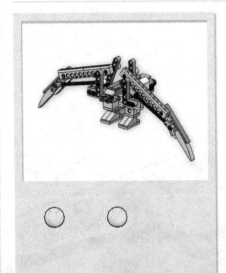

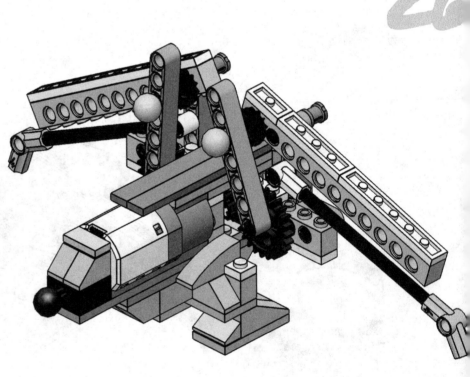

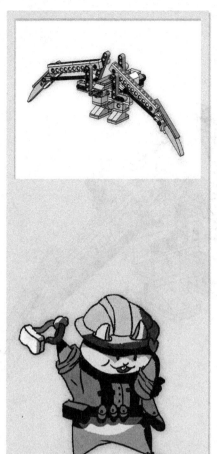

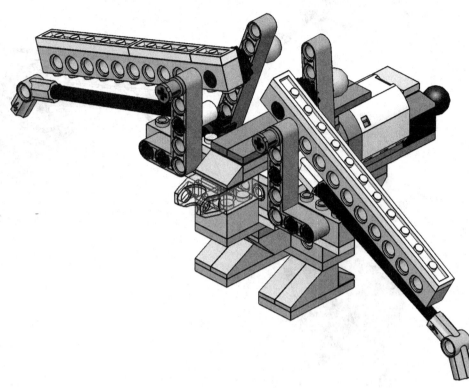

28

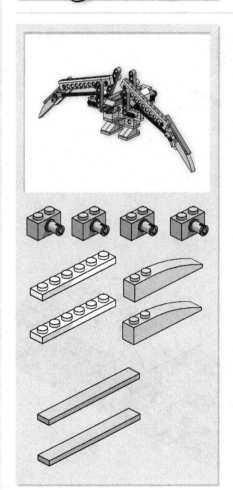

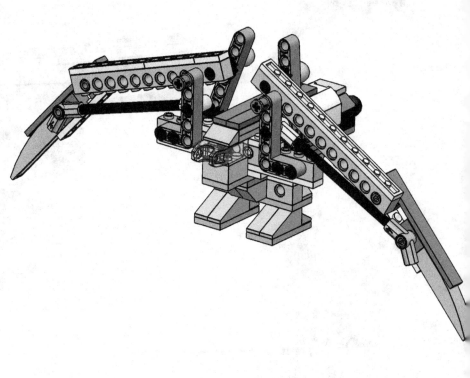

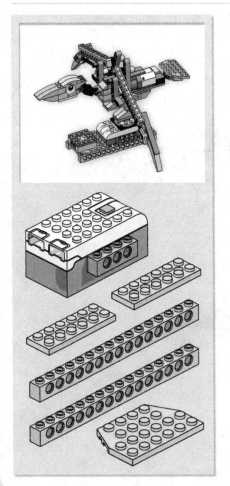

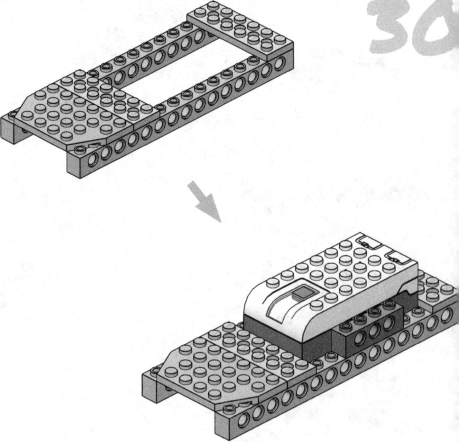

31

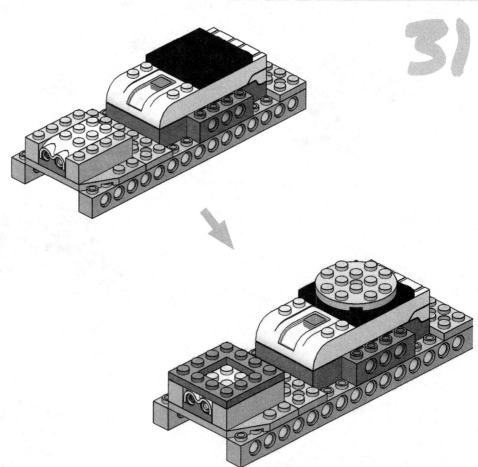

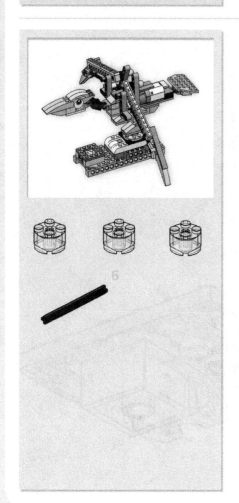

6

32

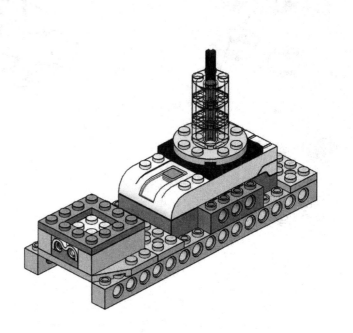

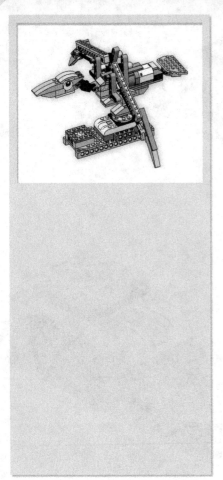

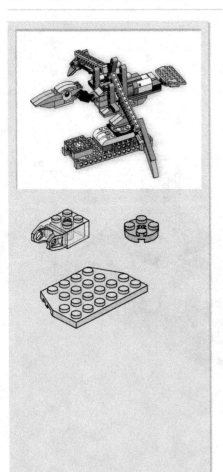

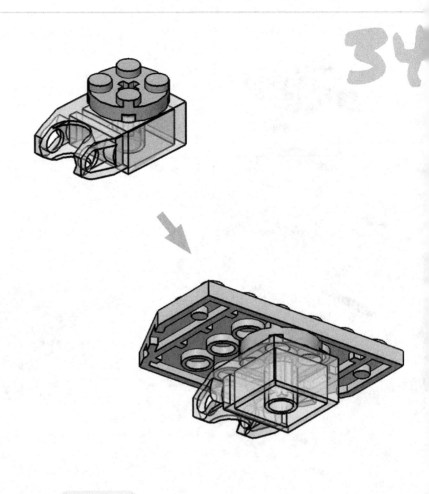

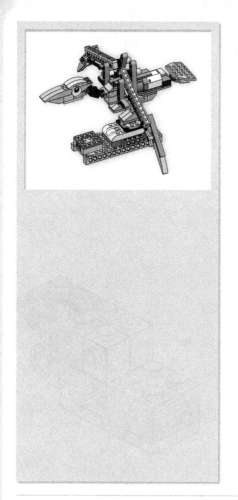

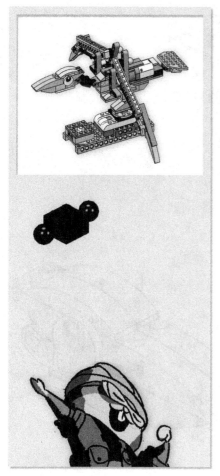

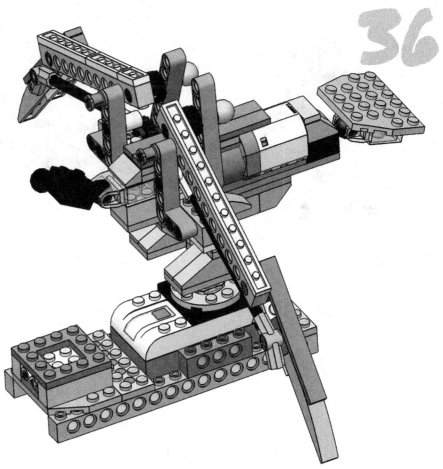

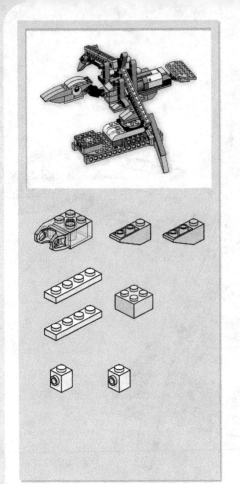

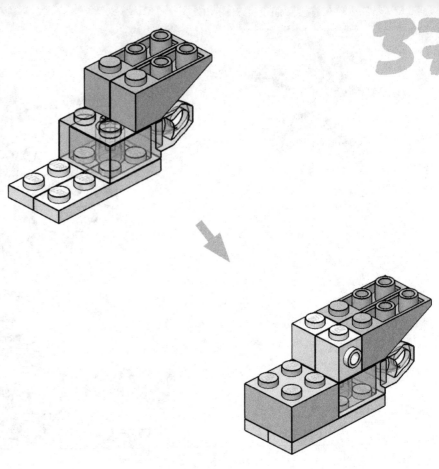

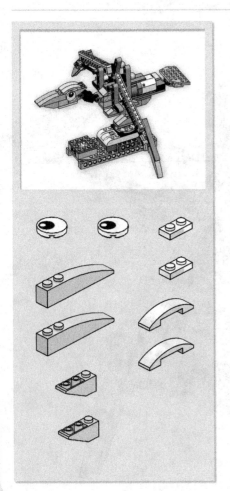

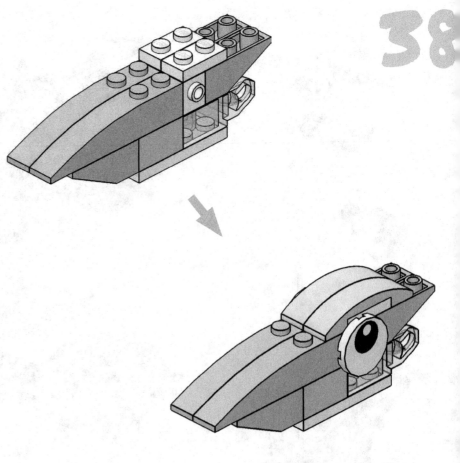

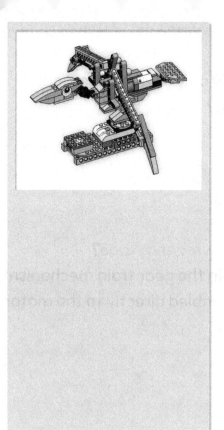

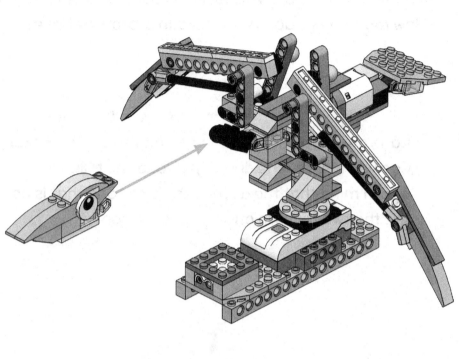

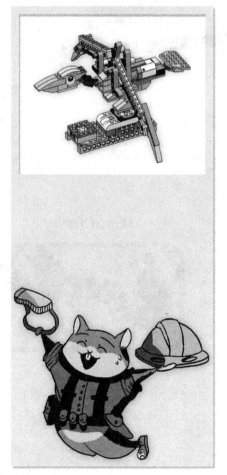

• Before going to the next phase, you can identify the mechanisms you are using in y
pelican prototype.

• Can you predict how your pelican prototype will move by only seeing the model?

• How many gears are you using in your pelican prototype?

• How many wings does your pelican prototype have?

Design features

• Your pelican uses the motor to drive its two legs.

• Can you identify the gear train and the crank–rocker four–bar linkage?

• Can you identify the driver gear and the follower gear in the gear train mechanism?
Keep in mind that the driver gear is the one that is assembled directly to the motor.

• Are the two wings in an in–phase motion?

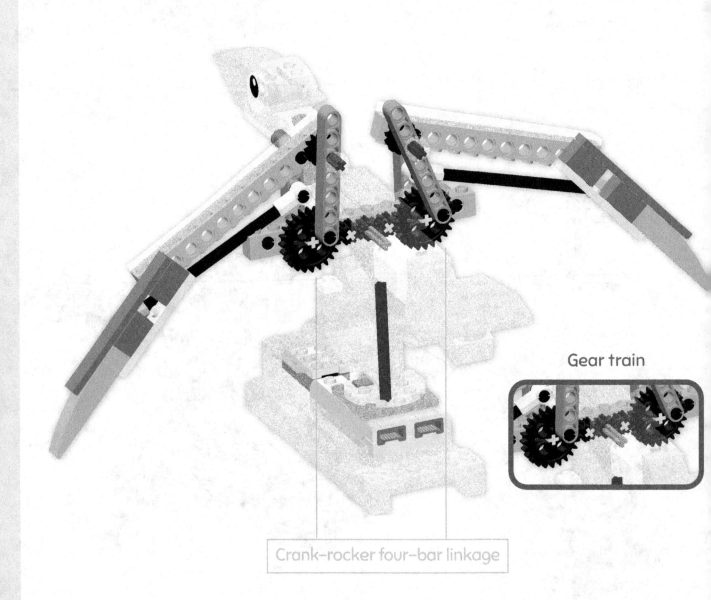

Gear train

Crank–rocker four–bar linkage

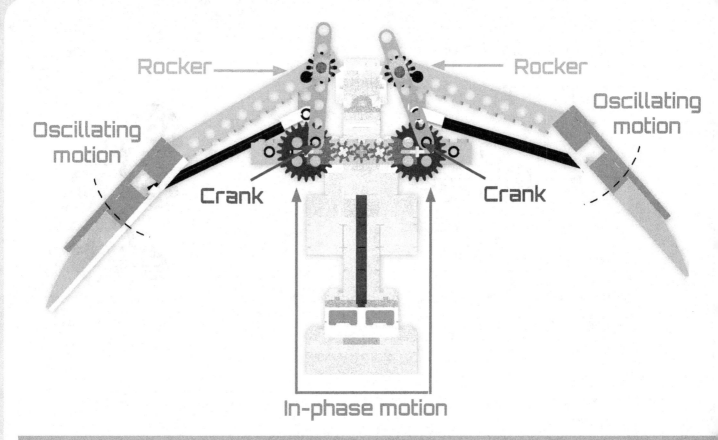

Rocker   Rocker

Oscillating motion   Oscillating motion

Crank   Crank

In-phase motion

Program phase: Power control by sensor

· In this section, you will explore the use of the distance sensor to control the motor power of your prototype.

· The **program idea** consists of moving the wings of your pelican depending on the value of your sensor.

· In a more detailed way, your pelican will move their wings slower as an object (your hand) approaches the distance sensor. The wings will move at maximum power when there is no object in front of the distance sensor.

Flowchart

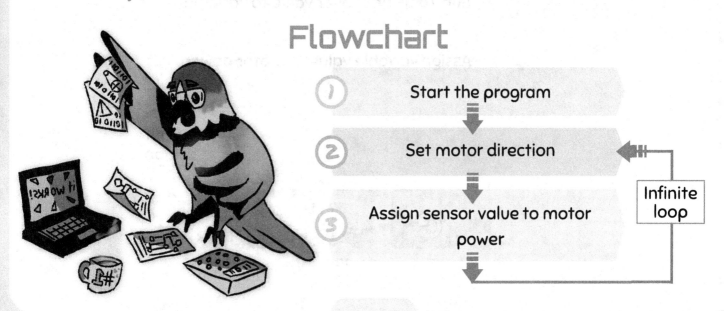

① Start the program

② Set motor direction

③ Assign sensor value to motor power

Infinite loop

- The flowchart indicates **three tasks**. Therefore, you can assign a **programming block** for **each task**:

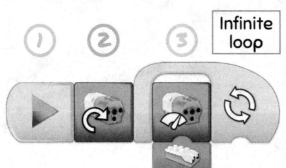

① ② ③ Infinite loop

How should I modify the progra... if I want the pelican to perform an opposite behavior?

Changing the logic

- What should you do to program your pelican so it can perform an opposite behavior?
- The **new program idea** is: your pelican will move the wings faster as an object (you hand) approaches the distance sensor. The wings will stop when there is no objec in front of the distance sensor.
- You need to use a **variable** to develop this new program. As usual, let's start with th flowchart first:

Flowchart

① Start the program

② Set motor direction

③ Set variable to 10

④ Subtract the sensor value to variable

⑤ Assign variable value to motor power

Infinite loop

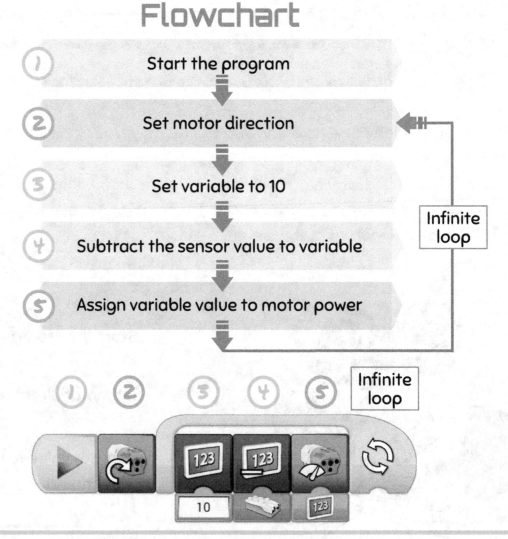

① ② ③ ④ ⑤ Infinite loop

123 10 123 123

Test phase: Getting closer and further

· Remember to verify the **communication** between your WeDo software and your WeDo hub before you start testing your prototype.

· Start testing your prototype by executing the program developed in the **program phase** by clicking the "Start" block.

TEST 1: Does the motor direction matter?

· Do the wings of your pelican move differently if you change the rotation of your motor from clockwise to counter clockwise?

TEST 2: Changing the logic

· Execute the first program developed in the program phase. Then, execute the second program developed in the program phase. How differently does your pelican perform in both programs?

TEST 3: From in-phase motion to out-phase motion

· Modify the position of your pelican wings to perform an out-**phase motion** and execute your program. Is the motion more similar or different from an actual wings motion observed in birds?

Document & share phase

· Remember to collect all your **notes**, **videos**, and **photos** to report your **findings and results**.
· Record a video of your pelican performing the two programs developed in the program phase. How different are they?
· Record a video of your pelican moving using an out-phase and an in-phase motion to compare the wings motion.

Enhancing the experience

· **Build:** Instead of using the distance sensor to control the wings motion, you can replace it with the tilt sensor.
· **Programming:** Program different motor power depending on the position of the tilt sensor. The flapping wings motion can be used when your tilt sensor is facing down. To emulate gliding motion, just set the motor power to 0.

You have learned different motions observed in animals and were able to replicate them to create robotic prototypes; so, what's next?

WHAT'S NEXT?

· Some of the prototypes featured in this book have been designed since 2011 using the WeDo 1.0 kit.

WeDo 1.0 prototypes

Sea lion

Dog

Frog

Pelican

Skier

American rhea

Caiman

· Can you notice the differences with the WeDo 2.0 versions?
· Which prototypes do you think have undergone the greatest changes?

Extra WeDo 1.0 prototypes

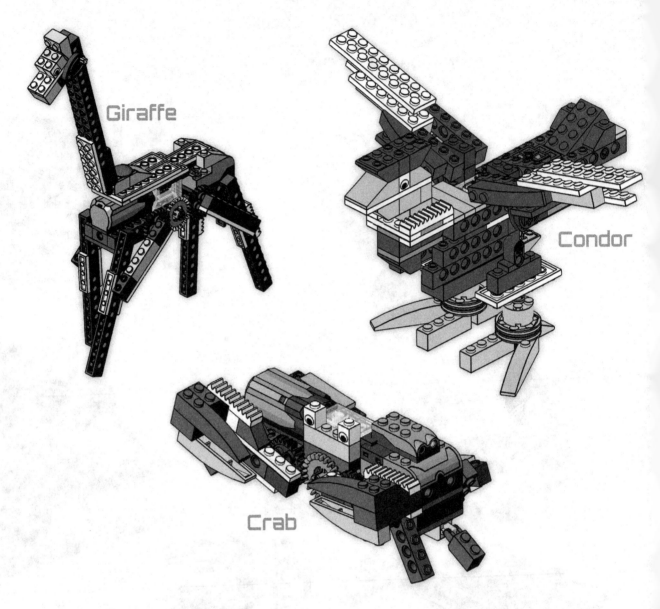

Giraffe

Condor

Crab

· Would you try to build the extra WeDo 10 prototypes using your WeDo 20 set by o
observing the preceding images?

Improvements in prototyping

· Each prototype implied a process of continuous improvement. There were prototype
that did not come out very well in the first version and have been improved. The improvement can be done in two ways:

· **Functional improvements:** Motion of your prototype
· **Aesthetic improvements:** How your prototype looks like

· The prototyping process encourages your **creativity** and allows you to learn throug
research and experimentation. **You learn to build your ideas.**

Review

· All the prototypes were designed following the five phases we proposed in the first chapter. Do you remember all the phases?

Phases in prototyping

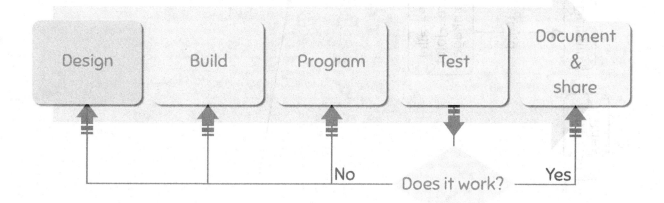

Design → Build → Program → Test → Document & share

No — Does it work? — Yes

Mechanisms: Gears

· In the development of the prototypes, you explored different gear mechanisms. Here is a review of all of them:

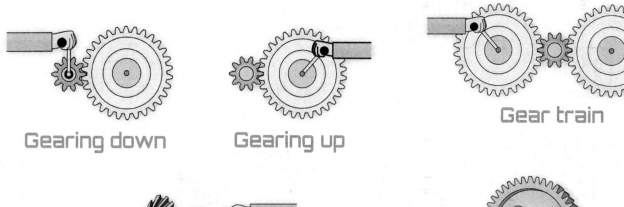

Gearing down   Gearing up   Gear train

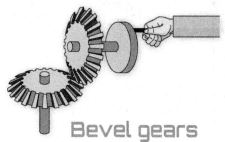

Bevel gears

Worm gear

· Can you remember which ones were used in each of all the prototypes?
· In several prototypes, more than one gear mechanism was used to create more complex motions.

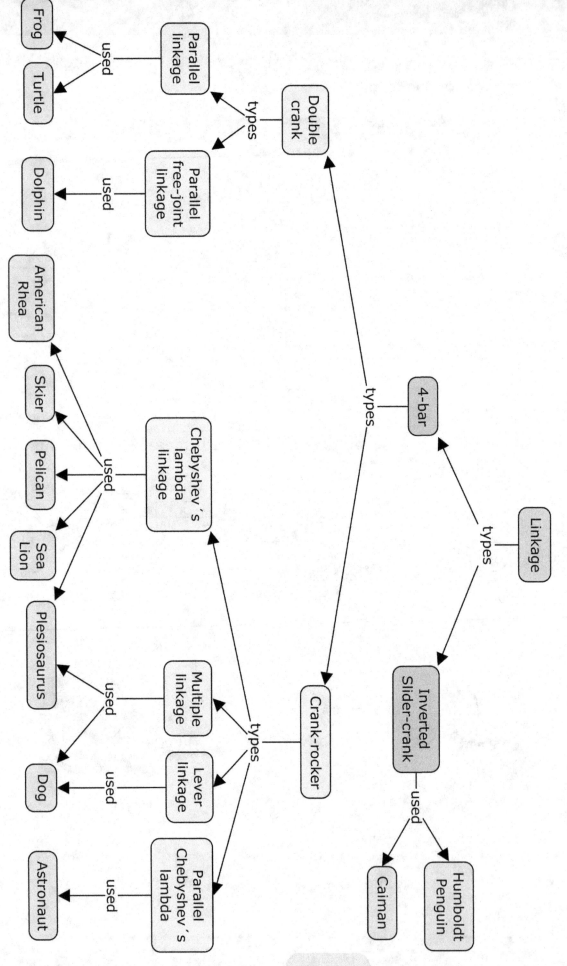

Animatronics

· It is the construction of prototypes with the **appearance** and **behavior** of **living beings**, which can move. You have built several; let's check them again:

Swim

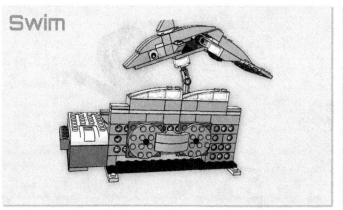

Fly

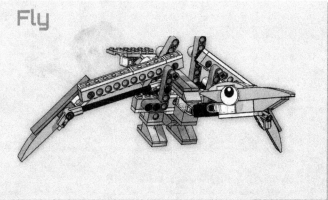

Crawl

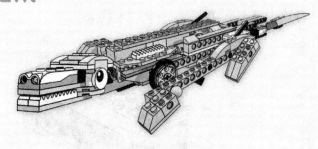

Bipedal walking

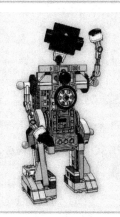

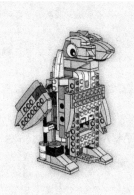

Quadrupedal walking

Sensors

· They are like the **senses in the human body**; they serve to realize what is around u
We have worked with two sensors: tilt sensor and distance sensor.

Actuators

· They are devices that allow the generation of events in nature. For example, **somethin moves** by using a motor or **something lights up** by using an LED.
· In your WeDo set, the LED is in the hub.

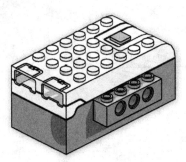

Locomotion and movement

· **Locomotion** refers to the **displacement** of a whole body voluntarily, for example, walking swimming, running, flying, crawling, and so on.
· **Movement does not necessarily involve displacement**; it can refer to a part of th body, for example, when a bird just flutters or when you move your neck or your arms.
· Almost all of the prototypes you have built have locomotion, meaning that they ca move from one place to another. Can you identify which ones do not have locomotion?
· Can you indicate which prototype is the slowest and fastest in **displacing**?

Movement

Locomotion

Where to go?

· If you like to build, design, and program, maybe you might like a career in engineering. Note that the original meaning of the word engineering was: **person who solves problems using ingenuity.** From that point of view, we are all potential engineers.

· Engineers transform an **idea into reality.** They invent!

· Engineering is based on **science, mathematics, and technology.**

Science

· Scientists use the so-called scientific method for "**the search of the truth.**" If you compare it with your "**phases in prototyping,**" you will see that they are very similar, right?

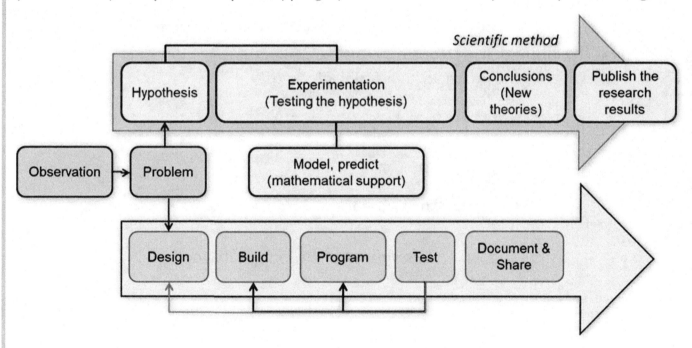

· Technology and engineering constitute the **application of knowledge** obtained through science to produce practical results.

· Scientists work with science ("**seeking the truth**"), and engineers work with technology (**seeking to solve problems**).

Mathematics

- Logic, calculations, and **measurements** are used to understand the phenomena of the universe and summarize it in mathematical formulas that allow us to predict its behavior.
- **Mathematics** is the **tool** that science uses to "**seek the truth.**"
- Mathematics is the search for the **symmetry and patterns** of things.
- You can play around with numbers and find interesting things, for example, what happens if you arrange the digits of the number 6174 from greatest to least and then from least to greatest and subtract them from each other?
- The result is: 7641–1467 = 6174.
- You get the same number again: 6174. This was discovered by the Indian mathematician **Dattatreya Ramachandra Kaprekar** (1905—1986) who was characterized by living playing with riddles.

Technology

- Technology is the **set of instruments**, **methods**, and **techniques** designed to solve a problem.
- Today, we use **various technologies** to carry out our work, such as computers, programming, the Internet, and so on.
- Technology is the practical knowledge of things.

Remember that work today is more mental than physical.

Intelligence is the main work tool.

How do you train your intelligence? Drawing, painting, building, programming, being happy.

Concept maps are graphic tools that allow you to organize and represent knowledge in an organized way. Concept maps are didactic summaries of a topic. They help to have a holistic view of a developed topic and highlight the important parts.

The concept maps of each of the book's chapters are presented in the following pages.

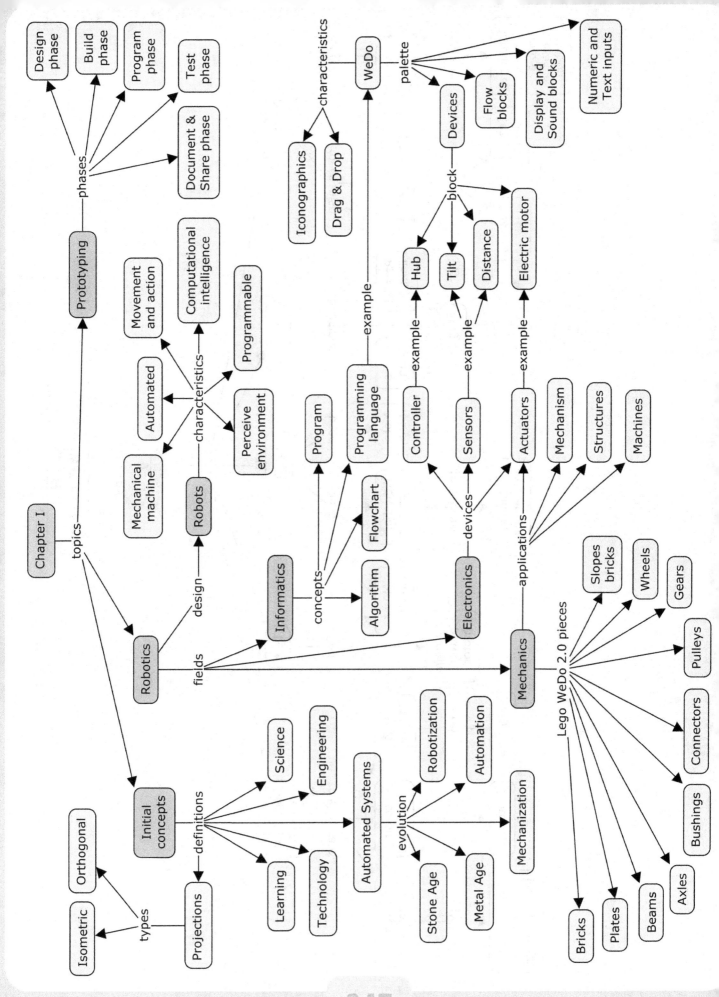

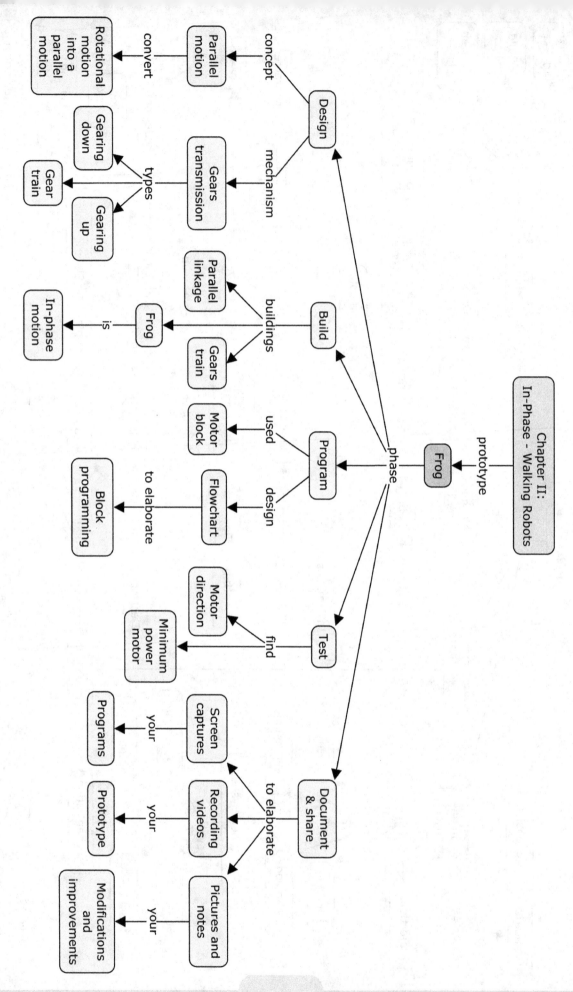

Chapter II:
In-Phase - Walking Robots

Frog

prototype

phase

Design
- concept → **Parallel motion** → convert → **Rotational motion into a parallel motion**
- mechanism → **Gears transmission** → types → **Gearing down** / **Gearing up** / **Gear train**

Build
- buildings → **Parallel linkage**
- **Gears train** → **Frog** → is → **In-phase motion**

Program
- used → **Motor block**
- design → **Flowchart** → to elaborate → **Block programming**

Test
- find → **Motor direction** / **Minimum power motor**

Document & share
- to elaborate → **Screen captures** → your → **Programs**
- **Recording videos** → your → **Prototype**
- **Pictures and notes** → your → **Modifications and improvements**

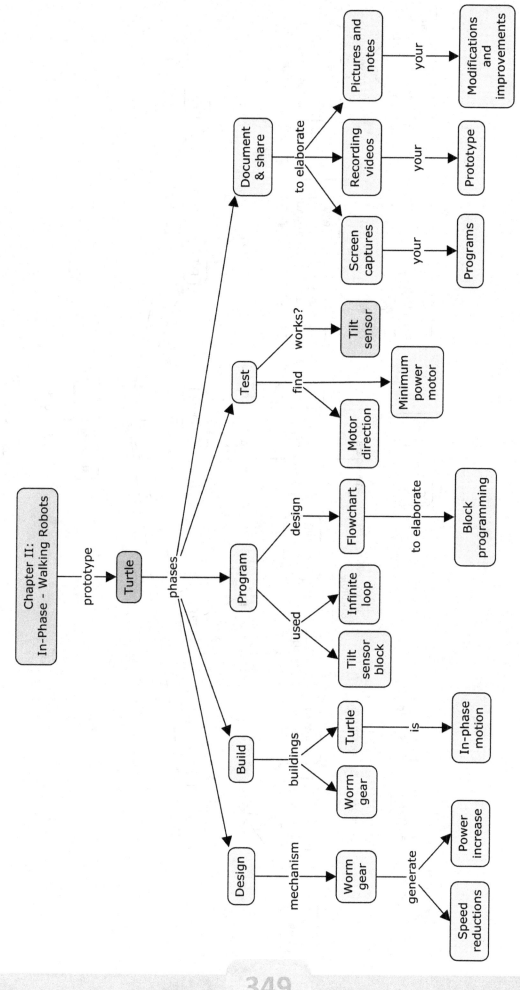

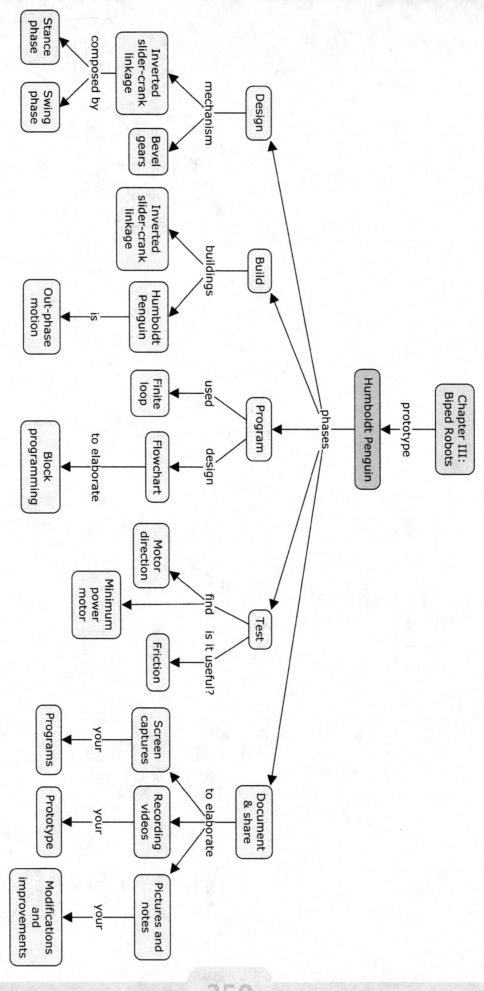

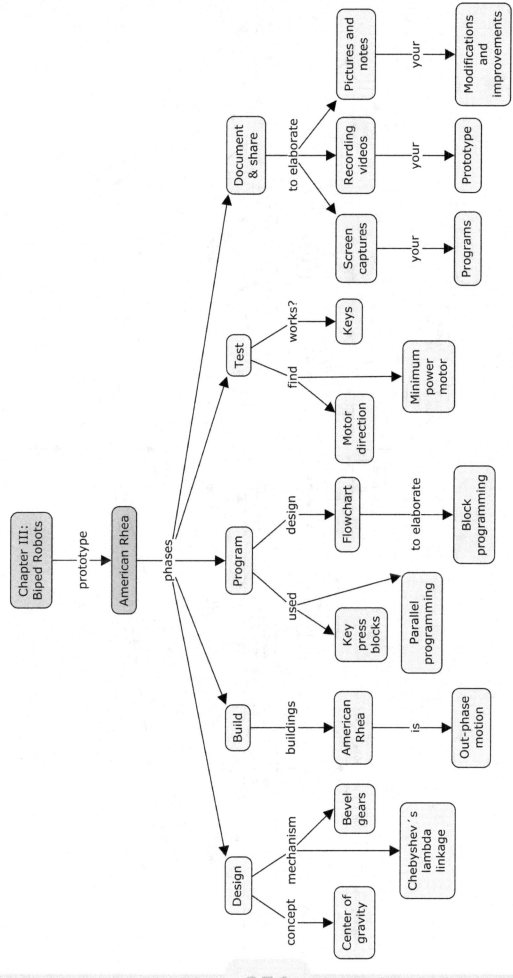

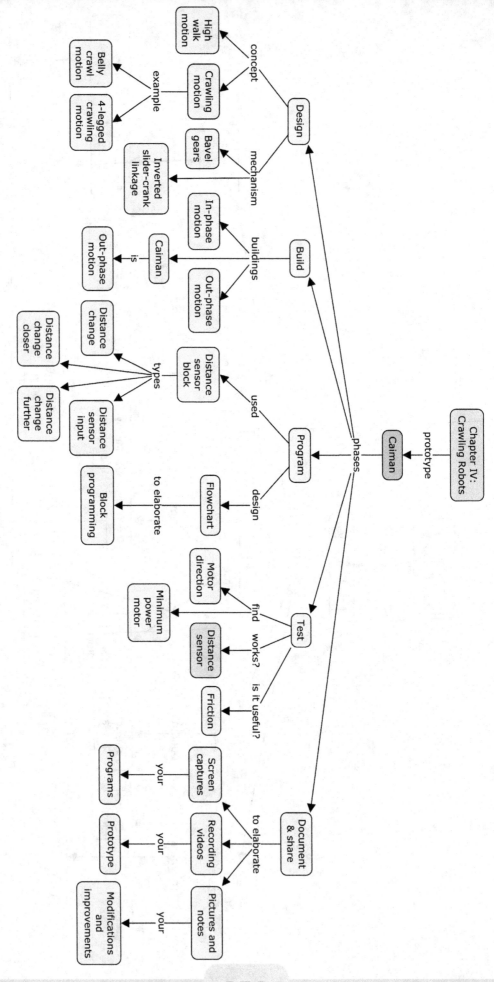

Chapter IV: Crawling Robots

prototype → Caiman

phases →

Design
- concept → High walk motion
- concept → Crawling motion
  - example → Belly crawl motion
  - example → 4-legged crawling motion
- mechanism → Bavel gears
- mechanism → Inverted slider-crank linkage

Build
- buildings → In-phase motion
- buildings → Out-phase motion
  - Caiman — is → Out-phase motion

Program
- used → Distance sensor block
  - types → Distance change
    - Distance change closer
    - Distance change further
  - types → Distance sensor input
- design → Flowchart
  - to elaborate → Block programming

Test
- find → Motor direction
- find → Minimum power motor
- works? → Distance sensor
- is it useful? → Friction

Document & share
- to elaborate → Screen captures
  - your → Programs
- to elaborate → Recording videos
  - your → Prototype
- to elaborate → Pictures and notes
  - your → Modifications and improvements

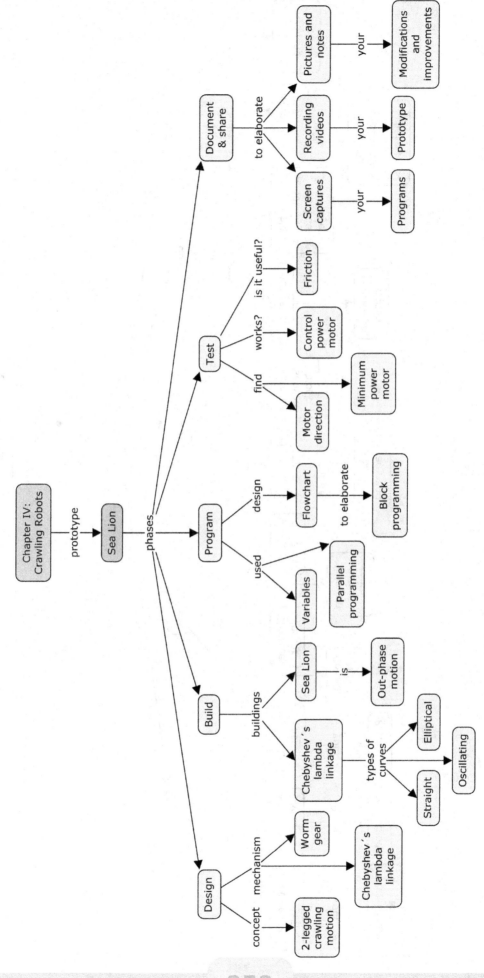

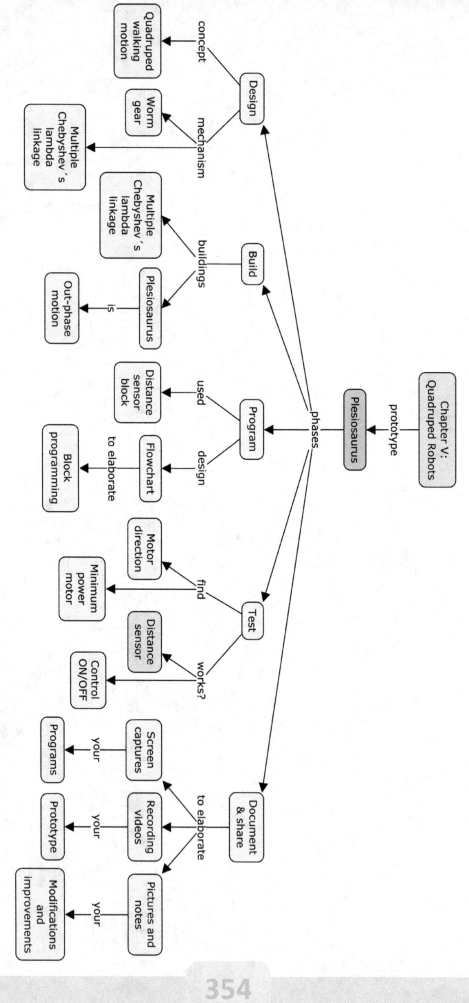

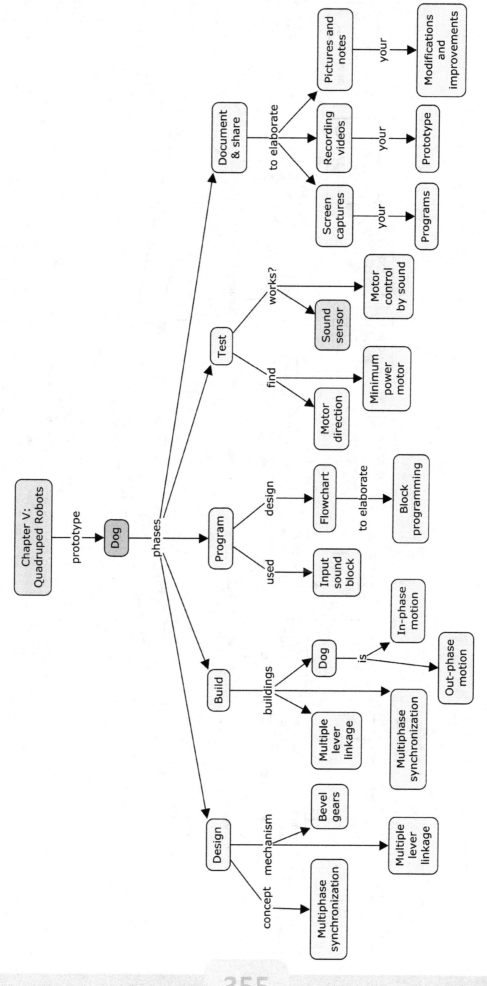

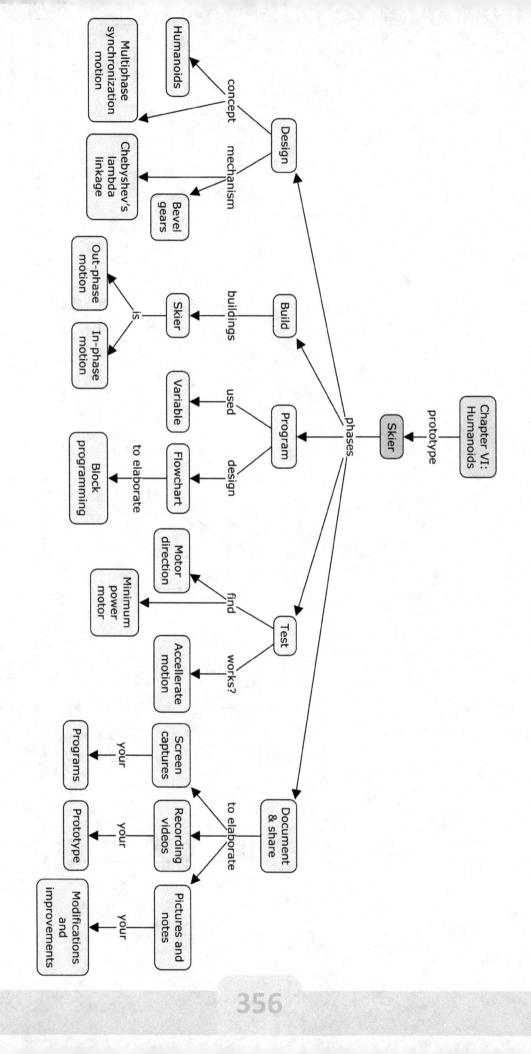

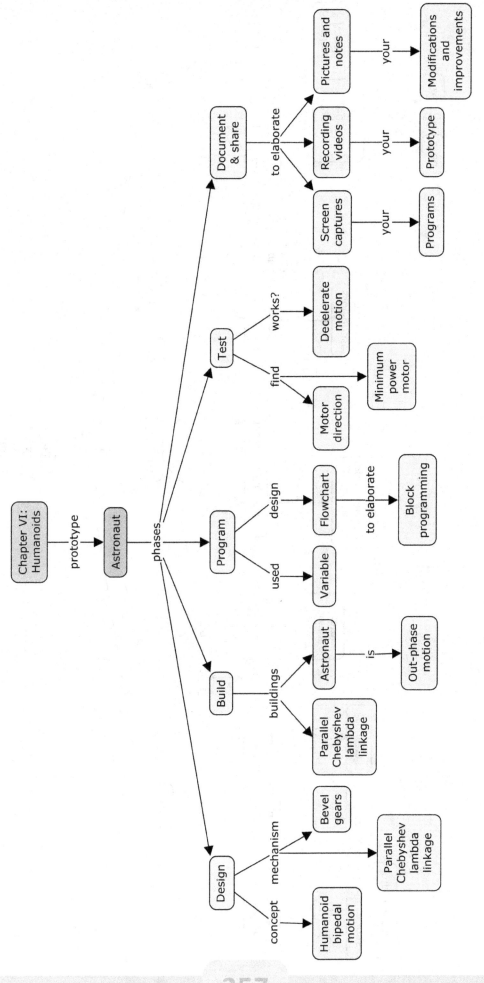

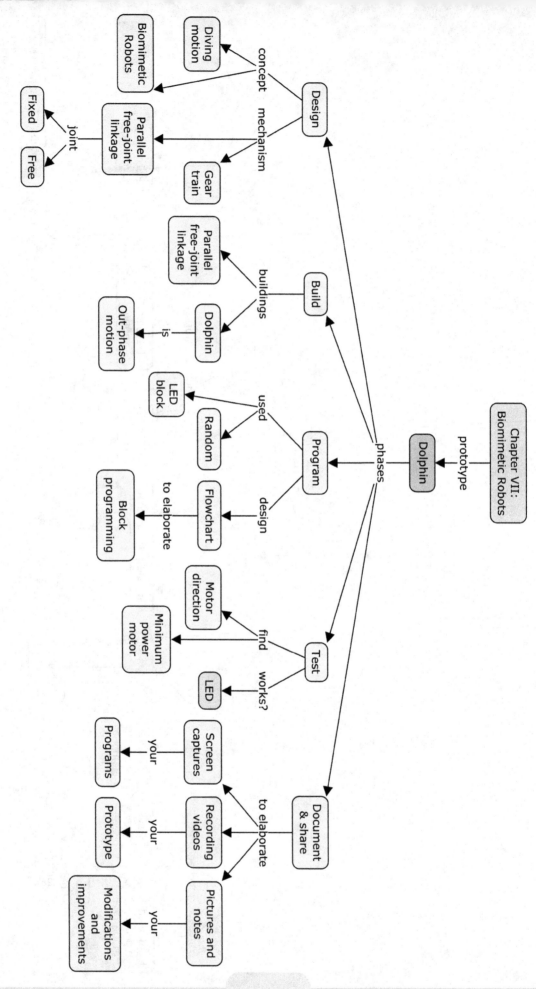

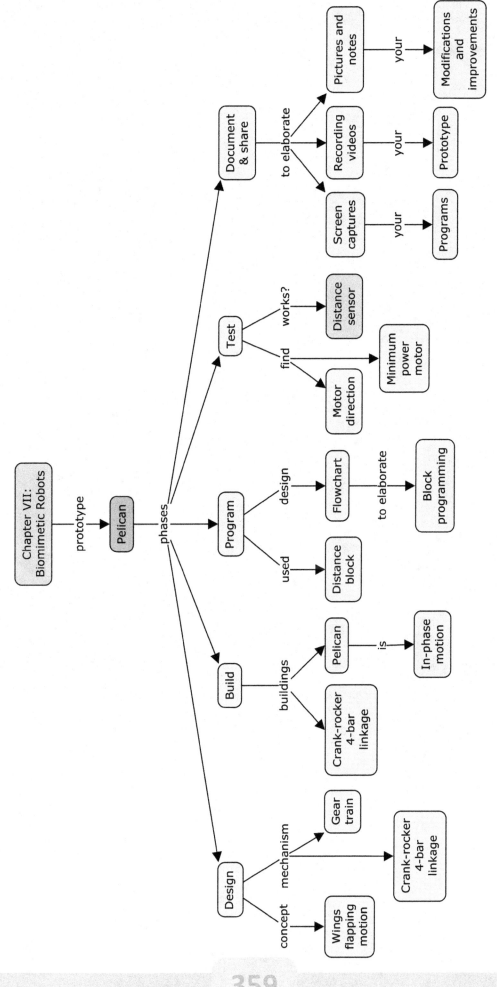

INDEX

Printed in the United States
by Baker & Taylor Publisher Services